Also by Pete Brown

Three Sheets to the Wind
One Man's Quest for the Meaning of Beer

Hops and Glory
*One Man's Search for the Beer That
Built the British Empire*

Pete Brown used to advertise beer for a living before he realized that writing about it was even more fun, and came with even more free beer. He contributes to various newspapers, magazines and beer trade press titles, writes the annual report on Britain's cask ale market, sings beer's praises on TV and radio, and runs an influential blog.

In 2009, Pete was awarded the Michael Jackson Gold Tankard Award and named Beer Writer of the Year by the British Guild of Beer Writers.

(No, not that Michael Jackson, the other one.)

PETE BROWN

Man Walks Into a Pub

A Sociable History of Beer

Second Edition
Matured for longer to give a thicker body
and a touch of extra bitterness

PAN BOOKS

First published 2003 by Macmillan

First published in paperback 2004

This updated edition published 2010 by Pan Books
an imprint of Pan Macmillan, a division of Macmillan Publishers Limited
Pan Macmillan, 20 New Wharf Road, London N1 9RR
Basingstoke and Oxford
Associated companies throughout the world
www.panmacmillan.com

ISBN 978-0-330-41220-9

Copyright © Pete Brown 2003, 2010

15 17 19 18 16 14

A CIP catalogue record for this book is available from
the British Library.

Typeset by SetSystems Ltd, Saffron Walden, Essex
Printed and bound by CPI Group (UK) Ltd, Croydon, CR0 4YY

Visit **www.panmacmillan.com** to read more about all our books
and to buy them. You will also find features, author interviews and
news of any author events, and you can sign up for e-newsletters
so that you're always first to hear about our new releases.

To my dad Ron,
and to my wife Lizzie,
who would have got on
like a house on fire

I liked the taste of beer, its live, white lather, its brass-bright depths, the sudden world through the wet brown walls of the glass . . . the foam on the corners.

Dylan Thomas, *Portrait of the Artist as a Young Dog*

Beer! Beer!
We want more beer!
All the lads are cheerin',
Get the blooming beers in.

Anon., traditional drinking song

Contents

Contents

Preface to the Second Edition

I've done some stupid things while under the influence, but I never thought drink would drive me to this.

In 1998 I was an advertising executive – working as a 'planner' in a big London agency on a salary considerably higher than the national average, with good career prospects.

Now I spend my life touring breweries, drinking beer and making other people thirsty.

While I believe my new career contributes in some infinitesimal way to the sum of human happiness, rather than detracting from it like my old one did, the high salary – indeed the concept of a regular salary of any description – is a distant memory. But boy, was it worth it.

This book was the turning point.

In my old job, one of my responsibilities was to organize market research focus groups, where you get eight people in a room and ask them why they buy a particular brand of washing powder or margarine. Then you might show them roughs of potential new adverts to see if you might change their minds if you spent several million quid making them and sticking them in the ad break in the middle of *Coronation Street*.

I'd worked on some pretty interesting stuff by that point. I'd been in the studio with Chris Tarrant and Tony Blackburn for Capital Radio; I'd helped launch Blockbuster Video in the UK; and I'd done my time on the washing powder and margarine ads. In each case, the focus groups had been fascinating: snigger at the thought of middle-aged northern ladies talking about stubborn undergarment stains if you must, but it was fascinating and at times humbling for a twenty-something middle-class advertising wanker to hear first hand the tiny tragedies and triumphs that make up everyday life for people whose existence doesn't revolve around the latest Soho bar.

But then I got to do the same for Heineken and Stella Artois, and something happened.

Twenty-one-year-old Stella drinkers would knuckle into the room with Liam Gallagher-modelled monkey swagger, all gelled hair, bleached denim and sportswear, and lean back with their legs splayed, defying the group moderator to impress or even engage them.

After ten minutes, they'd be leaning forward, talking passionately about why they drank the beer they did, how they swore they could taste the difference between Kronenbourg and Heineken, how the choice between Becks and Bud in a club said something important about the kind of person they were, how when they visited their parents they would buy a pint of real ale in the pub with dad, and bond with him over it, talk to him openly, share feelings, in a way they never could before they reached drinking age.

What was so special about beer?

I'd always been an enthusiastic beer drinker, but never

considered myself an aficionado. I drank lager most of the time, switching to John Smith's or Tetley's Cask when I went back to Yorkshire, where I grew up.

Now, I wanted to know how beer had gained such a hold over the British male psyche. I knew it was tied up in the evolution of British drinking culture and the unique nature of the pub. So I decided to look for a book that would give me a social history of beer and pubs, that would tell me why we carried on drinking bitter a century after the rest of the world had switched to lager, why a pub was so different from a bar, why we had such stupid licensing hours, and why people felt their choice of lager brand said as much about them as what they did for a living, or what football team they supported.

When, after a year searching, I couldn't find that book, I decided to write it myself. Beer slowly became an obsession and, gradually, my advertising career waned. *Man Walks into a Pub* was finally completed in June 2002, and published a year later.

Since then much has changed. The ownership structure of Britain's pubs and brewers has altered beyond recognition, with huge implications for what we can drink and where. There's been a global revolution in flavoursome, craft-brewed beers, and a wholesale revival in Britain's own real ale, which is rapidly shedding its beard-and-sandals nerdy image.

At the same time, the British government and the British media have seemingly declared war against the beer drinker. Astonishing rises in beer duty, a smoking ban, ever-tightening regulations and red tape and rock-bottom booze prices in supermarkets are helping to close thousands of pubs every year, and I'm regularly invited on TV and radio shows to answer the question, 'So Pete, is the English pub dead?' Meanwhile, tabloid hacks (and broadsheet reporters who should know better) are trying to convince you that binge drinkers are burning our town centres to the ground, while the medical profession asserts that if you drink a second pint of Stella in one day, you are officially a 'hazardous drinker' with an 'alcohol use disorder'.*

And for me personally, my knowledge of and relationship with the industry has changed. I'm now established in the old guard of a world I gently mocked (not so gently in the case of the Campaign for Real Ale) when I first wrote this book. But the beer industry draws you in, becomes a source of endless and multi-faceted fascination, and when that happens, your perspective changes.

I'm amazed that this book still sells reasonably well so long after it was published. But I started to feel increasingly guilty that anyone buying it at the end of the noughties was being shortchanged. That first edition was out of date. It contained some basic factual errors. And worst of all, some of the jokes were really, really shit. It's time to remedy all this.

I wouldn't write *Man Walks into a Pub* the same way if I started it today. But in this new edition I've decided to keep the naïve outsider tone it had, while correcting it, expanding it slightly, and bringing it up to date. If you're reading it for the first time, I hope you find it informative and entertaining and I promise you it's now all as accurate as it can be. If you've read it before and bought it again because of the fantastic new cover, I hope you find the footnotes less annoying this time around.

Cheers,
Pete Brown
London
2010

---

* I promise I'm not exaggerating or making this up. I really wish I were.

Acknowledgements to the
First Edition

My interest in beer grew when it was my job to advertise it. Probably the best job in the world. Thanks to Lowe for giving me this job, and for continuing to employ me even when I talked about the book endlessly instead of doing any work – special thanks to Laurence Green, John Lowery, Alison Hoad, Simon McQuiggan and the Bitches. For places of work, thanks to the British Library – surely one of the greatest ideas in the world – and Vicky Grinnell for the cottage.

For all sorts of help along the way thanks to Conrad Bird, John Crofts, Allan Crosbie, Chris Gittner, Charlotte Haynes, Lucy Howard, Jill Macfarlane, David Miller, Charlie Parkin, Kate Shaw and James Scroggs. Thanks and deepest apologies to Joan Ingle, who never used to swear, for meticulously gathering all the synonyms for drunkenness. As a result Joan now speaks like a nineteenth-century navvy and has the foulest mouth in Haringey, which really is saying something. Thanks to the General Picton, where we spent an enjoyable morning shooting the cover. Thanks to everyone at Pan Macmillan for being so kind, keen, and so damn *nice*, especially my editor Jason Cooper, who taught me how to actually *write* a book once I'd written it, if you see what I mean.

Most of all, thanks to Lizzie, for being my other half in every possible sense, and without whom I simply could not have written this. And thanks to Fatbert, the evil, selfish, scatalogical cat, for unwittingly keeping her endlessly amused while I was locked away writing.

Acknowledgements to the
Second Edition

I've made many new friends in the beer world since this book was published – some of them people I took the piss out of in these pages before I'd actually met them and found out how sound they really were. Thank you to everyone who has helped make the last seven years of my life so life-affirmingly pleasurable.

Thanks to Pan Macmillan for indulging me with this new edition, particularly Bruno Vincent, Jon Butler and Chloe Healy.

And thanks as always to Liz, who accepts the status of Beer Widow with astonishingly good grace and forbearance.

Introduction

'You should have seen us last night!'

On becoming bladdered
(Names have been changed to protect the guilty)

Dave lives in Leeds and works as a lawyer. One Friday night, he squeezes into a fake Irish pub and fights his way through shouting, tightly packed bodies to buy a pint of strong Belgian lager. He could have chosen a pint of strong Dutch lager or a pint of strong French lager, but he thinks the strong Belgian lager is the best quality lager on offer, the most 'genuine' lager. Over the next ninety minutes he has three more pints of the genuine Belgian lager. Time slurs, and he's in the Majestyk nightclub with his mates. The same Belgian lager is available here in bottles, but Dave ignores it now. He's at the bar, ordering a round, and it doesn't even cross his mind. Instead he opts for a watery American lager, because it's what everyone else is drinking. Another four of them and, at some point – exactly when, he's not too clear – he calls it a night.

He didn't think this too large. Quite large, yes, but not exceptional.

The next thing he knows it's Sunday lunchtime, and he's sitting under fake oak beams and prints of fox hunting, nursing a pint of 'real' ale born and bred less than twenty miles from where he sits, sipping, looking to take the edge off his hangover.

Dave likes to keep his head clear through the week for work. He doesn't drink again until the following Thursday, when he goes to Squares for a drink with some people from work. He has four pints of his Belgian lager, then ends up back at Majestyk where he has another three bottles of the American beer.

•

Matt lives in London. On Sunday, when Dave was nursing his hangover, Matt went to the gym and then the Green Man, a large theme pub full of students. He had three pints of Castlemaine XXXX then moved on to Beck's, drinking two bottles. Unlike Dave, Matt drinks most days. On Monday he stayed in and cooked a meal and had a bottle of red wine. On Tuesday he had to go to Newcastle because of his job. That night he went out with a work colleague for a curry, which they washed down with a couple of pints of Carlsberg, before discovering a lively bar. They drank mainly Beck's – probably about four – then retired to the hotel where they had a couple of pints of Caffrey's each before turning in. Matt didn't drink again until Friday evening, which he spent in his local. He had four pints of London Pride which, despite his behaviour through the week, he claims is his usual drink.

•

Matt and Dave are real people who kept diaries of their drinking for a normal week as part of a research project. You should try it. You might surprise yourself.

•

This is a book about why we drink beer: Matt, Dave, you, me and the rest of us. More than that, it is a book about *how* we drink beer and about why we drink the beer we do, the way we do. And it's a book about why, throughout our entire history, the British love affair with beer has endured.

Seventy per cent of men and fifty-five per cent of women drink at least once a week. Seventy per cent of those men and thirty-seven per cent of women include beer in that, and in total we drink an average of eight litres of pure alcohol each every year, more if you strip out those people who don't drink at all. This doesn't make the British the biggest boozers in the world, but we do seem to go at it with a little more bravado than most other people.*

Thinking about drinking

Within British culture, beer and its spiritual home, the pub, occupy a much bigger space than even the huge amount we

---

* Those consumption figures have declined significantly since the first edition of *Man Walks into a Pub* was published. Despite what politicians, the media and the medical establishment are telling us, Britain's reputation for notorious pissheadedness is increasingly undeserved. But if the *Daily Mail* isn't going to let mere facts get in the way of a good story, I'm not either, although my story is a little more positive than theirs. Alcohol and beer in particular still mean a great deal to us, even if we are drinking less these days.

drink would suggest. The pub itself defines this country, remaining a focal point for our social lives even among non-drinkers, and if we're not in there getting drunk we're talking about the last time we did, or the next time we hope to. Look at it this way. Everybody knows how the Inuit supposedly have ninety or so words for snow; it forms such a large part of their lives that they have specific terms for all the different types and textures.* Taking this principle forward, a cursory analysis of the English language and its colloquialisms reveals the extent to which we enjoy getting:

addled
annihilated
arseholed
barrelled
beggared
bellied
bevvied
bladdered
blagged
blasted
blathered
blitzed
blootered
blotto
bollocksed
boohonged
caned
comatose

---

* You develop a similar knowledge of mud if you go to Glastonbury.

crapulent

croaked

cunted

dagged

damaged

dionysian

dipso

dizzy

drenched

drunk

ferschtinkenered

floored

fucked

fuddled

gattered

giffed

greased

guttered

guzzled

half seas over

half-cut

hammered

honking

hoonered

inebriated

intemperate

intoxicated

jagged

jiggered

jolly

kaylied

laced
lashed
leathered
liquored up
loopy
lush
mashed
maudlin
mellow
merry
mizzled
monstered
mortal
newted
numb
obliterated
paralytic
pasted
pickled
pie-eyed
pissed (as a fart, bastard, cunt, parrot, newt or twat)
plastered
pot-valiant
raddled
rat-arsed
reeling
riotous
roistered
rotten
sauced
scammered

'You should have seen us last night!'

schwallied

scoobied

scuttered

senseless

shattered

shedded

shit-faced

skunked

slammed

slashed

slaughtered

sloshed

smashed

soaked

sotted

soused

sozzled

squiffy

stewed

stoated

stocious

stupid

tangle-footed

tanked up

temulent

the worse for wear

tight

tipsy

tired and emotional

trashed

trolleyed

trousered

twatted

under the influence

wankered

wasted

wazzed

well-oiled

wrecked

zonked*

The point is not the number of different expressions; it's why we need to make so many distinctions. Just as the Inuit do with snow, we identify subtly different types of drunkenness. Given that it's a social phenomenon, many of these terms relate to who is drunk and in what context, rather than just how drunk they are and on what. Only women get squiffy, whereas you're probably a big fella if you're getting bladdered regularly. Everyone knows that being annihilated is more extreme than getting tiddly. You grow out of getting paralytic after your early twenties, apart from at Christmas, whereas you probably won't get soused unless you reach a particularly embittered middle age. 'Tired and emotional' is a gentle euphemism which carries an undercurrent of *Private Eye*

---

* I was well into writing this book and had about 250 of these words when I came across Jonathon Green's *Cassell Dictionary of Slang*, and found a further 800-odd words and phrases. This is a very funny book. It is also a very, very scary book. He's gone through and listed nearly every slang word in the English language, past and present. It is clearly the work of an insane genius. Just so you know, the only other subjects that come close to having as many different slang terms as drunkenness are bonking, jobbies, wabs, the front bottom and the old chap. In itself, this says more about our culture than most books could ever hope to.

smugness, whereas 'cunted' and 'wankered' aggressively confront and challenge.

It has been argued (by my cynical mate Chris) that you could make this list of words as long as you wanted simply by taking any word at random and sticking an –ed suffix at the end of it. Thus you could claim that last night you got curtained, or you were absolutely tabled, or scruffed or railed, and you would get away with it; everyone would know exactly what you meant.* Well, I didn't do that – every word in the list above is in common usage somewhere in the country – but there is an element of truth to Chris's claim, and this makes a point in itself. Drinking is such an important part of our culture that it compels us to push our facility with language to new limits. After a serious night on the beer, existing words just aren't adequate and we are driven to create new ones in order to express just how bad we were. We are cosmonauts of the comatose, on a lifelong mission to seek out and explore new limits of oblivion.

The world through a pint glass

So again, why do we do it? Obviously, we drink to excess because beer is a very nice drink and we greatly enjoy the experience of drinking it. This is the answer you'd probably get from a beer drinker such as Matt in the pub on a Friday

---

* Comedian Michael MacIntyre arrived at the same insight, entirely independently and coincidentally, five years after this book was first published, and used it to great effect in his stand-up routine. Isn't that nice?

night, but it would make for a short and ultimately unreward-
ing book. Even if there were lots of pictures.

And anyway, there is a little more to it than that. Why do
so many of us prefer to get drunk on beer rather than anything
else? And why do we drink beer for so many other reasons
than just to become intoxicated? Why have we drunk beer
throughout our entire history? Why do we drink the beers we
do, in the places we do, at the times we do? And why do some
habits, beers and places steadily change over time, while other
basic drinking motivations and customs stay the same for
centuries? Why does Britain have a pub culture that is unique
in the world? Where did it come from? Why are we alone in
thinking that it's the ultimate sign of real manhood to be able
to drink loads of pints, and turn up at work the morning after
the night before with a sheepish grin and say something like,
'Ooh, you should have seen us last night'?*

You probably wouldn't get a full set of answers to questions
like these from the bloke in the pub on Friday unless he was
already quite hammered, and then they would be lost in a
torrent of opinion covering any and every subject. You could
get some answers from sociologists and psychologists, but they
would probably come with much dull theorizing and probably
a bit of preaching. So in the late 1990s, not having anything
better to do, I decided to try and find out for myself.† What

---

*   OK, maybe not totally alone – the Australians think it's a great thing
to do as well. But unlike the Brits, most cultures around the world do tend
to think they look somewhat cooler if they can take their drink and indulge
in moderation, rather than going for temporary lobotomies that result in
the wearing of traffic cones and the delusion that kebabs are edible.
†   I work in advertising – I'm not saying I wasn't busy, just that I *really*
didn't have anything better to do.

started off as a search for answers about why we love getting beered up led me to discover the extraordinary history of beer and pubs in Britain. Sure, I learned why we like to get pissed, but that was only the start of it. Beyond that, I discovered an epic tale of desire, joy, hardship and ingenuity. What I'm going to do here is try to relate this incredible story in a way that has a bit more of a sense of humour than the sociologists can manage, and is a little more lucid and coherent than the bloke down the pub after a few pints – although I'll probably retain some of his enthusiasm, most of his crap jokes, and a smidgen of his unshakeable belief that what he has to say is really, really interesting.

The story is an odd one, spanning five thousand years, several continents, and starring, at various points, people such as Isambard Kingdom Brunel, John Noakes, the Egyptian goddess Hathor, Louis Pasteur, David Lloyd George, a bear in a yellow nylon jacket and a pork pie hat also called George, the Canadian bloke who invented toasters, and some monks. It's a social history of Britain itself, albeit an incomplete, warped and utterly subjective history. Come to think of it, maybe it's not that different from the kind of story you'd get from the bloke down the pub after all.

Chapter One

'My liver is full of luck'

The ancient history of beer drinking

A long and glorious tradition

So we're in Sumeria, and it's the dawn of time. The world is a playground, and death does not exist. Men and gods live together, free of worry. Gilgamesh, one of the first men, is enjoying life. Enkidu, on the other hand, is a savage man, raised in the mountains by wild animals. Curious, Gilgamesh sends a whore to find out what he's like, and she ends up teaching him the ways of the world. She gives him bread to eat, because that's what humans do, and beer to drink, because that's what *civilized* people do:

> 'Drink beer the custom of the land.'
> Beer he drank – seven goblets.
> His spirit was loosened.
> He became hilarious.*
> His heart was glad and his face shone.

---

* Or at least, if he's like most of us, he thought he was at the time.

The two subsequently meet, and after a bit of a ruck they become firm friends, getting up to all sorts of adventures, killing monsters and so on, as you do. Their exploits catch the eye of the goddess Ishtar, who decides she wouldn't mind seeing what Gilgamesh has under his loincloth. Gilgamesh, however, turns her down.

Big mistake.

Ishtar doesn't take rejection well – she is a goddess after all – and in a fit of pique sends the bull of heaven down to kill Enkidu and Gilgamesh. They defeat the bull and, just to rub it in, Enkidu rips off its hind leg and throws it in Ishtar's face. Well, that does it. Within days Enkidu is dead.

This, the first human death in history, comes as something of a shock to Gilgamesh. Extremely upset, he seeks out the gods and asks them why they have done this, creating the precedent that men must die while gods live for ever. The gods, using that special divine logic gods always seem to have, explain that this is because men are men and gods are gods, and because gods are better than men and live for ever, men must ipso facto be mortal. It simply took Enkidu's appalling behaviour to make this clear to everyone:

> The life thou pursuest thou shalt not find.
> When the gods created mankind,
> Death for mankind they set aside,
> Life in their own hands retaining.

This is obviously a bit of a bombshell for poor Gilgamesh. It takes the sheen off his position as the father of the human race. The gods, to give them credit, feel a bit bad about the whole business, and tell Gilgamesh to cheer up and party, because worse things can happen:

Thou Gilgamesh, let full be thy belly,
Make thou merry by day and by night.
On each day make thou a feast of rejoicing,
Day and night thou dance and play!

Gilgamesh does exactly that – with the help of beer, the gift of the gods. The rest – in its widest and truest sense – is history.

Let's hear it for micro-organisms

I don't know about you, but when I'm musing on things and trying to persuade myself that, overall, life isn't actually that bad, when I'm thinking about all the great things in the world and counting my blessings, chief among them is the existence of families of microscopic, single-celled fungi. You know, *Saccharomycetaceae* and all that. I simply can't imagine what life would be like without them.

The thing about these fungi (better known as yeasts) is that they are obsessed with sugar. I'd like to say it's all they think about.* They float around in the air looking for warm, damp places with sugar in them. When they find such places they descend and have an orgy, eating sugar like it's going out of fashion and reproducing by the million within the space of a few hours. It's a good life. Oh, and when yeasts get to work, what goes in one end as sugar comes out of the other as carbon dioxide and alcohol. This is one cool fungus.

The sugars that drive these little fellas so wild occur

---

* But that would be silly. They aren't capable of conscious thought because they're microscopic plants.

naturally in plants, particularly in fruit. The skin of a fruit or grain is designed specifically to keep the greedy bastards out, because all that sugar is intended by the plants in question as food for the kids – the seeds which will hopefully fall to the ground before growing up into plants themselves. But, as the fruit becomes ripe and ready to fall it goes a bit mushy, the outer skin softens and, if the conditions are right, yeasts muscle in, turning sugar into alcohol and gas. That's how it works. That's what we now call fermentation.

Of course we didn't know this until about a hundred and thirty years ago, although by the Middle Ages we had figured out that there was something in the air, referred to as 'godisgoode', that caused the reaction. We had also worked out that we could keep back some of the mush from one brew and use it to ferment the next. But before this the transformation of grain and grape into beer and wine appeared nothing short of miraculous. And if it was a gift from the gods, it must have been given for a pretty good reason.

The *Epic of Gilgamesh* is the oldest known narrative poem in the world. It is just one variation on a theme common to the mythology of virtually every culture: humanity's first, awful realization of knowledge. In Christianity, God placed knowledge in an apple, hanging tantalizingly just within reach, and told Adam not to touch it, no matter what. Eve couldn't resist, and got us chucked out of the Garden of Eden. In Greek mythology, Pandora was charged with guarding a box full of really interesting secrets and told never to open it. When she succumbed to her curiosity, disease, famine, death and all other sorrows and miseries were unleashed from the box into the world, but she was left with one thing in the bottom of the box: hope. There is an African myth very similar to the Pandora legend, in which, remaining at the bottom of the empty casket, is not hope but a gourd of beer. The pattern is clear. In the oldest stories ever told, there came a point in our birth as a species where we realized we were mortal. Some of us simply had to deal with it, or pin our hopes on things looking up in the afterlife. But others were happier with their lot. Because they had beer.

Have brain, will mash it

The sinking of a few pints to drown your sorrows is as old as civilization itself, but where stories like that of Gilgamesh and the African Pandora stray from the truth is that we were larging it in one way or another long before beer came on the scene. Archaeological evidence shows that we have been getting high since we first started forming tribes of hunter-gatherers in the Upper Palaeolithic period, or the later Stone Age (about 38,000 to 45,000 years ago). It's easy to imagine primitive bands spending every waking minute hunting for food, trying to keep the rain off and attempting to scare away sabre-toothed tigers, but the consensus among archaeologists and anthropologists now is that our ancestors probably only worked a five-hour day at most, and spent the rest of the day chilling out, enjoying far more leisure time than most of us do today.* Once Stone Age man clocked off, it seems he had

---

* Two centuries ago John Stuart Mill declared that there had never been a labour-saving device invented that saved anyone a minute's labour. Computers today mean we can work far more quickly than we used to.

enough time on his hands to invent language, crafts and art, not to mention indulging in a little mind alteration. Every human society, throughout history, has known and used one or more intoxicating substances. Whether they were taken sparingly or liberally, with religious associations or without, for as long as we've been carrying these big brains around we have been trying to alter the way they make us think and behave by taking drugs to change our mood, our perception or both. And we do this because, for most people, the truth of everyday life is an unbearable, harshly lit reality of pain, compromise, work, disappointment, taxes, Simon Cowell, and inexorable ageing. Richard Rudgley, opening his book *The Alchemy of Culture: Intoxicants in Society*, sums it up perfectly:

> The universal human need for liberation from the restrictions of mundane existence is satisfied by experiencing altered states of consciousness. That we dream every night – whether we remember it or not – shows that we have a natural predisposition to these altered states, but people also pursue them in more active ways. Some follow the paths of prayer or meditation in their quest for spiritual insight, whilst others are transported to the higher planes by way of ecstasies induced by art, music, sexual passion or intoxicating substances.

Humans have always been an omnivorous race as well as an experimental one, and the first intoxicating substances we used were those that occur naturally in plants. We figured

---

Does this mean we have more leisure time or does it mean we do twice as much work?

out pretty quickly which ones were food, which were poisonous, and which were somewhere in between. Berries and leaves have since been used for their energy-giving qualities, for a psychological lift, and – every now and again – for intoxication.

The first person ever to get pissed probably did so on a forerunner of wine, given the ease with which fruit can ferment. No one really knows when we first took control of fermentation and started making it happen deliberately, or where it began, but it is safe to assume that we stumbled across it by accident not long after we started walking upright, by inadvertently eating fermented berries and realizing that they took the edge off a bad day's hunting and made us feel a little bolder down the watering hole.*

Fermentation also happens naturally with grain – it just requires conditions that do not occur as readily. Grain is a little more shrewdly designed than fruit. The outer coating is much tougher and the sugary food for the seed is stored as starch. It won't ferment in the open because the process that softens the skin and turns the starch to sugar won't happen while it's still on the stem. But if grain is harvested and stored in pots, and the pots get left out allowing the contents to get damp, the grain can be fooled. It's warm and wet and the seed thinks it's in the ground, so the skin softens, the grain germinates and sprouts, the starch inside the kernel turns to fermentable sugar and the yeasts come gleefully charging in like microscopic Viking raiders. They plunder the seed pod and ferment the sugars, producing a husky mush that vaguely

---

* Even elephants eat fermenting berries deliberately to get plastered. And we're much cleverer than them.

resembles beer. These ancient beers would often have other flavourings such as herbs added to them. They also contained grapes or honey, which added much more than flavour: both are rich sources of sugar, and are natural environments for *Saccharomyces Cerevisiae*, the dominant yeast strain in beer before modern science allowed us to mess around with it. Of course, the ancients didn't know this – but they would have seen that fermentation carried out with grapes and/or honey worked much better.*

Again, this process was probably discovered accidentally, but it does require the grain to be gathered and stored. This means that for beer to become widespread, we had to settle down into fixed communities and begin storing grain in heavy clay pots, as opposed to merely picking leaves off interesting-looking bushes while we wandered across the plains. Archaeological evidence of booze dates back to the first stable communities, a mere four or five thousand years. So which came first: the desire to settle down and put a roof between ourselves and the sky, or the urge to brew beer? Many archaeologists have little doubt: it is now widely believed that one of the main reasons we founded stable communities in the first place was so we could get down to the business of brewing. If this is true, it would of course mean that beer is the root cause behind the emergence of civilization.†

---

* American brewer Dogfish Head has created a beer called Midas Touch which is based on such ancient recipes, brewed with honey, white Muscat grape and saffron. While it echoes the flavours of stone age beer, I'm pretty certain that advances in brewing technology mean it tastes much, much nicer.

† Which would allow you to argue rather tenuously that drinking beer is

Getting drunk and the meaning of life

Once alcohol was on the scene, it seems to have quickly displaced most other drugs in settled societies. In addition to its primary role of cheering us up because we are going to die, it was significant in a wider spiritual sense. The story of Gilgamesh was only the first of many examples of a connection between beer (or wine) and the gods. As we didn't have a clue about yeasts and how alcohol occurred, the state of inebriation was regarded as a divine experience. The body feels possessed by spirits which bestow not only confidence and euphoria, but also inspiration. Such was the transformation produced by booze, so magical did it seem, that everyone naturally assumed it must be of divine origin. This idea occurs repeatedly across cultures that, as far as we know, had no contact with each other.

This spiritual dimension meant that in many societies the

---

the meaning of life. And you could go even further than that. Astronomers have detected the presence of vast clouds of alcohol in space, measuring billions of miles across. One cloud – Sagittarius B2N – is located near the centre of the Milky Way. Scientists believe alcohol molecules cling to interstellar dust particles. Did such particles arrive on earth in the frozen head of a comet? Is alcohol truly a gift from outer space? All we can do is speculate, but sod it, let's speculate: 'archeo-botanist' Patrick McGovern muses, 'It's a gigantic leap from the formation of ethanol to the evolution of the intricate biochemical machinery of the simplest bacteria, not to mention the human organism. But as we peer into the night sky we might ask why there is an alcoholic haze at the centre of our galaxy, and what role alcohol played in jump-starting and sustaining life on our planet.' Alcohol as the source of life on Earth? By Jove, it's an argument that works for me.

use of alcohol was tightly controlled. The Romans are famous for their enjoyment of wine, but it only flowed freely for those in power. In this great civilization, one of the two grounds on which a man could legally kill his wife was if she had been drinking (the other being adultery), and it was customary for men to give female relatives a kiss on the lips to check that they had not been tippling on the sly. The Aztecs in pre-Columbian Mexico were very harsh on anyone found drinking to excess when they shouldn't have been, because drunkenness was a sacred state. You could be put to death for getting blagged socially, but at religious celebrations it was compulsory. If you didn't get absolutely senseless the gods would be displeased, because drunkenness was, again, their gift to mankind and should therefore be honoured.

Beer Culture BC

The ancient Mesopotamians, Egyptians and Babylonians all left records describing how they took the happy accident of fermentation and made more of it. There was more rain then in the Middle East than there is now, and it is believed that it was here that cereals were first cultivated for food, from around 6000 BC. It's not clear exactly when people started deliberately fermenting these cereals into beer, but they were writing about it at least as far back as 3000 BC. Stone tablets dating back to at least 1800 BC contain the Mesopotamian hymn to the Sumerian goddess Ninkasi. She was the queen of the *abzu*, fresh water springs that were regarded as holy by the Sumerians. Borne of 'sparkling fresh water', she was the goddess who could 'satisfy the desire' and 'sate the heart', because she turned that water into beer. The hymn on those tablets is actually an incredibly lyrical guide to brewing – the earliest known recipe for a beer in which 'the waves rise, the waves fall' during fermentation, and the finished brew pours like 'the onrush of the Tigris and Euphrates'.* 'Sweet aromatics' and honey are added, again demonstrating how yeast was introduced to the brew.

The Babylonians also hired the first barmaids, a job which was taken far more seriously than it is now; the penalty for serving a short measure was death by drowning.

Translations from ancient stone tablets reveal one of the earliest drinking songs ever written, a song that should surely be revived and included in the repertoire of any self-respecting rugby team:

> Sweet beer is in the Buninu barrel.
> Cup-bearer, waiter-waitress, servants and brewer
>   gather around.
> When I have abundance of beer,
> I feel great. I feel wonderful.
> By the beer, I am happy.
> My heart is full of joy, my liver is full of luck.
> When I am full of gladness, my liver wears the dress
>   befitting a queen.

The Sumerians had one style of beer called *Kash*, which meant 'sweet beer'. The fact that centuries later, the Egyptians paid workers in beer has inevitably given rise to the story

---

* Sumer was a region of Mesopotamia, widely believed to be the cradle of civilization. It occupied the land between and around the Tigris and Euphrates rivers and is now – ironically given modern attitudes to alcohol – part of Iraq.

that this is the origin of the English word 'cash'. Sadly it isn't, but that does nothing to undermine the incredible import-ance beer had in many ancient societies.

Why the confusion though? Well, while the Sumerians may have been the earliest drinkers, they were left standing at the bar by the *really* big drinkers of ancient times.' If we believe the records they left behind, the ancient Egyptians remain matchless to this day as world-class boozers. Forty per cent of all grain harvested went into making beer. Drinking practices, beliefs and customs were meticulously recorded. Popular phrases and sayings from the time of the pharaohs such as, 'The mouth of the perfectly happy man is filled with beer,' and: 'Do not cease to drink beer / To eat, to intoxicate thyself / To make love and celebrate the good days' only start to hint at how seriously they took their drinking.

More food than drink, a thick, porridge-like substance that had to be drunk through straws made from reeds, beer was more important in ancient Egypt than it has ever been to anyone since; it was a cornerstone of the entire culture and society. It had its own hieroglyph – the symbol for food was a loaf of bread and a jug of beer – and records discovered in Tutankhamun's tomb clearly show him and Nefertiti enjoying a few jars. Nefertiti's temple actually had its own brewery, complete with wall frescoes depicting courtiers vom-iting after getting bombed on the stuff it produced.

Beer had its own goddess, Hathor, who often appeared in the guise of a fearsome bull. According to legend, Ra the sun god was feeling a bit pissed off with humanity in general and had decided to wipe us out. Hathor was the bull for the job. But after Ra had sent her on her way, he relented. He flooded the plain where Hathor was due to arrive on earth with beer, dyed red to look like blood. Hathor drank the whole lot and fell into a stupor. When she awoke, she had forgotten all about her task and went back to heaven to nurse her hangover. Henceforth she was praised in hymns:

> We soothe your majesty daily (with offerings of beer),
> Your heart rejoices when you hear our song.
> Our hearts exult at a glance of your majesty.
> You are queen of the wreath
> The queen of dance
> The queen of drunkenness without end.

There was a whole array of types of beer, some of which were so influential they seem to have influenced language. One particular type brewed for everyday use was known as *bouza.**

Apart from a jar to wind down after a hard day's pyramid building, there were special beers drunk at feasts and offerings. Beer formed the basis of most medical remedies, treating ailments from scorpion stings to heart conditions. The *Papyrus Ebers*, the single greatest medical text of ancient times, gives 600 prescriptions for every known ailment of the time, and beer is an ingredient of 118 of them. They even had a beer which was used for enemas, an experience which we can only speculate upon in wonder. However, there were some Egyptian physicians who insisted beer was bad, and Egypt gives us the earliest known description of death by alcoholism, dating to around 2800 BC: 'His earthly abode was

---

* *Bouza* is an Arabic word and, sadly, has no direct relationship with the English word 'booze'. A wheat beer named *bouza* is still popular today in Egypt.

25

torn and broke by beer. His ka escaped before it was called by God.'

As with all big drinkers, the Egyptians were quite dogmatic about how you should treat a hangover. Eublus, a writer living around 400 BC, wrote:

> Wife, quick! Some cabbage boil, of virtuous healing,
> That I may rid me of this seedy feeling.

In the second century AD Athenaeus still swore by the same cure:

> Last evening you were beer-drinking deep,
> So now your head aches. Go to sleep.
> Take some boiled cabbage when you wake,
> There's end of your headache.*

You may laugh, but recent scientific research has established that cabbage contains chemicals that help neutralize acetaldehydes, an unpleasant by-product of the liver's attempts to metabolize alcohol.

Beer also played an important part in Egyptian death rituals. It went into the tomb with the dead along with meat to provide sustenance for the long journey into the afterlife. For good measure, once the body had been mummified, the Liturgy of Opening the Mouth was performed: the body was

---

* Or at least, several books on beer assure me this is the case. But it's funny how millennia later, when you translate it into English from an ancient language, it still rhymes. That's all I'm saying.

unwrapped and beer was poured into the mouth just before it was sealed into the tomb.

The symbolism of beer was widely debated in Egypt. People dreamt about beer, and these dreams were taken to mean something. During the Nineteenth Dynasty (about 1300 BC) an entire book was written on the dream language of beer, which included such pronouncements as:

> When he dreams of sweet beer he will become happy.
> When he dreams of bakery beer he will live.
> When he dreams of cellar beer he will have security.

Beer was the celebrity endorsement of its day. If you had beer in your blurb, whether you were trying to sell ass's milk or the latest deity, people listened.

Ancient beer would have been very sweet, and various herbs were added to it to take the edge off. A few years ago, the brewer Scottish & Newcastle (as they were then) collaborated with archaeologists on a project to rediscover the exact formula for a typical Egyptian beer with the intention of recreating it. With his customary panache and imagination, Mohamed Al Fayed launched the beer through Harrods as Tutankhamun Ale. Surprisingly, it doesn't seem to have caught on.

•

Beer, then, is as old as civilization itself, and is intimately linked with the earliest great cultures in our history. And yet this probably comes as something of a surprise. That's because beer culture suffered at the hands of people who were not keen on it and had its place in history marginalized retrospectively. On the one hand, the conquest of the Middle East by the teetotal Muslims put an end to Mesopotamian and Egyptian brewing culture. On the other, the Mediterranean has a climate ultimately more suitable for the cultivation of grapes than barley, and the Greeks and Romans had already made sure that wine was the preferred drink of the region. Wine has remained the 'civilized' drink ever since.

But throughout its history beer has proved a great survivor, taking advantage of circumstances and popping up in new places and forms as old ones are suppressed. Above a certain latitude, vineyards don't grow too well, whereas grain is suited to a cooler climate. Also, the Med was a busy trading area, and good ideas spread quickly. The seagoing Phoenicians are thought to have introduced barley (the most common grain now used in brewing) to northern Europe, but the art of brewing was already well known to Nordic, Finnish and Celtic tribes. When their vast empire reached British shores, the wine-loving Romans would find that beer had beaten them here.*

---

* Although, it has to be said, the practice of beer enemas doesn't seem to have travelled well.

Chapter Two

'Pissing under the board as they sit'

Two thousand years of British boozing

'You smell of goat'

You had to admit, as pubs go, this place was something special. The regulars were, to a man, the hardest guys who ever lived. They drank beer from huge, ornately carved horns which seemed never to empty, despite the fact that they partied morning, noon and night, without end. The gaffer had done something really quite special with the place too. At the centre stood a massive tree, so big that some said its roots supported the earth. And you just had to love this gimmick: tethered to the base of the tree was a goat. And God knows what they were feeding it, but when they milked it, the goat produced the finest beer you'd ever tasted. Sadly, it's not there any more. Not because it's been turned into an All Bar One or an O'Neill's or anything like that. No, the thing is, the hall in Valhalla, the place where the dead spent eternity feasting with Odin, the father of the gods, just seems to have disappeared somewhere in history.

Northern European mythology is full of ale drinking. Not unreasonably, beer was pretty central to any representation of paradise. The Vikings went on about it more than most, but then again, as the above shows, that's because they had the best story.

Beer was pretty important in the real world too. It was used to pay fines, tolls, rents and debts, as well as being the cornerstone of the northern European diet. The Vikings may have made the biggest song and dance about beer, but it was playing an important role centuries before they rose to prominence. The Romans found beer culture firmly entrenched when they came north. Pliny the Elder, the orator and writer, huffed:

> The nations of the west have their own intoxicant from grain soaked in water; there are many ways of making it in Gaul and Spain, and under different names, though the principle is the same.

The Emperor Julian felt that this 'wine made from barley' was an insult to the god of wine and revelry himself, who clearly was altogether far too classy for these savages to appreciate, and wrote an ode of disgust to beer which just might have given the future authors of Viking legend a bit of defiant inspiration:

> Who made you and from what?
> By the true Bacchus I know you not.
> He smells of nectar
> But you smell of goat.

The Romans brought wine with them from their sunnier homeland, and stuck doggedly with it, but in Britain they were swimming against the tide. As we'll see in this chapter, from then until now, beer has defined us as a nation.

Early British brewing

When they reached Britain, the Romans found brewing as established here as it was everywhere else in northern Europe. The difference was that the early Brits favoured mead and cider rather than beer.

Essentially, anything that has naturally occurring sugars can be fermented to produce an alcoholic drink of some kind. Britain was heavily forested at this time, and the population clearly saw no point clearing the trees to plant fields for grain when they could just as easily get leathered on stuff that grew without them having to go to all that effort. This only began to change when, not for the last time, the Germans taught us what proper drinking was all about. In the fifth century AD the Germanic Angles and Saxons began to colonize Britain, the Angles eventually giving England its name and identity as distinct from the Celts in Wales, Scotland and Ireland. They loved to drink *ol* or *ealu*, words which evolved into 'ale', and the country had its national drink. The hard, beer-drinking tribes of north Europe forced the wine-loving Romans to withdraw, and we never looked back.

While 'ale' was the most common name for our beloved beverage, 'beer' was also used by the Anglo-Saxons from about the sixth or seventh century. This word derives from the Latin *biber*, 'a drink', which in turn comes from *bibere*, 'to drink'. Beer was so vital, its very name was synonymous with drink in its broadest sense.

Brewing remained a simple process. Malt was made by boiling barley grain to get the fermentable sugars, then straining out the grain husks. Yeast was then allowed to do its job, and finally a variety of flavourings and preservatives such as rosemary and thyme might be added. This routine was followed in most households, an everyday activity just like baking, and it became the responsibility of the woman or 'ale-wife'. But there is more to the ale-wife than Dark Ages sexism. In almost all ancient societies, mythologies state that beer was a gift given specifically to women from a goddess (never a male god) and women remained bonded in complex religious relationships with feminine deities, who blessed their brewing vessels. Recently, anthropologists have reported the amusement of contemporary isolated tribal societies upon learning that the men who had come to their villages to tell them how great the modern world was actually claimed that beer was kind of a male thing. Within Western culture, the ale-wife was to remain the key figure in brewing until the sixteenth century, when the general trend towards male dominance in all aspects of society, driven in no small measure by the patriarchy of the Church, meant that beer was inevitably claimed from women and improved by men – in God's name of course.

Several centuries of sousedness

The history of beer drinking gallops along at a fair crack through the Middle Ages, to the extent that we're about to cover several centuries over the course of a few pages. That's not to imply that beer was unimportant – on the contrary, it was absolutely central to life. The problem is, medieval Britons were somewhat less forthcoming than, say, ancient Egyptians. They didn't document their relationship with beer as meticulously, so we know much less about what they got up to. This may be down to the fact that in this case, beer was not accorded any spiritual status by the Church or state. Or it may quite possibly be that they were simply too wazzed to write about it.

Nothing was more embedded in British culture. Beer was an integral part of all diets, medical practitioners prescribed it, it was an essential aid to heavy, agrarian labour; and it was essential in any religious or civil celebration. Beer was not just an intoxicant, it was a valuable source of nourishment at a time when food supplies could be scarce and unreliable. Even when food was plentiful, for most people it was a monotonous and heavy diet of bread, vegetables, salt fish and, if you were lucky, a bit of cheese. Beer livened it up and made it all go down a little easier.

Beer was also a safe alternative to drinking water. As concentrated population centres grew up, water purity became a real problem, and diseases like cholera and typhoid were widespread. Compared to water, beer was relatively safe because it had been boiled during its production and contained vitamin B, which helps stave off disease, as well as calcium and magnesium. Having said that, there was beer and there was beer. When the first, strong brew was made, the grain would be recycled and mashed again to produce a weaker beer known as small beer or table beer, which was lower in alcohol and more common for everyday use rather than festivities. For centuries small beer would be drunk by women and children and was served with any meal including breakfast.

All this is interesting enough, but there is no getting away from the simple truth that, even back then, we loved getting trousered. We always have. If the British have a reputation for drunkenness now, it is only a continuation of our historical infamy throughout Europe. The modern-day nasty, drunken minority of travelling football 'fans' who supposedly spoil it for the nice, peaceful majority are merely carrying on a centuries-old tradition. As early as the eighth century, St Boniface, a missionary who was born in Devon but spent most of his life travelling the Continent, wrote to Cuthbert, Archbishop of Canterbury:

> In your dioceses the vice of drunkenness is too frequent. This is an evil peculiar to pagans and to our race. Neither the Franks nor the Gauls nor the Lombards nor the Romans nor the Greeks commit it.

In the twelfth century the historian William of Malmesbury, in his *History of the Kings of England*, wrote that at the time of the Norman Conquest:

> Drinking in particular was a universal practice, in which occupation they passed entire nights as well as days ... They were accustomed to eat till they became surfeited, and drink till they were sick.

According to Malmesbury, this proved our downfall. Remember how in 1066 England was being attacked by the Vikings as well as the Normans? Harold pulled off a victory against the Viking Harald Hardraade at York. We all know how hard the Vikings were, so this was a victory worthy of riotous celebration. Hung-over, the army then had to march back down south to meet the Normans near Hastings. We all know what happened there. Malmesbury reckons the battle was lost by the English partly because they turned up on the field completely arseholed, which led them to engage the Norman army 'more with rashness and precipitate fury than with military skill'.*

A hundred years after the battle, another travelling intellectual expat, John of Salisbury, wrote in a letter to a friend that, 'The constant habit of drinking has made the English famous among all foreign nations.'

One problem was that there was no way to measure the alcoholic strength of beer, as there is now. Small beer was produced by re-fermenting the stuff so you could be certain it would be weaker, but things were much less certain with the first brew. And yet the British somehow seemed to brew theirs stronger than anyone else. In 1598, Paul Hentzner, a visitor to Britain, commented with fear and admiration, 'Beer is the general drink and excellently well tasted, but strong and what soon fuddles'. Another 'problem' was that many drinking vessels, such as horns and bowls, couldn't be put down without their contents spilling everywhere. The only solution was to down them in one. By the end of the twelfth century, drinking was done in bouts. In 1236 Archbishop Edmund complained of, 'the ill practice by which all that drink together are obliged to equal draughts, and he carries away the credit who hath made most drunk and taken off the largest cups'.

The Magna Carta instituted standard measures for ale

---

* When you think about it, this could explain a lot: the famous arrow that pierced the King's eye was probably fired by some blethered idiot on his own side.

and wine, and Church and State called for moderation in drinking; the populace were too drunk to notice. Society revolved around popular celebrations known as 'ales': bride-ales, church-ales, midsummer-ales and lamb-ales were gatherings where plenty of alcohol was drunk, and they frequently degenerated into mayhem. Bride-ales, or bridals, were particularly famous. The word 'bride' can even be traced back to the same root word as 'brew'. The bride's mother would brew a batch of ale for the wedding, a reception would be held on the village green and the beer would be sold. Passing travellers would buy it at a standard rate, but wedding guests paid a ludicrous amount, thereby helping to provide the bride's family with the dowry. Scenes of utter drunken carnage were common across medieval England, and although laws were passed to curtail such celebrations they had little effect.

Another popular custom was the wonderfully named 'groaning-ale'. When it was known that a woman was pregnant, the local ale-wife would brew a batch of particularly strong ale, timed to mature for the time of groaning, or childbirth. When labour began the beer would be cracked open, midwife and labouring mother drinking heartily to help them through the ordeal. Records even tell of the newborn baby being washed with the beer.* Beer was the stuff of life itself, and British citizens were baptized in it. Clearly, something so fundamental to our lives could not be left in the hands of women.

---

* Before you throw your hands up in horror, this is where you have to remember that beer was pure and germ-free, much safer than water.

Habits and hops

Following the decline of the Roman Empire, the Catholic Church gradually became the dominant power across Europe. Via the monasteries, the Church came to dominate brewing in much the same way as it did many other aspects of life. Initially it may seem odd to think of the Church being so enthusiastic about beer, but alcohol and religion have been intimately connected throughout history. This relationship reveals a lot about how booze became the one drug it's legally OK to get scunnered on in Western society.

Booze has never had any shortage of people eager to condemn it, but on the whole it has been regarded throughout most of its history as a good thing. Partly this is because there is more to alcoholic drinks than just getting drunk, but even as an intoxicant, alcohol escaped censure for a long time in European, Christian society. Drugs which persuaded people that they had a one-on-one relationship with God, or any other deity for that matter, posed a direct threat to the Church, which relied on centralized, patriarchal power where the word of God came through the priest, and ultimately the Pope. But the Church didn't have to worry when it came to booze. Alcohol may alter the conscious state, but not to the same degree as other intoxicants. Even if we entertain the idea that it heightens perception and brain activity, alcohol doesn't provide the gateway to new worlds that other drugs can. The overall depressant effects of alcohol suited the Church just fine. Overindulgence in booze doesn't impart understanding; it takes it away. As Brian Inglis puts it in his history of drugs, *The Forbidden Game*, it 'takes away the cares of one world without granting entrance to another'.

But the main reason the Church was happy with booze was of course that wine is pretty central to the Bible. In the Old Testament it is usually coupled with bread as being God's gift to man, and is prescribed as a treatment for disease. In the New Testament Christ's first miracle is to turn water into wine, and damn fine wine at that, the best of the feast at the wedding in Canaa.* Christ later tells the story of the Good Samaritan who treated the wounds of the man he found injured with oil and wine. At the Last Supper, Jesus blesses wine as his holy blood, and promises his disciples that they will all drink wine together again in heaven.† Paul advises Timothy to 'drink no longer water, but use a little wine for thy stomach's sake and thine own infirmities'. And so on. These are just some of the hundreds of references to wine in the Bible. We can all be subjective in our interpretations of Scripture, but it requires a highly developed faculty for selective blindness to dispute the fact that in Biblical times wine was very highly valued.‡ It has even been suggested that this was a decisive factor in the Prophet Mohammad's decision to ban alcohol among

---

* Well, it would be the best ever, wouldn't it? It's crucial to the story. You couldn't have the Son of God performing his first ever miracle and producing a £2.99 bottle of Liebfraumilch. It would be embarrassing. He had his reputation as The Saviour of All Mankind to think about.

† The communion transformation of wine into Christ's blood mirrors, and is possibly explained by, the 'miraculous' translation of grape juice into wine. Think about it. If that's not a miracle, then miracles don't exist.

‡ Not to mention very creative use of sentences beginning with words like, 'I think what Our Lord *meant* to say was . . .'

his followers – in order to distance them from the Christians.

Many Christians of course have had a problem with drink; we'll see when we get to the temperance story that the movement against drink was driven by organized Christianity. That's because, despite the intertwined history of drink and Christianity, there's that hoary religious chestnut of human free will, which leads us always to want too much of a good thing and to overindulge. Even in societies where drink was held in the highest regard, the state of drunkenness was usually condemned as a sin. But if drunkenness was a sin, wine could be held no more responsible for it than meat was responsible for the sin of gluttony. Writing in defence of wine in the second century AD, Clement of Alexandria said, 'It is not what entereth in that defileth a man, but that which goes out of his mouth.' Two centuries later, John Chrysostom, a Greek saint, attacked those who claimed wine itself was evil, saying:

> When they see any person disgracing themselves from drunkenness, instead of reproving such, blame the fruit given them by God, and say, 'Let there be no wine'. We should say then in answer to such, 'Let there be no drunkenness; for wine is the work of God, but drunkenness is the work of the Devil.'

Arguments like these allowed the Church to continue to reconcile itself to drink.* Of course, what the Churchmen

---

* Most Christians today can appreciate the distinction made by St Chrysostom, but there are still those who are selective about the bits of the Bible to which they choose to apply their literal, to the letter, interpretation. I've found it's not worth trying to argue with them. But if you get accosted were really into was wine, and here we're talking about beer. But what is important is that, once wine had won the argument, no one could really object to beer. Beer used to be a lot stronger than it is now, but it was still nowhere near as alcoholic as wine. If wine was an acceptable intoxicant, then beer could hardly be resisted on the grounds that it got you scoobied. Wine was what the arguments were over because it was biblically symbolic, as well as being the drink most prevalent in southern Europe and around the Mediterranean – most notably in Italy, where the power of the Church was based. But it won the argument on behalf of all non-distilled alcoholic drinks. In Northern Europe, where we had to concentrate on fermenting grain rather than grape, this helped beer prosper.

So it should come as no surprise that the monasteries felt that they should be the ones to control brewing. Originally they began brewing beer as part of a wider pattern of self-sufficiency pioneered by St Benedict. Everything Benedictines needed to survive was to be produced inside the monastery walls so that the monks would not have to venture out and face the wicked temptations of the world. So beer simply had to be a fundamental part of the monastic experience.* During Lent, many monks survived on beer alone, and they managed to pack away a fair amount all year round. And although it was a staple of healthy living, beer's intoxicating properties were not unappreciated. Records from Burton Abbey, founded

---

by a nice, polite, smiling person with a curious fashion sense who tells you you'll rot in hell if you take another sip, feel free, give it a go. Go on, I'm right behind you.

* Well, it would, wouldn't it? Cooped up in a draughty stone building doing calligraphy with no women around . . .

by one Wulfric Spot, Earl of Mercia, in 1004, show that the regular *daily* allowance for its monks consisted of 'one gallon of strong ale often supplemented by one gallon of weak ale'.

The monastic brewing tradition only survives today in Belgium's Trappist beers, but at one time extended throughout Britain. As a schoolboy I visited Fountain's Abbey in North Yorkshire where, if I hadn't spent the whole time engrossed in a game of Top Trumps with David Firth and Steven Hargate, I would have been fascinated to learn that in its heyday the abbey produced a quarter of a million pints of beer every year.*

Monasteries were often large communities. As well as the monks, there were all the people who looked after them and ran the place – the artisans and their families, not to mention the regular stream of pilgrims seeking shelter on their way to and from holy sites across the country – so brewing had to take place on a large scale. Being scholarly types, monks developed a scientific approach to brewing. In the eighth and ninth centuries, Bavarian monks discovered that the hop plant, a hardy perennial and a member of the same family as both cannabis and the nettle, contained oils and resins that were very effective in both flavouring and preserving ale. Hops had been used in Egyptian brewing as one of many flavourings, but the art remained lost until the monks rediscovered it. Until this point various herbs and other plants such as bog myrtle, rosemary and yarrow had been used to

---

* But then you have to appreciate that it is far healthier for ten-year-old boys to be more interested in the maximum altitude of jet fighter aircraft and the fright factors of the Werewolf versus Dracula than in the historic production of beer. Isn't it?

season ale, but the taste imparted by hops is quite distinct. Hops give beer as we know it today its bitter bite and wonderful aroma. By perfecting and popularizing the use of hops, the monks created the basic recipe for beer that has remained largely unchanged ever since: barley, yeast, water and hops.

But more than its flavour, the hop's preservative properties proved crucial. The process of brewing was still poorly understood, and people were unaware of the nature of yeast and the role it played. In many countries brewing was impossible during summer months because high temperatures spoiled the yeast, or competing strains of wild, airborne yeasts would interfere, and the brew would be ruined. This meant that beers brewed in spring often had to last through the summer, and hops greatly improved the chances of this. Before hops, the only way of making beer robust and long-lasting was to give it a high alcohol content. Hops permitted beers to be brewed less strong, introducing a new, more subtle taste to the drinker of strong, excessively sweet ale. Until the fifteenth century the words 'beer' and 'ale' had been used interchangeably, but hops created an important distinction between the two.

Britain resisted the lure of hops a little longer than the rest of Europe. They were finally brought here by Flemish traders who landed in Kent and Sussex and couldn't stomach the taste of heavy English ale. A long battle ensued between the advocates of the two drinks: the new-fangled hoppy beer and the old-fashioned strong sweet ale. On the Continent, this war had been going on for hundreds of years. In twelfth-century Bohemia, now part of the Czech Republic, King Wenceslas of Christmas-carol fame was a keen patron of brewing. The man so famed for his Yuletide generosity made it a crime punishable by death to export his prized hops anywhere else. Today Czech hops such as the Saaz variety are prized above all others, and are used in many of the best-tasting lagers such as Pilsner Urquell and Budvar. In the opposite corner you had traditional Brits, with Henry VIII instructing his court brewer never to use hops, and towns like Shrewsbury and Norwich banning the 'wicked and pernicious weed' outright. Andrew Boorde, writing in 1542, blamed hops for pretty much everything he could think of:

> Beer is made of malte and hopes and water; it is the natural drinke for a Dutch man, and nowe of late dayes it is much used in England to the detriment of many Englisshe people; specially it killeth them the which be troubled with the colic and the stone and the strangulation, for the drink is a cold drinke, yet it doth make a man fat, and doth inflate the belly, as it doth appeare by the Dutch-men's faces and belyes.

But the taste for bitterness spread, helped by the fact that hopped beer lasted longer. By the 1520s hops were being grown in Kent, and have been with us ever since. As the debate subsided, so did the distinction between beer and ale, and the two words became interchangeable once more. But there were still those grumbling about hops by the end of the sixteenth century, as this quote, which also reveals the long history of one of our favourite insults, illustrates:

> Ale made of barley malt and good water doth make a man strong, but nowadies few brewers doth brew it as

they ought, for they add slimy and heavy baggage unto it thinking thereby to please tosse pots and to increase the vigour of it.

Henry VIII's antipathy towards hops might have had something to do with his famous dislike of the monastic tradition, or it might just have been his equally famous sweet tooth. Whatever, his dissolution of the monasteries in 1536 had a significant impact on the development of British drinking patterns. He couldn't stop the eventual triumph of hops, but he did deal a body blow to the consumption of wine. Not satisfied with beer, monasteries also cultivated vineyards to produce the copious amounts of wine they consumed. Much of this was needed for the sacraments, with services involving communion occurring daily, but, like beer, the surplus was sold outside the monastery walls, where there was a small but lucrative market for it.

Ever since the Norman Conquest wine has been the preferred tipple of the French-influenced British upper class – just one of a set of class preferences that have survived to this day. Where there is a French alternative and a Saxon one, the French is superior. So while most people have a good laugh over a meal, the bourgeoisie enjoy bonhomie over their cuisine. But when Henry VIII dissolved the monasteries he effectively wiped out the English wine industry and cast the vast majority of the nation firmly as beer drinkers. Despite fashionable dalliances with various wines and spirits we have remained so ever since.

A trip north of the border

They do things differently in Scotland, always have, and beer is no exception. The origins of Scottish beer are tied up with arguably the most celebrated concoction in the history of beer, the lost heather ale of the Picts. The Picts were small, aggressive and heavily tattooed ('pict' and 'picture' are possibly derived from the same Latin root). They were also so hard that even the Roman legions couldn't conquer them.

It's sometimes claimed that Pictish heather ale was the first beer brewed in the British Isles. No one knows for sure because by the eleventh century, the Picts were more or less extinct. But as befits a people like the Picts, the legend is that this was an extraordinary brew. Heather was used for fermentation, but heather also harbours a naturally occurring white, mossy powder, known as *fogg*. *Fogg* has narcotic, even hallucinogenic properties, and it's reputed that the beer didn't just get you bevvied – it also made you trip.

The Irish claim it was the Vikings rather than the Picts who were the masters of heather ale. But whether it was Pictish or Viking, the legend behind the loss of the fabled recipe is always the same. The secret of brewing the beer was known only to the chieftains, and as they were hounded out of what is now Scotland (or Ireland) there came a point when only a father and son survived. They were threatened with torture and death if they did not reveal the recipe, and the father claimed he would reveal it only if his son were killed first, as he feared the son would murder him if he gave away their secret. The son was executed, and the father then revealed that they had fallen into his trap: the father had in fact feared his son would crack and reveal the recipe (or in some versions the father feared the son's torture would make him do the same). But now, with the son out of the way, there is nothing that will make the father reveal the recipe, and he takes it with him to his own grave.

Some brewing of heather ale survived in remote areas, and commercial production resumed in the mid 1990s, albeit without the hallucinogenic ingredients. Modern versions follow strict guidelines about the type of heather used, and about how it must be cleaned of any other substance before fermentation. I suppose it's just as well.*

The spirit of empire

By the fifteenth century water was regarded as a sign of poverty in Britain, and was drunk only as an act of penance. Somewhat later, even the Puritans depended on beer; to go without it was unthinkable. In 1620, the Pilgrim Fathers chose their landing spot in North America on the basis that they couldn't stay at sea much longer. The journal of the *Mayflower* reads, 'We could not now take time for further search or consideration; our victuals being much spent, especially our beere.'

It wasn't just the conviviality of a pint after a hard day's sailing they were missing. On top of the advantages already discussed, alcohol prevents bacteria from growing; and hops

---

* While you won't experience wild hallucinations (not on less than twenty bottles anyway), it's well worth checking out Fraoch heather ale, a bottled beer that's widely available.

have the added advantage of being a natural disinfectant, important benefits on a long sea voyage. These qualities didn't go unnoticed on land either. Records from St Bartholomew's Hospital and Christ's Hospital from the seventeenth century show that sick children averaged about three pints of beer a day.

For all these merits though, beer's ability to make you merry gradually became more important than the rest of its manifold benefits. In 1583, Philip Stubbes, a Puritan, wrote a pamphlet, 'The Anatomy of Abuses' in which he vividly described the denizens of the ale house who sat drinking:

> All day long, yea, all the night, peradventure all the week together, so long as any money is left, swilling, gulling and carousing from one to another, till never a one can speak a ready word ... How they stutter and stammer, stagger and reel to and fro, like madmen, some vomiting, spewing and disgorging their filthy stomachs, othersome pissing under the board as they sit ...

We have no accurate way of telling how strong beer was at this time, and we have to bear in mind the English talent for gross exaggeration, but much of it was almost certainly strong enough to put beers like today's Stella Artois to shame. In 1680 a Member of Parliament urged that, 'There must be a reformation of ale, which is now so strong that it is for a groat a quart. It is strong as wine and will burn like sack.'*

One of the most renowned drinkers of English beer was

---

* Sack was strong sherry or wine, rather than a bag made of fabric. But you never know. In this context perhaps he was looking for an unusual simile.

none other than Queen Elizabeth I, who was famous for liking her beer particularly strong. Demonstrating that rumours of royal boozing are nothing new, she described beer as 'an excellent wash', and would drink a quart for breakfast. When she visited Hatfield House the Earl of Leicester hastily wrote to Lord Burleigh, 'There is not one drop of good drink for her there. We were fain to send to London and Kenilworth and divers other places where ale was: her own beer was so strong as there was no man able to drink it.'

The demand for beer was insatiable, and kept increasing. Sure, the population was expanding rapidly, but that couldn't explain why per capita consumption of beer increased. In 1577 there was an alehouse for every 120 of the population. By 1636 this figure was one for every ninety-five. From 1684 the annual production of common brewers (wholesalers) and brewing victuallers (retailers) was recorded, and together with the estimated production from private brewing they were turning out nearly nineteen million barrels a year, or 2.3 pints per day for every man, woman and child in the country. At the end of the seventeenth century it was estimated that beer accounted for 28 per cent of the nation's total expenditure. When, about a century later, the Prince Regent proclaimed, 'Beer and beef have made us what we are,' he was boasting, not complaining, echoing sentiments felt in this eighteenth-century drinking song:

Ye true honest Britons who love your own land
Whose sires were so brave, so victorious, so free,
Who always beat France when they took her in hand –
Come join honest Britons in chorus with me.

Let us sing our own treasures, Old England's good cheer,
The profits and pleasures of stout British beer;
Your wine-tippling, dram-sipping fellows retreat,
But your beer-drinking Britons can never be beat.

The French with the vineyards are meagre and pale,
They drink of their squeezings of half-ripened fruit;
But we, who have hop yards to mellow our ale,
Are rosy and plump, and have freedom to boot.*

Beer drinking defined us: the places and occasions we drank beer, and the people we drank it with, were constant, unchanging pillars of British life. So when the nature of British life altered permanently, so did the way we drank beer. The sheer scale and speed of change in our society from the seventeenth century means we can only give the briefest of summaries here, but it's worth taking even a sketchy look in order to appreciate how the life of the ordinary beer drinker changed.

The fuel of a revolution

Following the feats and discoveries of the great explorers, all the large European powers went on a round-the-world boat race to 'discover' as much new territory as possible and claim it, its people and its resources, before the other lot got there. These voyages brought new products and new wealth back home. There was a sense of optimism, and a growing spirit of invention and industry.

---

* Al Murray, eat your heart out.

The growth of the British empire in India, America and Africa yielded great riches from trade in spices and cotton, not to mention slaves, and meant that there was a new class of merchants who became very rich indeed. The new, working wealthy wanted to prove they were just as good as the landowning aristocracy, and felt that buying up land themselves was the best way to achieve this. In France, the tension between old and new wealth led to revolution. In England, it helped produce the enclosures.

The fashion for land buying and the emergence of new methods of agriculture meant that the rolling, open landscape of Britain was transformed virtually overnight into tightly demarcated fields – private property – on which people who had lived and worked the land for centuries were no longer welcome. With nowhere to live and no means of making money, many people ended up in the newly built workhouses. But many more got on their carts and looked for work in factories, mills and mines in the rapidly expanding industrial towns. In the eighteenth century, we changed from a nation of farmers to a nation of factory workers.

This new wealth, technological change and tranformation of the landscape together revolutionized our drinking habits. Under the old agrarian lifestyle, people lived on the land they tilled; work and home were one, and drinking was a family thing. But the factory system threw large numbers of men together into artificial environments, free from the social constraints of having to behave in front of the wife and kids. They went to alehouses together to eat and drink, and did so to greater and greater excess.

Looking back, you can hardly blame them. Britain was the first nation to undergo industrialization, a process that brought with it some of the most appalling social conditions ever endured by any group of people not formally classified as slaves. The new industrial towns and cities grew rapidly and were poorly planned. Conditions in and outside work were grim. We all know about little urchins up chimneys and down mines, but perhaps these rote-learned stories actually prevent us from really appreciating the full horror of the time. Put simply, man and machine were treated as one. In 1832 J. P. Kay described conditions in the cotton mills:

> Whilst the engine runs, the people must work – men, women and children are yoked together with iron and steam. The animal machine – breakable in the best case ... is chained fast to the iron machine, which knows no suffering and no weariness.

For many, the only escape from this hell on earth was through drink.

When a society ends up with a chronic drinking problem its causes can usually be traced back to massive social upheaval coupled with a new injection of booze. Just as North American Indians were given cheap and nasty alcohol while white settlers were tearing their way of life apart, so in eighteenth-century Britain rootless people arrived in the cities, bewildered and traumatized, to find alcoholism waiting to welcome them with open arms. Excessive drinking had been a worry to kings and governments through the ages, but they hadn't seen anything to compare with the effect that the sudden injection of very strong, very cheap gin into this industrial nightmare was about to have. It was a catastrophe of their own making, and one that would pose the first major threat to beer and to the notion of Britain as a nation of beer drinkers. Not to mention to the actual existence of the British working people themselves.

'Drunk for 1d., dead drunk for 2d.'

Until the seventeenth century, distilled spirits were taken almost exclusively as a form of medicine. They conferred a feeling of warmth on those who drank them, and were ideal for fevers and other diseases. Spirits prevent organic matter in jars from rotting, so it seemed logical to some that they would preserve life. In 1450 Michael Schrick wrote, 'Anyone who drinks half a spoon of brandy every morning will never be ill . . . when someone is dying and a little brandy is poured into his mouth, he will speak before he dies.' Inevitably though, the proud imbibers of Britain started to drink spirits for intoxication rather than for purely medicinal uses.

In the late seventeenth century one of the most popular spirits in the country was French brandy. Then, Britain and France fell out with each other. Again. King and Parliament suddenly developed a desire for brandy to be much less popular. At the same time, they were worried about how powerful some of the emerging commercial brewers were becoming. Duties on gin were slashed to increase demand, and those on beer were simultaneously increased.

After 1694 gin cost less than beer. And we're not talking about the watered-down stuff we drink today either; this really was hard liquor, around double the strength of the gin we know. Consumption rocketed, and by 1742 a population one tenth the size of today's was necking around nineteen million gallons a year, ten times the amount we get through now. Anyone was free to open a gin shop, and it was estimated that in some parts of London one in every four houses sold gin.

Suddenly the whole population was mullahed. It wasn't just the blokes either, women took to drinking just as enthusiastically. Birth rates fell and mortality rocketed as people succumbed to 'gin drinker's liver'. People would drink themselves into a stupor, collapse on the floor of the drink shop, wake up and start drinking again. Some gin houses had cellars where comatose people could be dumped until they recovered sufficiently to drink again. This led to stories like the one about the apocryphal sign which hung above one Southwark gin shop, which sought to attract custom away from its competitors with: 'Drunk for 1d., dead drunk for 2d., clean straw for nothing'. Hogarth painted his famous *Gin Lane*, depicting a London with houses falling down, a blotto woman dropping her baby over a railing, the pawnbroker and undertaker the only happy people on the scene. People didn't need beer, couldn't afford it anyway, and were dying from alcohol poisoning. For the first time in its history beer was under threat.

Here was a population enduring terrible hardship, seemingly without end, with access to ludicrously strong, ludicrously cheap drink. Alcohol had become a narcotic rather than an intoxicant, enabling people to systematically remove themselves from the horrors they faced.

Taxes were nudged back up in a half-hearted attempt to deal with the problem, but the government soon became dependent on the huge revenue this produced. For a long time the rich didn't care what was happening in the slums. But they gradually realized that the gin epidemic was destroying their servants and the rank and file soldiers in the army, and finally this affected them. Eventually, pure self-interest resulted in a rate of duty which didn't prohibit gin consumption, but did make it impossible for the average working-class person to get bollocksed every day. Class suicide was averted.

Beer Street

Despite being comparatively expensive, beer was soon directly profiting from gin's bad press. In comparison, it could be promoted as a sensible and wholesome drink. *Gin Lane* is famous as a depiction of squalor, but it has a less well known sibling, another Hogarth painting called *Beer Street*, which is its complete inversion. The picture is a romantic image of happy, smiling people, with only the pawnbroker looking pissed off. Each painting came with an inscription, just in case the pictures themselves didn't make the message plain enough:

Gin! Curs'd fiend with fury fraught,	Beer! happy produce of our isle,
Makes human race a prey,	Can sinewy strength impart,
It enters by a deadly draught,	And wearied with fatigue and toil,
And steals our life away.	Can cheer each manly heart.

Beer consumption bounced back.

People were no longer drinking themselves into early graves, but they were still caning it big style. Cesar de Saussure was incredulous, and wrote home in 1726:

Would you believe it, although water is to be had in abundance in London and of fairly good quality, absolutely none is drunk? The lower classes, even the paupers, do not know what it is to quench their thirst with water. In this country nothing but beer is drunk ... it is said more grain is consumed in England for making beer than making bread.

Benjamin Franklin, the American revolutionary, spent some of his early days in London working in a printing house. He made the enormous social faux pas of drinking water, which earned him the nickname 'Water-American' at work.* At that time, they still couldn't calculate the strength of beer like we do today. However, by analysing recipes and processes, we can be pretty sure that it contrived to be, on average, far more potent than it is now, at around seven per cent alcohol by volume (ABV). Franklin wrote that his companion at the printing press drank:

> A pint before breakfast, a pint at breakfast with his bread and cheese, a pint between breakfast and dinner, a pint at dinner, a pint in the afternoon about six o' clock, and another when he had done his day's work.

The man insisted that this heavy consumption was necessary for him to be strong in his work – beer really was food as much as a means of getting pasted. At a temperance meeting in Warrington in 1830 an ex-drunkard expressed a desire to sign a teetotal pledge. One of his friends tried physically to restrain him, calling out, 'Thee mustn't, Richard, thee'll die.' In 1840, Robert Warner, a Quaker, applied for a life insurance policy and was told that as an abstainer he would have to pay an extra premium.

---

* Clearly, the sharp sense of humour that characterizes drinkers and pub culture today must be a relatively new thing.

Heavy labourers would continue to regard beer as an essential part of their diet until well into the twentieth century. It is a legitimate source of calories, as anyone with a beer belly can attest to. And it slips down so well. Anyone who has attempted to cut down on their drinking will have marvelled at how easy it is to drink a pint of beer, whereas a pint of any other liquid, even water, seems like a terrific amount. Workers could have got their calories elsewhere, but the amount of bread they would have had to eat to get the same energy, for instance, would have been indigestible.

Gradually, better food became available, and the physical demands of the average job simultaneously fell. Beer remains an important part of daily life, but it will never again be as vital to the working man as it was before the Victorian era, when it was the lifeblood of the nation, the fuel on which an empire was built. You could say it has been in gradual decline since the height of its fame in ancient Egypt. Yet somehow, that doesn't feel right. Over five thousand years its role may have changed, but in every society where it has been present it has been absolutely central to what people choose to do with their time. Next time you raise a pint glass, consider that you are carrying on a long and noble tradition without compare. You're not just drinking that pint for base, selfish reasons; you're doing it in tribute to the history of civilization. It's a great thing you're doing; you should be proud of yourself. And you can tell anyone thinking of criticizing your behaviour that they should be proud of you too.

Chapter Three

'An oblivion of care'

The evolution of the pub

Johnson nails it again

Any book about British social history cannot really take itself seriously unless it features a quote from Doctor Johnson. It's obligatory if you want to establish any credibility as a writer, because it suggests that you've done your research and are well-read, but also that you have a bit of humanity, an appreciation of wit.

So anyway, Doctor Johnson once exclaimed:

There is no private house in which people can enjoy themselves as well as at a capital tavern . . . You are sure you are welcome; and the more noise you make, the more trouble you give, the more good things you call for, the welcomer you are. No servants will attend you with the alacrity with which waiters do, who are incited by the prospect of an immediate reward in proportion as they please. No, Sir, there is nothing which has yet been

contrived by man by which so much happiness is produced, as by a good tavern or inn.

There's a particular reason why I chose this quote from
the ranks of eulogies to the pub over the centuries, but I'll
come back to that in a minute. For now, it's a pretty good
summation of how we feel about this bastion of our culture.
About a quarter of British adults still go the pub at least once
a week, and 27 per cent of us meet our future spouses there.
For 90 per cent of tourists visiting Britain, once they've
finished gawping at the Royals, the first thing they want to
do is get a traditional British pint in the appropriate surroundings. There's just something about the place. In 2000,
in a survey of why people choose a particular pub, 38 per
cent of the respondents said a key reason was 'my type of
atmosphere' and 26 per cent said 'my type of people go
there', compared with only 20 per cent who mentioned the
range or choice of beer. We go there for the *feeling* of the
place.

'Pub' is of course short for 'public house', and it's worth
dwelling on what that means. The pub is more than just a
shop that sells beer; it's a social venue. You feel you have a
little more ownership of the space, more of a right to be
there, than you do in any other commercial establishment.
The pub is comfortable, like home, and gives you a sense of
security. And yet it's public as well. You can regularly spend
time there with people whose company you quite enjoy over
a few beers, but who you'd never dream of letting into your
own house. There's a sense of freedom and excitement, and
you don't worry about whether you're making a mess as
much as you would at home. When a grumpy landlord asks,

'Would you do that in your own home?' well, no, you wouldn't. That's the whole point. Look at it this way: where do you most commonly find karaoke? Exactly. In a pub you feel safe enough to get up and bellow 'Pretty Woman' in the manner of a dying seal, but there's enough of a sense of excitement and 'being out' to inspire you to show off and be so outrageously cool in the first place.

Of course, there are elements of drinking culture that are common across the world. There are bars in most countries, and there'll usually be things that look familiar no matter where you go. I once had to visit Kenya to learn about drinking culture there. The salty snacks may have been goat meat rather than nuts, the lager may have been Tusker rather than Stella, but the conversation was all about women, work and football. OK, the bar was a square with a straw roof arranged around an open-air courtyard, but there was still a telly up in the corner showing highlights of Arsenal versus West Ham in the Premiership.

But these common elements come together in the English pub in a different way, under the benign but supreme authority of the landlord. He is most definitely in charge, but keeps completely at a distance unless he is asked, or forced, to intervene. And then he can be policeman, priest, arbitrator or family counsellor. If the pub is any good, he's a skilled psychologist and diplomat, and a natural leader.

Pubs look different from other kinds of commercial establishment in this country, and they look different from bars in the rest of the world. They are halfway between shop and home, often cosy, letting you know that here is a place where the cares of the world can be left on the doorstep.

And the pub, as opposed to that global concept, the bar,

has its unique customs which, if you look at them from the outside for a moment, seem pretty odd. In 1993 the Brewers' Society commissioned some anthropological research which revealed the amount of ritual in pub life. Everything, from, 'What's yours?' to, 'Time please, ladies and gents,' follows a complex, unwritten code.

For example, getting served in a pub is a unique experience. Bars around the world have table service, and in shops you have a simple queue. Far too straightforward for the pub. No, you have to stand at the bar, looking anxious and expectant – but not overly so. And to add a further quirk, a nation famous around the world for queuing decides to do something different in the pub. We have an *invisible* queue, where you take your place and the barman makes a note of who's next. But you have to be careful to keep your invisible place. Look too chilled and the bar staff will think you've already been served, too pushy and everyone will think you're an arse. So you lean forward, your money in your hand but not held up or waved about, because of course that would be *rude*. You don't speak until the barman acknowledges you, because good bar staff read your body language instead. We take it all for granted. But look at it from an outsider's point of view: as one Dutch tourist remarked to researchers who were detailing our pub behaviour, 'I cannot understand how the British ever manage to buy themselves a drink.'

We do things this way because going up to the bar gives us an excuse for social interaction. We're a reserved lot, and we need safe territory to initiate exchanges with other people, which the bar provides. Unless you're a sweet old lady standing in a bus queue, the bar is probably the only place in

Britain where you can start a conversation with a complete stranger and not be thought of as deeply odd.

This need for structured social interaction is even more manifest in the buying of rounds. There is a very serious social stigma attached to not getting your round in. 'He never buys his round' is a stain on one's character which few are prepared to live with. At the beginning of the century that stigma was regarded even more seriously than it is now. 'Treating' was all about obligation. People would use stealth and deception, buying drinks for their companions by devious means, simply to place those companions under an obligation, creating a vicious spiral of begrudging stociousness. Frederick Hackwood, in his 1912 book *Inns, Ales and Drinking Customs of Old England*, was particularly disgusted by this custom:

> It is the English practice of all others; for a meeting of friends on the common ground of a public-house is invariably celebrated by their drinking together, and, as a rule, an end cannot be put to the celebration till each man has acquitted himself by paying for 'drinks round' – and therefore the larger the party the larger the number of drinks taken, and all of them except the first quite unnecessary, either for the quenching of thirst or the celebration of a happy meeting.

Today the buying of rounds is still all about mutual obligation, but psychologists and anthropologists argue that this isn't just meanness masquerading as generosity. Gifts are constantly used in any society to create an obligation for something in return. This is an important aspect of creating social bonds. Again, in the pub this behaviour follows important, unwritten rules. If you were daft enough to keep close tabs on who had spent what and attempted to settle up at the end of the night, you'd very quickly find yourself drinking on your own. Contrary to Hackwood's experience, if you're in a large group you may not end up buying a round on that particular occasion and no one worries about it, but the obligation is still there, and next time you're out with roughly the same group of people you'd do well to get a round in first.* We trust that, over time, everyone buys their share. When I first started drinking in my local as a teenager, there was one lad who never bought his round. When that group of friends meets up at Christmas or at someone's wedding we still talk about it. I'd refer to him by name, but I hear he has managed to build a new life in a different part of the country, and I don't want to dig it all up and make a pariah of him. But he knows who he is.

Obviously, it would be far simpler if we all just bought our own drinks, but we don't. The point of going to the pub is not just to get a drink, it's to bond socially, and rounds are a vital part of that.

Even pub conversation is ritualized. The anthropologists I mentioned earlier identified two conversations in particular that happen every day in every pub in the country. The first is, 'Mine's better than yours.' It might be about cars, football teams or even lawnmowers, but it always starts in the same way, something like, 'Man United are shit and we are going

---

* Not the most popular person in the pub? Get your round in first. Psychological research has shown that, if everybody buys a round that is roughly equal in price, the people who get their round in early are regarded by the group as generous, and those who buy last are thought of as tight, even though everyone has spent the same.

to twat you on Saturday.' Now, you could even be a Barnsley fan* and still start this conversation. It would clearly be a ludicrous thing for a Barnsley fan to say,† but the point is to lay down a challenge to which the other person must respond in similar fashion, or else lose face. After a few initial exchanges one of the participants may even reveal that he agrees with the other, but only after the ritual has been satisfied by a few well-crafted insults and volleys of ridicule.

The other opening gambit for a bit of verbal sparring is 'Don't fancy yours much,' uttered when two women walk into the bar, one of whom is more attractive than the other. The fact that neither would give the two conversationalists a second glance is neither here nor there; the assumption that the men are in a position to choose is never questioned. It creates an illusion of manliness and superiority, which both players know, but never openly acknowledge, to be utter bollocks.

What you talk about matters less than how you talk about it. It's all about free association of subjects, a sense of the absurd, a determination never to take anything too seriously, an absolute obligation to take the piss out of your mates and insult them (in ways that, outside the pub, would be bizarrely

---

* Which is similar to being a football fan, but slightly different. It has more to do with a complex mix of fierce local pride and unresolved issues concerning masochism and self-loathing rather than an appreciation of the silky skills of talented athletes.

† Having said that, in 1998 Manchester United, at the height of their powers, were knocked out of the FA Cup by Barnsley, who beat them 3–2 in a fifth-round replay. I have video evidence to prove it. And Barnsley would have beaten them in the first game at Old Trafford if they hadn't had a blatant penalty denied. It's important that this fact is reiterated wherever possible. No one must ever be allowed to forget. Never.

cruel) and an absolute obligation to argue, preferably about something utterly irrelevant. Arguing allows us to express our beliefs, to be demonstrative and to get closer to each other, but in a way that still allows us to pretend we're undemonstrative and uninterested in each other, as all good English people should be.

Colin Dexter, the creator of beer-swilling detective Inspector Morse, had a good attempt at trying to encapsulate all this and sum up the pub's appeal: and is quoted in *Pub-watching*:

> The pub is a separate circle of existence. You have your job, your family, circles that intertwine and overlap, but the pub is somehow outside that. It's another little world – like going to another country, but not very far away. It's a different ambience, a sense of independence, and that sort of feeling is very valuable. Above all, for me, it is the magic combination of friendship, conversation and beer – that form together a sort of alchemy of a very enjoyable piece of existence.

OK, we've established that pubs are pretty special, but how did they come to be like this? If you've been paying attention to the trend of the story so far, it won't come as too much of a surprise when I say that it was a complex process with many different groups and factors coming into play, and that makes it a difficult story to tell. For a start, let's come back to that quote of Johnson's. See how he refers to 'a good tavern *or* inn'? That's because in Johnson's time they were quite separate establishments. They were not just synonyms for the pub, they were licensed differently, sold different drinks, and had different clienteles. Then there were alehouses, which were different again. In the nineteenth century these three types of establishment were joined by a fourth separate entity, the beer shop. Confused? I'm not surprised. The modern pub is the child of four parents. This is part of the reason why there is so much diversity in the types of pubs around, and also why pubs are so different from anything else.

Alehouses

As we've seen, brewing, like baking, began as a subsistence activity carried out in most households. In the Middle Ages everyone brewed beer using the same yeast with which they baked their bread. These were the necessities of life, and in difficult times people would pool their resources and make a common brew. Because brewing was such an imprecise art, some people were naturally better at it than others. Those who were more proficient would share their produce with their neighbours – for a price. But one individual would rarely have a constant supply of ale and it would often be brewed a batch at a time. When ale was ready an announcement had to be made, so aspiring brewers would place a pole covered with some kind of foliage above the door – an ale stake. In 1393 Richard II introduced legislation that made it compulsory for landlords to erect a sign. Ale was important – if you brewed good ale, you had to let people know: 'Whosoever shall brew ale in the town with intention of selling it must hang out a sign, otherwise he will forfeit his ale.' Naturally, the people who sold the best ale attracted regular custom, and their houses became known as alehouses.

The transformation of the alehouse from private dwelling

to commercial property was often not easy to spot. Much of what was bought from alehouses was taken away, but the conviviality surrounding the drinking of ale meant that people tended to hang around the alehouse longer than they did, say, at the baker's or the blacksmith's. There are still pubs around today that are essentially the front room of someone's house. Back then there would be no bar, just a small serving hatch through which pot boys would pass the ale in jugs, flagons, pints or bottles. Gradually, commercial brewers started to build bigger houses that became busy meeting places, hence the term 'public house'. By the thirteenth century, permanent alehouses were everywhere, and communal brewing had begun to disappear.

With the alehouse was born the landlord's reputation for watering down the beer and serving dodgy pints or short measures. In the Chester miracle plays of the fourteenth century, Christ redeems a bunch of characters from hell, all apart from the brewer who heads straight for eternal damnation after admitting:

> Some time I was a taverner,
> A gentle gossip and a tapster,
> Of wine and ale a trusty brewer,
> Which woe hath me bewrought.
>
> Of cans I kept no true measure,
> My cups I sold at my pleasure,
> Deceiving many a creature,
> Tho' my ale were nought.

Alehouses became the focal point of the community. If you needed to find someone, chances are that's where they would be. Alehouses served as polling stations, banks, court-rooms, theatres, even lawyer's offices. All human life was to be found there, most of it the worse for wear. In 1629 Bishop Fade gave a description of an alehouse that still rings a bell today:

> A house of sinne you may call it, but not a house of darknesse, for the candles are never out ... To give you the total reckoning of it, it is the busieman's recreation, the idle man's business, the melancholy man's sanctuary, the stranger's welcome, the Innes of Court man's enter-tainment, the scholar's kindness and the citizen's curtesy. It is the study of sparkling wits ...

As alehouses became more common their ale stakes started to cause problems. They often extended far out into the street and threatened to knock riders off their horses and wagons. Gradually, painted signs began to appear which, apart from being safer, allowed more creativity and individuality. Soon every tradesman had cottoned on to the idea: bakers, cobblers, and grocers all followed suit, until the whole high street was a riot of colourful signs. Alehouse owners became more elaborate to rise above the visual cacophony. Signs hung from gallows that allowed them to stretch across the road became the fashion until they got so heavy they started falling on people in the street.

For most of our history the vast majority of the population have been illiterate. Alehouse signs were therefore hugely important, initially as a way of differentiating your alehouse, but increasingly as a reference point for the community at large. By referring to the signs people gave names to the alehouses. As these names were rarely written down, many evolved over time, and the most popular ones now engender endless speculation as to their origin.

Many alehouses were named after monarchs or national heroes. This might have been the sign of a good patriot, but more often than not there would eventually be a spurious claim that the monarch in question had once popped in for a pint. Before Henry VIII broke with Rome and proclaimed himself head of the Church of England there were also many Pope's Heads around the country, as well as establishments named after various saints. Many of these were on monastery lands and had historical links with the monks who had done so much to further the brewing and selling of beer. When the Reformation happened and the monasteries burned, many landlords suddenly got the urge to change the name of their establishment to the King's Head, the Rose (after Henry's Tudor symbol) or the Rose and Crown, which remains one of the most common pub names. Those who wanted to retain a coded link to the Church would name their establishments the Angel or the Bells.

Decoding pub signs can be a fascinating game if you're a bit bored on a rainy afternoon. The George was probably originally the Saint George, until the Puritans of Cromwell's time insisted on the removal of any celebration of religious symbols in their campaign against popery. Of course, for much of our history Christianity was still competing with the pagan religions that had been here before it, and the Green Man became a potent symbol of a mystical Arcadian past, as we hurtled forward on steam and steel through the nineteenth century. Later, many alehouses were started and run by retiring soldiers. The Marquis of Granby was popular among those who served under him, reputedly because he was generous with pensions for his troops, and many of them used the money to set up in business with a pub. Some names are the result of the corruption of other phrases as the spoken language constantly mutated. The odd-sounding Bull and Mouth in Holborn (now the Ah King Chinese restaurant) was corrupted from the Battle of Boulogne Mouth in 1544, and in 1861 Anthony Trollope claimed that the Goat and Compass (there's one in Hull and another in downtown Wilmington, North Carolina) was derived from the phrase 'God encompasseth us', although alternative explanations include links to one of London's ancient livery companies, the freemasons, devil worship, or the medieval belief that if you stuck a goat in the house of an ill person they'd get better.

The best alehouses had reputations that travelled, and some enterprising owners would simply steal the name of a famous competitor to grab a share of their custom. Before there were branded pub chains there were thousands of alehouses all with the same name. Often the more established ones would add the prefix 'Old' to their name in response. If you're ever in Battersea High Street in London (not that there's any reason you should be) check out the Woodman, just a few doors down from where the Original Woodman used to be.*

Alehouse names were rarely chosen at random. They

---

* For over a century the 'Original Woodman' stood near the Woodman, a source of idle bar stool speculation until someone shut the pub and turned it into Le QuecumBar (sic), a copy of a 1930s Parisian brasserie where Django Rhinehardt played. Why anyone, anywhere, thinks any of this is a good idea is not made clear in Le QuecumBar's publicity.

were often intertwined with the history and culture of their locality, or the context in which they found themselves. The two Woodmen are in an area where there used to be lots of woodcutters. A publican who couldn't stretch to an elaborate painted sign might make do with a simple log of twisted wood, and his pub would become known as the Crooked Billet. A Green Gate probably marked the place on the road where travellers had to stop and pay a toll. In London, in districts such as the Angel and Elephant & Castle, drinking establishments even gave their names to the locality. This deep historical relationship between the alehouse and its community begins to explain the horrified reaction of pub purists to the recent trend of parodying traditional names without really understanding them – the Slug & Lettuces, Pitcher & Pianos, Rat & Parrots and Farrago & Firkins – as they replace names that had some individuality and meaning.

The joy of sport

As alehouses proliferated they turned to things other than the quality of their beer to compete against their rivals. As the place where everyone gathered when they were not working or sleeping, the alehouse became the venue for various forms of entertainment within the community. Bear-baiting and cockfighting were particularly popular. The importance of the latter to the life of the pub is shown by the fact that the Courage logo is a cockerel. In 1949 this logo was extensively researched among punters to decide whether the cockerel should be depicted dressed for fighting (trimmed) or not (untrimmed), despite the fact that cockfighting had been banned for over a century. Eventually these sports were discouraged and finally banned,* and the far more politically correct bare-knuckle fighting caught on instead. By the sixteenth century there were even games that didn't require anyone or anything to bleed for our entertainment. In the seventeenth century, someone came up with the idea of attacking inanimate objects instead of living beings, and invented darts. The noble art of shove-halfpenny became so popular that Henry VIII was a keen player. Court records show that on one occasion, 'Lord William won £9 of the King at Shouvilla Bourde,' but that in a subsequent game, the King won forty-five pounds off Anne Boleyn's brother, Lord Rochford.

As well as games that took place in the building itself, most alehouses would have owned the land immediately adjacent to them. Remember, in the Middle Ages most alehouses brewed their own beer, so many had fields for crops and would set some land aside for recreation. The pub gave birth to virtually every sport known to us, from cricket and tennis to bowls, skittles, boxing and wrestling.† Publicans would make money by arranging events, charging admission, and magnanimously acting as bookmaker into the bargain.

The links between pubs and sport explain another bunch of classic names, such as the Fox and Hounds, The Talbot

---

* Most of them over a century before the equally cruel but far more upper class sport of fox hunting was. I wonder why that could be?
† You didn't think it was just coincidence that most sporting trophies are cups, did you?

(a large hunting dog), and of course the Dog and Duck.* If it's a surprise that some of these reflect the genteel sport of hunting, it shouldn't be. The pub's reliance on farmland for brewing materials means that it has always been intimately linked with country pursuits; after all, the logo for Tetley's is a red-coated huntsman. Sport was an integral part of festivals that celebrated the end of the hardship of winter or the toil of getting in the harvest, and at these times beer was omni-present. During its early days in the nineteenth century, the temperance movement opposed sporting events as much as pubs, because people were just as sure to be stoated there.

Sport has remained absolutely central to pub life through the centuries. The plasma screens for the footie on Sky may be new, but it's safe to assume that throughout recent history, if people weren't playing sport in or near pubs, they were talking about it. In the 1930s the Mass Observation study recorded that 37 per cent of all London pub conversations were about sport. The two go together to define what it is to be male and British. A 2002 survey by Greene King revealed that men claim to be obsessed with football more than any-thing else, with beer in second place and sex beaten into third. So if men really do think about sex once every six minutes, there's no doubt about what we dwell on for the other five.

---

* Named after the noble and skilful sport of duck hunting. In one corner, a pack of spaniels. In the other: a duck. Clearly this was a totally unfair fight. Things were evened up a bit ... by pinioning the duck's wings to stop it from flying. Now we were talking. Should the fierce but thankfully restrained duck somehow come off worse against its adversaries, its only means of escape was diving to the bottom of the pond, which was invariably owned by the pub landlord. You have to admit, when it comes to entertainment, we've always been incredibly inventive.

Inns

It's clear then that there is a direct line of descent from medieval alehouses to the modern pub. And yet, pubs today look nothing like the true 'public houses' that alehouses used to be. When you close your eyes and think of what the typical traditional English pub looks like, you're probably not thinking of the alehouse at all, but of a different kind of establishment entirely.

The history of the inn is entirely different from that of the alehouse, and goes back to our old friends, the monks. Having developed beer as we know it, they went on to have a huge influence on the drinking establishment itself.

By the twelfth century, pilgrimages to important graves and places of religious significance were the package holidays of their time, as Chaucer revealed in the *Canterbury Tales*. In the early days monasteries provided rest and refreshment for the pilgrims, but soon there were so many travellers that a new type of commercial establishment emerged. Like an alehouse only bigger and more diverse, the inn provided food, accommodation, stabling and storage facilities for travellers as well as beer. The pilgrimage from London to Canterbury that has made so many schooldays so wretchedly miserable started at an inn.

While alehouses were continually being knocked down and rebuilt as larger, custom-built premises or destroyed along with the slums they served in cities, inns proved far more robust. As they became synonymous with the idea of travel, they became even more pronounced focal points within their localities than alehouses. Early inns served as recruiting centres for armies, and the allegedly oldest surviving pub in the country, Ye Olde Trip to Jerusalem in Nottingham, was an inn that served as a staging post for Richard the Lionheart's crusade in 1189.*

The Canterbury pilgrims travelled at a leisurely pace on horseback or on foot, which until the seventeenth century were the standard ways to travel. Even the best roads were simple dirt tracks which always seemed to be muddy in the English rain, and the only significant wheeled traffic consisted of farm equipment, merchants' wagons, army baggage trains and royal entourages. Coach travel was slow and expensive, out of the reach of most people because coaches required teams of six or eight horses to drag their burden through the mud. Central London was paved, but that was about as far as it went for decent road surfaces.

This changed in 1663, when the Turnpike Acts were passed to encourage the paving of roads. There was an economic boom and merchants, bankers and lawyers all wanted to travel more between thriving towns and ports. Public coaches were soon doing profitable business on key routes. Points were needed to rest en route as well as at final destinations, so journeys between towns happened in stages, with stops along the way. Public stagecoaches worked specific routes, carrying people and provisions from town to town far quicker than ever before. Coaching inns sprang up on

---

* While the stories are great, you do have to take claims like this with a pinch of salt. Often the small print will say 'a pub has stood on this site since . . .', but it's not the same pub. The 'Olde Trip' claims to have stood unchanged for over 800 years. All I'm saying is that the word 'trip' didn't enter the English language (in the sense of 'journey') until the seventeenth century – five hundred years after the 'unchanged' pub was allegedly built.

main roads up and down the country to serve the booming traffic.

But it was the introduction of mail coaches that caused the coaching era to really take off. Mail coaches competed to get their cargo to its destination as quickly as possible. With decent roads journey times were slashed, and timetables were regularized to the extent that rural villagers could almost set their clocks by the passing of the mail coach. Coaches travelled carefully specifed stages, changing tired horses for fresh ones at inns every eight to ten miles, and coaching inns became the points between which routes were planned.

Coaching inns varied in scale and grandeur. Some were merely changing posts for horses, but innkeepers with premises located precisely a day's journey from the last big stop were made. The road north from London saw large coaching towns develop at roughly equal distances: Dunstable, Market Harborough, Northampton, Loughborough, Leicester, Derby, Ashbourne and Buxton. Those inns that served as stages on less important routes might be little better than alehouses, whereas those on important routes could be massive. The Chequer in Northampton had a long narrow yard a couple of hundred feet long, lined on either side with stables, coach houses and warehouses.

In the overall timescale of the evolution of the pub, inns peaked fairly briefly. Less than two hundred years after the roads were made decent, the railways came and the dashing mail coaches were obsolete virtually overnight. On the most important and the longest routes coaching inns simply adapted and became railway inns, and some of these survive today. But as a widespread phenomenon, the coaching inn suffered a very sudden demise. In 1866 George Eliot summed up the nostalgia that people were already feeling for the coaching era in the opening paragraph of *Felix Holt*:

> Five-and-thirty years ago the glory had not yet departed from the old coach-roads: the great roadside inns were still brilliant with well polished tankards, the smiling glances of pretty barmaids, and the repartees of jocose ostlers; the mail still announced itself by the merry notes of the horn; the hedge-cutter or the rick thatcher might still know the exact hour by the unfailing yet otherwise meteoric apparition of the pea-green Tally-Ho or the yellow Independent.

The stagecoach era may have been brief, but it made a lasting contribution to the evolution of the pub, and we're not just talking about the coaching inns that feature every year on Christmas cards. Stagecoach passengers were divided into the wealthier ones who could actually afford to travel inside the coach, and those who had to sit on top or hang off the sides, risking death by tree or, more common in winter, by hypothermia. When they reached an inn the 'outsiders' were entertained in the bar room, while the 'insiders' were granted entrance to the innkeeper's private salon. 'Salon' was corrupted to 'saloon', and the division of pubs into a basic public bar and a more salubrious saloon eventually became commonplace.

So when you think of the traditional English pub rather than the town-centre boozer or style bar, it got its design and physical appearance from the inn. Much of the timbering, horse brasses, bedpans, lamps and lanterns might be fake these days, but this is the style that coaching inns created. Some of it was practical, some was just the fashion of the period. But our perception of what an archetypal pub should look like almost became frozen in time at this point.

Up until now we've talked about the pub as a place that sells beer. Understandable really, because that's the point of the book. But if you want a more complete history of the drinking establishment we've started a good few centuries too late. Places that sold drink were common before beer itself was established in Britain. And to the horror of any red-blooded geezer down the pub, the earliest commercial drinking establishments were not alehouses or inns, but were in fact the direct forerunners of trendy, European-themed wine bars.

Taverns

As Monty Python fans will appreciate, the Romans did quite a lot for us. As well as building the first roads across the country in order to get their troops more quickly to the nearest bunch of stocious Celtic rebels, they established places on these roads where the soldiers could stop to rest, freshen up and enjoy a glass of vino. The Latin *taberna* means shop, and in those days this usually referred to a shop that sold wine. Roadside *tabernae* appeared in towns and on major routes. They would hang pictures or some other reference to vines or bunches of grapes outside to show that these were places to get something to eat and drink. Alternatively, because chess was a popular way of relaxing among the Romans, they would hang chequerboards outside. So while they had nothing to do with the evolution of selling beer, these places were an important forerunner to the pub.

Taberna of course became corrupted to tavern. A few, more discerning Brits realized how trendy the wine bar concept would one day become, and hung on to it after the Romans withdrew. Taverns survived in a small but profitable niche, serving nobles and clergymen, or anyone else who had been abroad and become accustomed to fancy foreign wine-drinking ways. In the twelfth century the marriage of Henry II to Eleanor of Aquitaine opened up the trade in Bordeaux wine, and taverns, as distinct from alehouses or inns, began to grow in popularity again. By the end of the thirteenth century they were widespread in London and to a lesser extent in port towns on significant import–export routes.

Taverns bumped along until the reign of Elizabeth I. As we've seen, in the late sixteenth century it became fashionable to travel, see the world, and claim it and all its resources in the name of (insert name of European ruler with large navy of your choice here). There were vast resources in the New World just waiting to be exploited, and a huge boom in foreign trade occurred as a result. Walter Raleigh famously brought back the potato, and that's about as much as we learned when we studied the era in school, but there was trade in all manner of items. Merchants felt inordinately pleased with themselves at having made so much money and, on the back of massive imports of very cheap wine, taverns grew rapidly to give them somewhere to spend it.

As transport within the country became easier, beer became more readily available and the relative price of wine increased. Taverns began to sell beer as well as wine in an attempt to protect their business, but wine remained their focus, distinguishing them from alehouses or inns. As our old mates Cesar de Saussure and Benjamin Franklin have already shown, foreign visitors often provide the best descriptions of what life in a country was like, and in 1669 an Italian visitor described the drinking establishments of London:

> There are an infinite number of beer shops ... These places are not very extravagant and they are almost always to be found full downstairs, crowded with the rabble, and upstairs with every condition of man from artisan to gentleman. They differ in this point from the taverns namely that in those they drink Spanish wine which they call sack, wines of the Canaries, Malaga and Bordeaux and other valuable foreign wines, whilst in the beer shops there is nothing but cock ale, butter ale, Lambeth ale and the like.*

There was less of an air of necessity about taverns. They were only really found in the centres of prosperous towns, so they didn't need to act as community centres in the way of alehouses, nor provide shelter for travellers like inns. Johnson's eulogy to the tavern at the start of this chapter gives an

---

* Look, I'm not sure what they were either, but remember that these were times when people were very literal when it came to naming things. So I'm guessing that butter ale was brewed with butter, and Lambeth ale was brewed in Lambeth. I'm not sure what's special about Lambeth in the ale stakes, but Samuel Pepys used to swear by it, and he knew his ale. As for cock ale, forget double entendres, the truth is even funnier. They used to get a cock (i.e. a male chicken), stick it in a sack and bash it against walls until it was completely pulverized. It was important that the bones were shattered and the whole thing was a bloody pulp. Then they'd chuck in a load of spices, such as cloves and mace, and drop the bag into a vat of ale while it was fermenting, and age the resulting brew for longer than normal to produce a much richer, heartier beer than normal. Yes, I'm serious. No, I don't know why, nor what the person who first did it was thinking of. I don't think I want to.

idea of its boisterous, playground atmosphere; this was no centre of business. It was more aloof than the alehouse, which meant that the upper classes could feel comfortable there, but it didn't have the formality of the gentlemen's club. Inside the tavern, those who had to look responsible in public could kick back and let off steam. Warming to his subject, Johnson had another go at explaining the tavern's specific appeal:

> As soon as I enter the door of a tavern, I experience an oblivion of care, and a freedom from solicitude; when I am seated, I find the master courteous and the servants obsequious to my call, anxious to know and ready to supply my wants; wine there exhilarates my spirits and prompts me to free conversation, and an interchange of discourse with those whom I must love; I dogmatise and am contradicted; and in this conflict of opinions and sentiments I find delight.

This was where lawyers, Members of Parliament and other professional men, as well as people like poets and writers who didn't have to work for a living, congregated to pass the time. The tavern was the home of wits and scoundrels, aesthetes, sages and actors. André Simon, in his 1926 book *Bottlescrew Days*, quotes one eighteenth-century commentator who was referring to the tavern when he described the behaviour of the leading politicians of the day:

> Men of all ages drink abominably. Fox drinks what I should call a great deal, though he is not reckoned to do so by his superiors. Sheridan excessively and Grey more than any of them, but it is a much more gentlemanly way than our Scotch drunkards, and is always accompanied

with lively, clever conversation on subjects of importance.
Pitt I am told drinks as much as anybody.

It sounds like the essence of the modern pub: men who should know better getting pissed and talking bollocks. Taverns may have been distinct from alehouses and inns, and had much less to do with the selling of beer, but in their age they were closer in spirit to the modern pub than its more direct forebears.

Pubs

When Johnson died in 1784 the age of the tavern did not long outlast him. Wine was becoming more available through inns, coffee houses and wine merchants. At the same time, the problems caused by the gin epidemic meant that conspicuous drunkenness was increasingly frowned upon, and it became less acceptable for the prime minister of the day to get tanked up after a hard day's governing. In addition, the Industrial Revolution had created a new class of moneyed industrialists with a strong work ethic who frowned upon sottish behaviour.

Alternatives to beer were becoming common on the back of burgeoning trade within the rapidly expanding empire. Coffee had appeared in 1650, chocolate in 1657 and tea in 1660. With them came new places to challenge taverns, alehouses and inns. At first these drinks were very expensive, but coffee houses in particular eventually established themselves in cities, with a different character and atmosphere from that of pubs.

In the face of this competition, the nature of drinking establishments began to change. Running an alehouse in town was for a long time one step away from poverty, a secondary source of income or something to tide you over until you got a proper job. Now alehouses were no longer the only places people could go to eat or drink, they had to buck their ideas up if they wanted to stay in business. But with the industrialization of Britain, new thinking was emerging which suggested an alehouse keeper could do far more than just survive. In 1776 Adam Smith published his *Wealth of Nations*, which signalled the growth of economics as a proper subject worthy of study, debate, idle banter and making up as you went along. People began to think about the work they did on far more commercial lines. Leisure was a business, and the provision of booze was no exception. Sheriff's officers, justice's clerks, constables and bailiffs, after careers trying to make alehouses more respectable, retired and became landlords in increasing numbers. Investors who speculated in property began to invest in alehouses, and their character began to change.

The new wealthy – merchants and industrialists – needed ways to ensure that their status was recognized. As class distinctions became more fluid following the demise of feudalism, it became all the more important to demonstrate to which class you belonged – or aspired. Dodgy drinking shops abounded in the cities, catering for the large, displaced work forces looking for places to drown their sorrows. More respectable alehouses moved upmarket, and new ones were built which had separate rooms for different classes of people and for different purposes. Ironically, these new places, which bore much less resemblance to houses opened to the public and looked a lot more like taverns or inns, were now referred to as public houses. The upper classes, who didn't want to be associated with such base places, moved away to coffee houses, many of which eventually became exclusive gentlemen's clubs. Taverns and inns either declined or became less distinguishable from alehouses, and in time all three types of establishment came to be referred to as public houses.

If you look at pubs today, you can see the community aspect that is the legacy of the alehouse, the architecture and sense of national heritage of the inn, and the tavern tradition of spending the evening with your peers getting slowly rat-arsed and talking about nothing with increasing conviction as the night wears on. Once you pick the pub apart into its various historical strands, it kind of starts to make sense. You can see why, thanks to the nature of our communities, our empire, our towns, our industry and our religions, the British pub has ended up quite unlike anything else. And this is only the start of it. The pub has always been so linked to society that any change in the way we live is mirrored by changes in the nature of our drinking establishments. And there were many such upheavals just around the corner.

Chapter Four

'The universal Cordial of the Populace'

Science, fashion, and the birth of modern beer

Local brewing

If you were to Google 'beer' or 'brewing',* the majority of links you would get back would be to microbreweries or home-brew enthusiasts rather than the big commercial brewers who dominate the supply of beer around the globe these days. OK, so there are bound to be more home brewers than commercial brewers simply because the commercial brewers are so huge, but the enthusiasm and buzz around beer that you get on these sites, not to mention the sheer number of them, reflects the strong rise in recent years of small-scale brewing. The modern craft brewery scene in America grew out of the home brew revival in reaction to faceless corporations brewing identical, tasteless beers. In recent years the British brewing industry has grown increasingly similar to its American cousin – both in terms of the

---

* Indulge me – imagine you were really bored or something.

scale and uniformity of the biggest brewers (many of the same companies now dominate on either side of the Atlantic) and the excitement and flavour explosions among what are often called microbreweries.

Among the very smallest micros are brewpubs, who brew and sell their own beer, just like the alehouses of a thousand years ago. One level up micros, who supply a handful of pubs within an area of thirty miles or so, echo beer production as it was for centuries, before industrialization gave us the giants we have today. We'll talk some more about the resurgence of the micros later. But the historic upheaval of the original journey from micro to mega forms the next part of our story.

The birth of commercial brewing

Once the use of hops had become commonplace, the way beer was made remained unchanged for centuries. Any large community or organization brewed its own beer. Some brewers operated on a commercial basis, brewing beer to sell to locals or passing travellers through their inns and taverns, but these were all small concerns serving a tightly defined area. This resulted in a massive variety of types and qualities of beer across Britain and the rest of Europe. Nobody sold beer to anyone who lived more than a few miles away, and each region had its own speciality of which it was fiercely proud. A small amount was traded but beer is a bulky product to move, and the poor roads meant a bumpy ride that would probably spoil the precious cargo. Anyway, there wasn't much point. If you did take your beer all the way to the next town, they'd tell you in very plain terms that it was in no way as good as the local brew.*

At the start of the seventeenth century, one in twenty of the English population lived in London; by the end of the century this figure was one in nine. The concentration of population brought with it a massive rise in the commercial demand for beer. Remember, this was a time when beer was a food as well as an intoxicant, and the working classes needed more of both; forgemen and foundrymen worked in temperatures from 90 to 140°F and could lose up to twenty pounds of sweat in a day. To replace this they would drink up to twenty pints of weak beer in a shift.

The effect of sheer numbers was compounded by the upheaval and added stress the new urban environment created for people moving into it. There was a market for beer much larger than anyone had seen before, and the preservative properties of the hop made it possible to brew larger batches that would keep for longer. Commercial brewers began to prosper, first in London and then in places such as Edinburgh, Burton, Hull, York and Nottingham.

Brewing is mentioned rarely in accounts of the Industrial Revolution. Temperance pressures meant it was impolitic for brewers to boast of their achievements and innovations, and few accurate records exist of exactly how it performed in the nineteenth century compared to those glamorous, sexy indus-

---

* This strong allegiance to local styles survives even today. For example, ale drinkers in the south will try to tell you that their pint should have a thin head that gradually disappears, whereas any idiot knows that the northern fashion for a thick, creamy head that lasts the whole pint down, lacing your glass with a delicate, gossamer lace of foam as you drink, is infinitely superior. (Not that I'm biased or anything.)

tries like coal mining and steel making. But the huge demand coupled with the innovations that were coming along to help meet it, meant that brewing was one of the success stories of the age. In fact, while brewing is rarely if ever mentioned in history books and school lessons about the golden age of Victorian industry, contemporary accounts suggest that in terms of contribution to the economy and numbers of people employed, it was second only to cotton.

It's difficult to comprehend now just what a revolution it was. Britain led the way in innovation. As the British empire reached its peak we were a proud and boastful lot, and size really was everything. One emphatic illustration of this is the famous photograph of Isambard Kingdom Brunel looking very pleased with himself standing in front of what seems to be a wall of chain. Each link in the chain seems almost as big as he is, even in his ludicrous stovepipe hat. The chain itself is an awesome thing, but *it's only the chain* – you look at this picture and you think, *Shit, how big must the thing be that's attached to the chain? What did they manage to build?* This scale of ambition was just as notable in brewing as it was anywhere else. It all started, predictably enough, in London, where the particularly large demand for beer gave the brewers a head start over everyone else in terms of rapid growth.

The most accomplished London brewer of the age was Samuel Whitbread. He began brewing in 1742, and in 1750 moved to the famous Chiswell Street brewery in the heart of the City of London. I know this sounds strange now, but at the time this was an ideal location because of its proximity to a great source of pure water that could be drawn straight up for the beer – yes, I'm talking about the Thames. Whitbread was passionate about his business. A workaholic, he was always looking for the next new thing that could increase production. In 1785 James Watt installed a steam engine at the brewery to replace men and horses; it was such an impressive bit of kit that it became a must-see on the London tourist route, and even the king came to have a look.*

There were plenty of other brewers whose premises were not quite as impressive as Whitbread's, but whose desire to expand was just as keen. During the 1780s and 1790s the biggest brewers grew rapidly, and an increasing share of beer production was concentrated in ever fewer hands. The biggest brewers churned out enough beer to benefit from economies of scale which meant they could sell cheaper, take a bigger share of the market, make even more profit, invest it back in

---

* The brewery still stands in Chiswell Street today, but doesn't brew any beer. In fact, neither does Whitbread plc – it now describes itself as 'the UK's largest hotel and restaurant group'. Their 'restaurants' include Beefeater pubs, Brewers (sic) Fayre pubs, Table Table pubs and Taybarns pubs, but they insist on calling them restaurants instead of pubs. Taybarns' strapline is 'The ultimate eatery, suggesting if you eat there, it will be your final meal. And yet according to their website: 'Our fans have been known to travel the country for a taste of Taybarns!' Whitbread's 'hotels' consist mainly of the Premier Inn chain, which is apparently 'award winning'. I can only let my imagination run riot over what those awards might be for. Why am I being so grumpy and sarky about this? Because I love pubs and beer, and Whitbread is a company built on pubs and beer. They still run pubs, but refuse to admit that they are pubs. You might expect this from some poncey gastropub in Hampstead, but even then it's still annoying. For one of the biggest pub groups in the UK to pretend they don't do pubs makes me rather vexed. But anyway, we were talking about Chiswell Street – a piece of brewing history. Whitbread sold it in 2005, throwing the irreplaceable brewing archive into a skip. 'The Brewery' is now a conference centre. Apart from the hint in the name, there is not a single mention of beer or brewing – or Whitbread's achievements – anywhere on the venue's website.

the business and grow ever bigger. In 1748 the twelve largest brewers brewed 42 per cent of London's beer. By the end of the century this figure stood at 78 per cent. Smaller brewers gamely tried to hang on, but the trend was already clear when war delivered a fatal blow.

At the beginning of the nineteenth century Britain was embroiled in the Napoleonic Wars, and the government was becoming desperate for revenue to fund the war effort. They increased tax not only on beer itself, but also on the malt and hops that went into it. Only the biggest brewers could absorb this punitive increase in costs. Even if you could afford the expensive new equipment and the taxes on the raw materials, fuel for boiling was far more difficult to come by now most land had been enclosed. In 1795 David Davis commented, 'Where fuel is scarce and dear, poor people find it cheaper to buy their bread of the baker than to bake for themselves.' The same was true of beer. Not only the nation's home brewers, but also taverns, ale houses and other small brewers realized that they could actually buy beer from the big brewing companies much cheaper than they could brew it themselves. And if that wasn't enough, thanks to the investment the big boys had made, chances were their beer would be much better quality too. By necessity, people moved to buying rather than brewing their beer.

From leather pants to glass tubes

For most of its history, brewing has been a process of trial and error. The end product was terribly inconsistent from one batch to the next. Relying on something as unstable and unknown as yeast meant that anything could go wrong, and often did.*

Fermentation itself was a very difficult process to measure, and there was no precise way of saying when the beer was actually done. For centuries, the quality of beer was

---

* If you really want to get a hint of the yeasty delights that faced the beer drinker a few centuries ago, and in the spirit of the oft-repeated maxim that you should try everything once except incest and morris dancing, you should definitely try a Lambic beer. Lambic, brewed mainly in Belgium, has no yeast pitched into the brew. Instead, fermentation happens solely with the help of natural airborne yeasts and anything living in the rafters of the brewery. It's not quite the same as mainstream brewing used to be, because yeast multiplies as it feeds and excess yeast has for centuries been kept back from one brew and pitched into the next. But that yeast would have been a complex substance with wild strains mixed in, and Lambic gives those wild boys free rein. When I first wrote this book, I described Lambic as being like 'lager, cider and bitter all mixed together'. Since then I have visited Cantillon, the world's most revered Lambic brewery, several times. Their 'Rose de Gambrinus' has been variously described by beer connoisseurs as the 'Champagne of beers' or even the 'Laphroiag of beers'. Someone I gave a glass to recently described it as 'some beer that you've just sicked back up'. Last time I tried Cantillon beers my own impressions ranged from – just let me check my tasting notes here – 'aaaoooooeerrghhhh!' to 'yeeeaaaiiiizzzerhhaaaaa'. Fans reckon that to taste Lambic properly, you have to take three sips. The first produces reactions like those in my tasting notes, but by the third sip it starts to taste OK and you might even enjoy it, although when you realise for the first time that you are enjoying it, you might start giggling uncontrollably and have to ask someone standing near you to slap you hard across the face. Whether this is because Lambic creates a degustatory black hole in your mouth and drags your taste buds through to an alternate dimension such as Superman's Bizarro World, or whether it just completely destroys them and leaves a smoking ruin where your finely tuned palate once stood, has not yet been scientifically determined.

judged by a man known as the ale conner, an officer appointed by the Crown to ensure that the quality of beer being sold commercially was of an acceptable standard. The ale conner was easily recognizable: he'd be the bloke striding into the pub in his leather trousers, the most important part of his attire. According to completely unsubstantiated and unverified popular pub legend, this wasn't some weird fetish – the trousers were vital to judging the quality of the beer. A small amount of beer would be poured onto a bench. The ale conner would then sit in this puddle for half an hour, trying his best to look dignified and important. When he rose, if he got a clean break from the bench he would pronounce the ale fit to drink. However, if his leather keks stuck to the bench this meant there was still residual sugar in the brew and, having not yet finished fermenting, it was unfit to drink. Although he looked daft, not to mention possibly perverted, the ale conner was an important figure in society. None other than William Shakespeare's dad joined the august brethren who sat in puddles of beer for a living, when he was appointed ale conner for Stratford in 1557.

Keeping the brew at the right temperature was another headache. Too hot and you'd kill the yeast and the beer would spoil; too cold and the yeast would be too lazy to attack the sugar and the beer wouldn't ferment. Like the three bears' porridge, it had to be kept just right. The problem was, if you couldn't measure temperature, you couldn't really control it. The best anyone could do was the old elbow test that parents use to check the baby's bath water. The growth in the scale of brewing initially made the problem even worse, as demand for beer was driving brewers to make it in bigger vats, and the bigger the vats, the higher the temperature in the centre of the brew.

For a while this last problem in particular frustrated the plans of even the biggest and most advanced brewers, and there seemed to be a natural limit to how far beer production could progress. This was welcome news to some, who still regarded good beer-making as something more like alchemy or artistry than a subject for modern science and industry. But, sadly for the Luddites, the big brewers invested and researched and experimented until finally the innovations came through that allowed better understanding and control of the brewing process.

First, brewers adopted the thermometer, invented by Daniel Gabriel Fahrenheit in 1714. If temperature could be measured accurately, it could be controlled better. Brewers still had a while to wait before the invention of refrigeration, which would allow them to control the brewing temperature, but once they could measure it, they could install large networks of pipes to run around brewing vessels with cold water pumped through them, making a reasonable attempt at keeping the temperature within optimal limits. Like everything else at the time, nice if you could afford it.

The next innovation to have a significant effect on brewing was the hydrometer, invented in 1780, which provided an accurate measure of the amount of fermentable sugar in the wort (the fermenting liquid that would become beer), otherwise known as the specific gravity. Sadly perhaps, the ale conner and his leather breeks were out of business. The trend towards large-scale brewing gathered pace.

The phenomenal allure of entire butt

It wasn't just science and technology that drove the growth of big brewing. As always happens when people are exposed to new ideas and new surroundings, tastes changed. And one such change transformed the steady trend towards larger-scale brewing into a stampede that created a modern industry.

It's a defining feature of drinkers that we love to experiment. We don't need to reminisce for too long about the lethal cocktails we all bolted down and promptly threw back up in our youth. But we were never unique in this respect – in a corner of the same pub, there were probably a couple of old men pouring a bottle of sweet stout into a half of bitter. With this experimentation as with so much else in beer, we are merely carrying on a centuries-old trend, and this trend was another factor in the growth of the huge breweries we know today. It prompted a wholesale change in what we drank, and gave birth to a beer that remains one of the most famous in the world even today.

Late seventeenth- and early eighteenth-century pubs offered a variety of beers and ales, and drinkers experimented according to their tastes. The wonderfully named (but almost certainly pseudonymous) Obadiah Poundage told readers of the *London Chronicle* in November 1760 that Londoners enjoyed a 'sweet heavy drink, in general used ale mixed with beer, which they purchased from the Ale draper'. While breweries sold their ale as soon as it was brewed, the 'Ale draper' would age some stocks for six to eighteen months, which would produce a sharper, sour taste.* In the early 1700s, pale ales brewed for country houses were becoming popular with the gentry, but when yet another war with France led to taxes on malt rising faster than taxes on hops, unhopped sweet ale became more expensive than hoppy, bitter beer. This pale beer was too bitter for London tastes, and so, according to Poundage, while some drinkers opted for 'mild beer and stale mixed', others became more adventurous and went for 'ale, mild beer and stale blended together'.

Eventually brewers realized that 'beer well brewed, kept its proper time, became racy and mellow, that is, neither new nor stale', and that with such a beer they could make more profit for themselves and make life considerably easier for London's reluctant early beer cocktail mixologists. After a slow start, this new brown beer 'succeeded beyond all expectation' thanks to the enthusiastic patronage of London's working people. Many of these were employed carrying goods and messages across town, and were called porters. Demonstrating yet again the imaginative flourish so prevalent at the time, the beer was soon dubbed 'porter' in their honour, or 'entire butt', as it used beer from all three mashings of a brew, not just the first mash for the strongest beer. In Hogarth's *Beer Street* a street or ticket porter – identifiable from his badge bearing the arms of the City of London – can be seen drinking from a quart pot after resting his heavy load of books.

By the middle of the century everybody was drinking it, prompting Henry Jackson to comment in 1758 that, 'Beer,

---

* You can get a good impression of what this aged ale would have been like by sampling a Belgian 'oud bruin' beer today, if you're feeling adventurous. Prepare to pucker.

commonly call'd Porter, is almost become the universal Cordial of the Populace'.

Legend has it that a Shoreditch brewer called Ralph Harwood 'invented' porter, but there's no direct evidence to back this up. As is usually the case with beer styles, the truth is that it evolved over time. Old Obadiah tells us that early porter was 'far from being in the perfection which since we have had it'. But the obituary of Ralph Harwood's son James in 1762 described him as 'an eminent brewer in Shoreditch, and the first that brought porter to perfection', so Harwood's brewery may well have been the one to finally bring the style to fruition – even if it took more than one generation.

But perfect or not, it certainly took off quickly. In 1726 our old friend Cesar de Saussure encountered porter, which left him as gobsmacked as ever by the English and their beer. He wrote home that porter was 'a thick and strong beverage' and that 'the effect it produces if drunk in excess is the same as that of wine'. In reality it wasn't quite that strong, but probably about 7 per cent ABV, still way stronger than premium beers today.

Porter was originally a brown beer, but was brewed darker over time. It had to be aged for four of five months, and was often kept much longer than that. When beer ages it grows darker, and as porter was often aged for up to eighteen months, brewing a darker beer to start with would have been a short cut to suggesting a quality brew. Stronger beers of any style were often referred to as 'stout' beers, and strong porters gradually became referred to simply as stouts.*At the

---

* For much of the twentieth century porter was by any meaningful

height of porter's popularity in London, a certain Arthur Guinness, an Irishman, figured there was definitely a future for this particular brew, and took the recipe for it back home to his brewery in Dublin.

Although porter was a better beer in many respects than its predecessors, it was actually quite troublesome to produce. It needed to be matured for up to eighteen months and required careful brewing, so it actually had to be brewed in larger vessels if anyone was going to make any money out of it.

Again, this meant that only the biggest London brewers had the scale necessary to brew porter commercially, and the impressive steam engines and cooling systems adopted by the breweries so far were only the merest hint of what they were about to get up to. Just like Brunel with his big chain, the brewers were about to try to symbolize the scale and ambition of the entire Industrial Revolution. In the shape of a beer vat. And like many of the most grandiose schemes of men throughout history, it would end in tragedy.

Porter explodes – no, really

Of course, it was Sam Whitbread who led the way. In 1760 he made his already impressive Chiswell Street brewery even

---

definition extinct as a beer style, but it's made a spectacular comeback on the crest of the latest craft beer revolution (oops – spoiler alert – in case you didn't already know, there's a craft beer revolution towards the end of the book). Porter is a London beer style, and you can't do much better than to try the offerings from two great London brewers – Fuller's in Chiswick and Meantime from Greenwich.

more fantastic with the addition of the Porter Tun room. The room was a feat in itself, with tourist guides at the time marvelling, 'the unsupported roof span ... is exceeded in its majestic size only by that of Westminster Hall'. And it was dominated by a giant beer vat.

The gauntlet had been thrown down. Proving that phallic substitutes among powerful men predate the arrival of bright red sports cars, rival brewer Henry Thrale built a new porter vat and celebrated its completion by having a hundred people sit down to dinner inside it. 'Right then, you bastard,' thought the Meux brewery, who went off and built one sixty feet wide and twenty-three feet high. They had two hundred guests to dinner in that one. Just to make sure everyone knew who was boss, they soon added a second one which was almost as large.

The contest reached its conclusion with the Meux's Horse Shoe Brewery tragedy in 1814. The brewery's main porter vat stood twenty-two feet high. On Monday, 17th October 1814, it was about nine tenths full, holding 3555 barrels (just over a million pints) of porter, which had been ageing for ten months. In the afternoon of that day George Crick, a storehouse clerk, noticed that one of the iron hoops binding the vat had burst and flown off. He reported this to the brewery management, but as this had happened many times before without causing any problems – largely because it was one of 29 hoops, each of which weighed at least a third of a ton, seven of them over a ton – they agreed that there was no immediate danger.

Later, while working a short distance from the vat, Crick claimed, 'I heard the crash as it went off, and ran immediately to the storehouse where the vat was situated. I found myself up to my knees in beer.' His brother was trapped under the wreckage of the vat; the brewery cellars and the wells within them were full of beer, and one of the walls seemed to be missing. After rescuing his brother, Crick and brewery employees devoted themselves to saving as much beer as they could, completely unaware of any wider ramifications of the exploding vat until the body of Ann Saville floated past them among the ruins, together with the remains of a private still from one of the neighbouring houses. With unintentional and – let's be honest – inappropriate comic effect, Crick would inform an inquest two days later that 'he [was] quite certain neither [the body nor the still] were there before' and realized he was standing in the middle of a monumental disaster.

The explosion had knocked the cock out of a second vat containing 2400 barrels, starting a chain reaction. In total, the brewery later calculated that between 8000 and 9000 barrels – between 2.3 and 2.6 million pints – had been lost in a tidal wave of beer that engulfed the surrounding area.

The force of more beer than you could possibly imagine* had 'burst with great impetuosity' through the brewhouse, according to the following day's *Morning Chronicle* newspaper. It demolished the 25-foot high, one-foot thick brewhouse wall, and 'so great was the force of the explosion, that the bricks of the brewhouse were thrown over the tops of the houses of Russel-street'. The surrounding houses were home to poor families, and densely packed, with many of the residents out of work and therefore at home.

---

* Yes, I'm sure you can imagine an awful lot of beer, but trust me – this was more.

Mr Goodwin, a poulterer who lived in the street, was in the yard behind his house with his family when the wave picked them up and carried them through the house, out of the front door of their shop and deposited them in the street without injury. Many others were not so lucky. One young girl was sitting in a first floor room with her mother when the wave swept them out through a window. The mother survived, but the girl was 'dashed to pieces'. In one house about thirty people were assembled for the wake of a small girl when the house was flattened. 'The cries and groans which issues from the ruins were dreadful,' said one newspaper, 'and it is feared a great number of them may have perished.'

Confusion reigned for a couple of days, with reports that 'the extent of the mischief done by this dreadful and extraordinary event, can scarcely be ascertained. Great numbers of individuals were in the most distressing state, in the uncertainty of the fate of persons connected with them.'

Stories abounded of people flinging themselves into the torrent and hampering the investigation effort, of people collecting beer in any utensil that would hold it, of drunken riots and people drinking themselves to death.* But *The Times* told a different story of 'several Gentlemen who were

---

* In recent years, one of the most scurrilous, ill-informed sources of tall tales about the Great London Beer Flood of 1814 was, um . . . me. It was such a great story and it has been embellished so vividly over the years, that when I wrote the first edition of this book I simply repeated the most exciting account I could find. Turns out there was no documentary basis to that story whatsoever. Sorry about that. By way of restitution, the above account is now as accurate as the newspapers of 1814 reported it. Which means it simply *must* be true, right?

drawn to the spot to prevent any noise among the crowd, that the persons who were employed in clearing away the rubbish might, in pursuing their work, direct their ears to the ground, in order to discover whether any of the victims were calling for assistance. The caution and humanity with which the labourers proceeded in their distressing task excited a strong interest, and deserve warm approbation.'

Two days after the incident the official inquest was held on eight bodies. There were rumours that others were missing, and that a ninth man had succumbed to alcohol poisoning, but there is no contemporary account of any further casualties after the inquest, and one week later a newspaper declared that no further fatalities had occurred.

The brewery itself almost became the final victim of the tragedy. But after a verdict of accidental death 'by calamitous accident, but the most probable [being] the violent escape of air generated in the liquor', the government agreed to waive the duty on the beer that was lost and Meux survived to brew another day – though it's doubtful that they continued to boast about the size of their porter vats with quite as much bravado as before.

This inconvenient setback may have curtailed the fashion for huge expressions of brewing prowess, but not the desire to grow as businesses. The pattern was now established. In times when demand fell, such as when people decided they preferred tea, coffee or gin, the biggest brewers had the cash reserves to weather the storm. When times were good, they benefited from economies of scale. From this point on, the story of British brewing was increasingly the story of fewer and fewer companies growing ever larger on the back of increasing demand.

High fashion in Burton-on-Trent

Throughout most of the nineteenth century, people were drinking more and more beer. The population increased rapidly, but the sketchy figures that do exist suggest that beer consumption was growing even faster, so per capita consumption was also rising. This was driven by more than just changes in technology and licensing laws; the Victorians were developing a taste for the good life.

We tend only to remember the repressed, puritanical traits of the Victorians – with the temperance movement and a philosophy of abstinence when it came to any form of sensual pleasure. But this kind of moral self-flagellation was largely confined to the middle classes, and even there it was never universal, particularly before the 1870s. Also, while the Industrial Revolution may be remembered chiefly for the misery of factories and mines, you don't get that degree of progress and change without there being a significant increase in wealth and living standards somewhere. Although it was a very unequal society with a grossly unfair distribution of wealth, some of that wealth filtered down through society at large. Overall, the hardship faced by the Victorian poor wasn't nearly as bad as had been endured by earlier generations, and by the mid 1840s the employed working classes had enough money to spend on food and drink, even a little left over for the more pleasurable things in life.

Victorian Britain may not have measured the rise and fall of fashion and celebrity in the microseconds we use now, but you could be forgiven for thinking that they were just as shamelessly fashion-obsessed as the most ardent glossy mag reader of the early twenty-first century.* The Victorians were always looking for the next big thing, and a very big thing indeed was about to sweep porter aside, shooing it out of the nation's pubs as dramatically as it had arrived.

The trigger was the abolition of excise duty on glass in 1845. Cheap glass production allowed beer to be packaged attractively in bottles, and it began to be served in glasses rather than ceramic mugs and pewter tankards. At some point the big porter brewers must have thought this was a fantastic idea – dead stylish and all that – but because drinkers could now see what they were getting, the appearance of beer became much more important, and dark, mysterious porter suddenly looked less appetizing than it once had. People had never noticed before how strongly the liquid resembled a muddy puddle. There were also the innovations in pasteurization and filtration which meant beer could be bottled and shipped much further afield with a far greater degree of consistent quality than ever before, and the invention of refrigeration in the 1880s meant the temperature during the brewing process could be better controlled. Brewers no longer had to rely on the dark, burnt malts that characterized porter to get consistent good quality.

'Mild', a term that had been used for centuries to describe ale that was fresh from the brewery rather than aged, evolved into a specific style. Sweeter and lighter in both alcohol and character than porter, it became the dominant beer style during the 1830s, especially in the beer heartlands where industrial workers were looking for quantity rather than

---

* If you don't believe me you've never read any Oscar Wilde.

alcoholic strength. And then, the railways started to link London to the provinces.

The brewers in Burton-on-Trent, particularly Bass, were gathering a growing reputation for their fine pale ales. The water around Burton is rich in gypsum (calcium sulphate) and other minerals, and brewing required substantial hopping to get a beer with a balanced flavour. The end result was a light, bright, sparkling beer that looked so much more pleasant and appetizing than murky old porter. The hopping gave it an edge of bitterness over other beers, and it was Burton-style beer that first came to be called bitter.*

While London porter brewers had the domestic market sewn up, the Burton brewers had been quietly developing a lucrative export trade. If beer was important in British towns and cities as a source of nutrients and clean water, it was essential in harsher climates such as India and Australia. The local beverage in India, *arak*, was made from rough, fermented palm juice and played a significant role in reducing life expectancy for Europeans in the subcontinent to a mere three years. Clean drinking water was just as difficult to come by as it was in London, and apart from that, those serving in the colonies experienced lives that consisted of long periods of extreme boredom punctuated by – in the case of the troops in particular – short bursts of extreme violence. To

---

* Hops also affect the mouth in a very particular way. The taste buds on the tongue are grouped so that different parts of your tongue pick up different flavours. The bits that soak up bitterness are concentrated towards the back of the tongue and the top of the throat. If you drink a particularly hoppy beer, the back of the tongue is quite buzzy, puckering your mouth and creating the desire to keep drinking. People drink hoppy beers faster, and therefore drink more.

relieve the crushing boredom the Anglo-Indians built their lives around booze, exhibiting extremes of gatteredness that put their homebound rivals to shame.

The trouble was, the climate in India made it impossible to brew, so beer had to be imported. This meant a six-month sea journey that normally included two transatlantic crossings, one navigation of the notorious Cape of Good Hope, and two crossings of the equator. Only the hardiest beers could survive, and while porter was strong enough to make the journey successfully, the dark, murky brew didn't seem quite as appealing on a verandah in Calcutta as it had in a smoky Shoreditch tavern. A London brewer called Hodgson eventually perfected a version of the pale 'October ales' brewed for country houses and cornered the Indian market with it. Being paler, Hodgson's beer – after being chilled with ice harvested on the Indian hills during the cold season and stored in underground ice houses – was perfect over dinner after a hard day shooting tigers or stringing up Indian servants for some perceived slight (such as not chilling the beer properly). What's more, that rigorous sea journey actually improved the beer, the extreme conditions creating an accelerated approximation of the long cellar ageing that October ales were used to.

In the 1820s the Hodgsons got greedy, imposing restrictive trade terms, which upset the East India Company. This was not a great idea given that 'John Company' was the most powerful corporation the world had ever seen, had its own army and navy, controlled many of the ships making the passage from England to India and was run entirely by ruthless, corrupt and vindictive evil bastards who were by far and away the richest and most powerful merchants in the world.

These bastards coolly destroyed Hodgson by approaching the brewers in Burton-on-Trent, who had built a reputation for brewing beers that survived long sea journeys by exporting sweet, brown Burton Ale to the Baltic States and the Czar's court in St Petersburg. Burton's brewers recreated Hodgson's beer, added more hops, and found that Burton spring water made it far superior to the original. This 'East India Pale Ale' became the fuel that powered the glory years of the British Empire, the world's first global beer style.*

As troops and families returned from the subcontinent, India Pale Ale (IPA) brewers began to sell their beers (cellar aged rather than shipped to India and back) at home. Brewers across the country all had a go at the style, but none could match Burton. And when the modest Midlands town got its rail connection in 1839, it became viable for Burton brewers to sell their beers in the biggest market of all: London.†

They didn't waste much time. Bass and Allsopp, two of the biggest brewers in Burton, used the railways to their

---

* Check out my third book, *Hops and Glory*, for (a) a fuller account of the India Pale Ale legend, and (b) a stark warning of how an obsession with beer and the recreation of, say, a historic journey from Burton-on-Trent to India by boat can drive you to the brink of madness if you're not careful.
† IPA changed over time, and by the mid-twentieth century was a weak session bitter. Greene King IPA, which at 3.6 per cent is half the strength of a traditional IPA, is often pilloried as some kind of fake, but it's simply the most successful survivor from this time. American craft brewers have revived traditional IPA as a style and created their own version of it, with brands like Goose Island IPA beating Kiwi Sauvignon Blancs at their own grassy, citrus flavoured game. Worthington White Shield is the only remaining authentic survivor from the golden age of British IPAs, but new creations such as Meantime IPA, St Austell Tribute and Marston's Old Empire are worthy inheritors of the style.

fullest extent. They offered railway workers rewards and incentives to make sure their beers got to London as quickly and in as good condition as possible. It paid off. The Victorian skilled artisan and middle classes went for the bright, strong distinctive Burton ales, and porter quickly became the stuff poor people drank. Burton's output increased tenfold between 1850 and 1880. Bass and Allsopp became the leaders in innovation and scientific research. Not only was IPA more appealing than porter to fashionable London, described as a 'wine of malt' and endorsed by the medical profession, Burton's brewers reinvested their profits and developed a lighter, less potent version that could be served fresh, without the ageing process required by both porter and IPA. These 'running ales' were essentially the first cask conditioned 'real ales' as we know them today.

At first, the reaction of the leading porter brewers to Burton bitter was to ignore it. Having built their fortunes on people's evolving tastes a century earlier, they refused to believe this new change was anything other than a passing fad. As far as they were concerned, switching production would have meant substantial rebuilding of the breweries, and anyway they didn't have the water in London to get the same effect the hard water in Burton produced.

It would perhaps be nice to think that the lumbering, old-fashioned brewers disappeared and the bright, thrusting Burton breweries and all their contented bitter drinkers lived happily ever after. But even a wholesale change in what we drank couldn't shift them. Bass and Allsopp merely joined the ranks of the big brewers, who all took a knock but eventually switched their production away from porter to mild and

Burton-style bitter. All, that is, apart from the descendants of that Irishman we mentioned earlier.

Pure genius

Arthur Guinness began brewing ale, the old-fashioned kind, in Dublin in the eighteenth century. When the London brewers started turning out porter in huge quantities, the craze swept out across the country and over to Ireland, and imports of London porter took large chunks out of Arthur's Dublin market. He decided to get in on the act and began brewing porter himself. He became very good at it. By 1799 he had switched over completely to producing the dark, heavy beer, and had turned the tables on London by beginning to export his stuff back there. It became so popular that at the Battle of Waterloo in 1815 wounded English officers supposedly cried out for it by name.

When the popularity of porter began to decline and the big London brewers switched to ale, Guinness, now run by Arthur's son (the imaginatively named Arthur II) had different ideas. While all the English brewers were developing lighter, paler beers, Arthur was perfecting his darker, more robust 'extra stout' porter. It was a distinctive beer, almost black thanks to the use of heavily roasted malts. Guinness wasn't the only brewer of stout, but it was certainly the most successful. Soon the Dublin brewery was the largest in the world, and Guinness was selling around the globe.

But while Guinness ploughed its unique and very lucrative furrow, the rest of the big brewers carried on producing a range of the most popular beers of the time. Seemingly, there was nothing that could stop beer production being consolidated into ever fewer, larger hands. They had economies of scale so huge that they could handle trifling matters such as everyone suddenly deciding to drink a product they didn't make with relative ease, especially when there were further inventions and innovations to come that would transform the industry yet again.

'Études sur la bière'

OK, I'm sorry to have to bring the French into this very British narrative, but one particular Frenchman is about to make a major contribution to it.

People had long since figured out that glass could be used to magnify images – microscopes had been used to discover cells as early as the seventeenth century – but the science was crude and imprecise. Lenses, at a certain level of magnification, will break up white light into its constituent parts, so instead of seeing a magnified image you see a kaleidoscopic effect. This limited the development of microscopic research until the nineteenth century, when research into the properties of light and lenses solved the problem. By the latter half of the century, we could study things to a far more – well – microscopic level than had previously been possible. Obviously, this led to all sorts of useful scientific and medical advances that transformed our lives. But never mind all that. It allowed us to make better beer.

Louis Pasteur was without doubt the man who made the most of the new technology. He solved the mysteries of rabies, anthrax, chicken cholera and silkworm diseases, and contributed to the development of the first vaccines. He debunked the widely accepted myth of spontaneous generation – that living organisms could appear from nowhere – thereby practically inventing modern biology and biochemistry. He was single-handedly responsible for some of the most important theoretical concepts and practical applications of modern science. And, just for fun, he established the scientific basis of fermentation, wine-making and the brewing of beer.

It all started with the Franco-Prussian War of 1870–1. Napoleon III wasn't too popular at home, and was advised that he needed a good war to sort this out. These same advisers told him the German state of Prussia would be easy pickings. Wrong. Bismarck, the Prussian chancellor, formed a coalition of German states and inflicted a painful and humiliating defeat on France which marked the end of French hegemony in continental Europe and resulted in the creation of a unified Germany.* Pasteur was a patriotic Frenchman and was not too happy about this turn of events. He decided that, in his own small way, he would use his immense scientific brain to redress the balance in a petty but immensely satisfying manner.†

German beers had long been acknowledged as superior throughout Europe but, following his studies of microorganisms, Pasteur suspected he understood far more than anyone else in the world about how and why beer turned out the way it did. He resolved to share and develop his knowledge of beer with anyone who was interested in enhancing

---

*   I'm guessing these advisers were subsequently 'downsized'.
†   He was French after all.

their reputation as a brewer of top-quality beers. Anyone, that is, except the Germans. Pasteur began his research into brewing and the actions of yeast in his beloved home country, and just in case anyone felt like giving him the benefit of the doubt by pretending that this was about anything other than knocking Germany off its beery pedestal, he insisted that any brews resulting from his methods should be dubbed *Bières de la Revanche Nationale*, or Beers of the National Revenge.

By August 1871 Pasteur realized that he needed a bigger canvas to work on, and came to London where the breweries were bigger and more scientific. He turned up at Whitbread's Chiswell Street brewery, badgered them into buying a microscope, and proved that bad brews were due to the yeast becoming infected by competing strains or other micro-organisms. Pasteur returned to France to continue his work, where he established beyond doubt that all kinds of fermentation were caused by micro-organisms. In 1876 he published his findings in *Études sur la bière*, a book that was quickly translated by all major brewers, revolutionizing their methods.

Initially there was some resistance to the new, scientific way of brewing. Horace Brown was a brewer who studied at the Royal College of Chemistry in the 1860s. When he started work at the Worthington brewery people shunned his new-found knowledge and tools 'due to the fear that the display of any chemical apparatus might suggest to customers the horrible suspicion that the beer was being "doctored"'. But soon every brewery had a microscope. In 1895 the *Journal of the Institute of Brewing* celebrated the fact that the days when any moron – even those the army rejected – could find a job in the brewing industry had now disappeared. Now, they claimed, the modern brewer should be, 'essentially a chemist, as brewing is practically the conversion of certain substances into certain chemically different substances by what is more or less a chemical process'. Godisgoode, the magical breath of air that transformed base liquid into beer, had been revealed scientifically as the work of microscopic organisms. Brewing had made the transition from mystical gift from the gods, via natural but mystical process which mankind could perform but never fully control, finally to science over which we had some pretence of mastery.

The Scots. Different. Again.

At this time Scottish beers were still quite distinct from their English cousins, but the same processes of consolidation and scientific advancement were happening. The expenses of production and the high transport costs involved in distributing beer from Edinburgh and Glasgow across a scattered, rugged country meant that the industry there consolidated just as quickly as in England. Robert Tennent, a publican, and William Younger, an excise officer, established the country's first commercial breweries. It was actually William Younger's son, Archibald Campbell Younger, who really made the difference though. He had the ambition to produce a distinctive Scottish beer that would rival those from England. He and Tennent imported the finest English malts to supplement the local variety. Hops were not grown locally and were expensive to import from the south of England, so they were used more sparingly. Scottish beers remain less hopped, and are still significantly less bitter than English beers as a result.

Scottish beer still goes under a range of different names which can be confusing at first. Mild is known as light and bitter is called heavy. With the disappearance of mild from most pubs this now leaves heavy with no apparent relation. Except there is something in between called special, which is also bitter. Confused? To clarify things, light is also known as 60 shilling, special as 70 shilling and heavy as 80 shilling. This system goes back to the 1870s when beer was graded according to the invoice price for a barrel, which was in turn determined by the gravity of the beer.

By the nineteenth century the big Scottish brewers were well established and were busy buying up the few remaining small country breweries. The railways allowed them to grab most of the local market and even export to England. Scotland's biggest export was people, and where Scots went to work – or fight – their beer followed. A 'magic circle' of wells around Edinburgh was discovered to contain water comparable in its mineral content to that in Burton. By the end of the nineteenth century Tennent's and McEwan's were globally famous names. The Scottish capital had eclipsed the legendary beer town as the greatest exporter of pale ales across the Empire, comparable in its day not only to Burton but also to Munich or the Czech town of Pilsen as one of the greatest brewing cities on the planet.

The birth of modern brewing

The late nineteenth century was something of a golden age for beer, with names such as Bass, Guinness and Younger's gaining international renown. Such was their success that everyone wanted a piece of it. By the mid 1880s there were thirty-one brewers in Burton-on-Trent looking for a share of the glory. In a nation with such a thirst on, there were large sums of money to be made by the unscrupulous. Some smaller, crooked brewers benefited from the reputations of the larger breweries by producing any old crap of low or variable quality, and passing it off as one of the leading beers. Some of this gut rot could even be poisonous – in Salford in 1900 seventy people died in a mysterious epidemic that would be traced back to a batch of beer contaminated by sulphuric acid.

Bass in particular was such a popular beer that countless brewers claimed their inferior products were actually Bass brews. The brewery came up with the bright idea of stamping their barrels with a distinctive bright red triangle, but many of their competitors simply copied it. In 1875 the Trade Marks Registration Act was passed to provide companies with some legal protection against this kind of practice. The act came into force on the first day of the following year. That's why the bloke from Bass spent New Year's Eve sleeping on the doorstep of the new trademark office. The next morning the Bass red triangle became the UK's first registered trademark. Others quickly followed suit. After the practice of burning recognized symbols of ownership into wooden barrels and crates, these marks became known as brands.

By the end of the nineteenth century a few large companies accounted for 90 per cent of total British beer output, and owned nearly 90 per cent of the country's pubs. The transformation of the brewing industry from quaint network of cottage industries producing local products for local people to huge business, with brands like Guinness and Bass famous across the world, was complete. The process had been haphazard and chaotic in places, but the trends had been set. From now on, beer would be produced by perpetually fewer and bigger companies, and drinkers would be faced with an ever-dwindling number of beers to choose from. So much had changed in the way beer was made. But that was nothing compared to what was happening to the places in which we were drinking. As all this was going on, the pub itself changed beyond recognition.

Chapter Five

'Those who are not singing are sprawling'

Pubs in the nineteenth century

Agitation over a glass of grog

You know what happens when women go away and men are left in the house on their own? How it doesn't merely become messy, or dirty, but acquires a deeper layer of grime and seediness, a smell of staleness, a thickness in the air? At the end of the eighteenth century, that's exactly what happened to the pub.

As working patterns changed it became common for men to drink together in groups, and by the nineteenth century, if you were a woman in a pub it was assumed that you were there for one thing only, and that you were probably going to charge for it.

The changes in the nature of drinking establishments reflected the increasingly hypocritical attitudes towards class distinctions which were developing in the newly industrialized world. While the profession of publican became seen as a respectable living, actually visiting a public house was increasingly something a gentleman simply did not do if he wanted to avoid adverse comment in polite society. The public house may still have been 'the primordial cell of British life', as Charles Booth put it, but it was starting to develop a serious image problem. In 1797 Sir Frederic Eden wrote that it was 'not the fashion for gentlemen and people of rank to frequent alehouses'. They were dirty and undesirable – or at least, they were in the minds of people who no longer visited them. Having abandoned the place themselves, respectable people looked at the pub from the outside and started to talk disapprovingly about what (probably) went on there.

There was a widespread belief that the pub was a haven of crime. Criminals? Pubs were full of them. Must have been. Just look at them. Once seen as a legitimate meeting place for people from all classes, the pub was increasingly regarded as a refuge for villains. As respectable people deserted the place, it stood to reason that a higher proportion of those remaining would be disreputable.

An even more serious concern, at least among the ruling classes, was the role of the pub in fomenting political dissent, causing disapproval of the place to develop into paranoia and outright hostility. In many areas pubs were the only places large enough for public meetings, so they were magnets for political groups. The American and French revolutions had shaken Britain, and meeting places full of commoners were seen as dangerous. Whereas it was perfectly understandable for gentlemen and politicians to congregate in city taverns to discuss the issues of the day, if the working class did likewise there was bound to be seditious plotting going on. This paranoia was nothing new. In ancient Babylon King Hammurabi (the same bloke who decided barmaids could be drowned for serving short measures) decreed that the introduction of political debate into beer shops was an offence punishable by – you guessed it – death. I don't think he was just trying to keep the atmosphere upbeat.

People in pubs talk more freely, out of sight of their rulers and bosses, and different trades tended to be centred around specific areas in towns and villages, so the local was a natural meeting place for people with a common grievance. Pubs therefore acted as midwives in the birth of the trade union movement. In the nineteenth century one temperance campaigner became quite exercised about what a bad thing this connection was:

> Nine tenths of the tyranny and violence of Trades Unions which sometimes exhibit themselves in overt acts, but are more frequently suffered in silence by individuals, arises from the intemperance of those who are in many cases more prominent members, and from the facilities afforded by the present iniquitous system for hatching secret plots over a glass of grog or a pot of beer in the public house.

The 1832 Reform Act extended the right to vote to any man living in a house with an annual value of ten pounds or more, and the Chartist movement was formed in 1836 to demand more constitutional rights for the working classes. Those in charge no longer had any idea what these people were discussing in the alehouses, because they couldn't possibly venture in there themselves. Of course, the government couldn't actually ban people from meeting and talking about politics (although, with the Anti-Combination Acts around this time, they did come close) but they could lean on people to stop it happening. Between 1807 and 1830 the Whig opposition had relied on public houses as crucial meeting places during years of Tory rule, but by 1839 a Whig government was threatening landlords with refusal of their licences should they allow Chartists to meet on their premises. The message to the newly enfranchised classes was very clearly, 'Do as we say, not as we do.'

Bars and beer engines

But, for all these pressures, the pub was still an essential part of everyday life. It had survived disapproval before, and would continue to adapt and prosper through increasingly turbulent times as the Industrial Revolution helped the serving as well as the production of beer, with the spirit of invention reaching the bar itself. I say bar, but the bar as such didn't really exist yet.

Beer had to be kept in cellars to keep it cool enough to remain in good condition in crowded, sweaty pubs. This meant pot boys were employed to run up and down from the cellar with jugs slopping all over the place, which, as urban pubs became busier, revealed itself as a pretty poor system. At the end of the eighteenth century people were experimenting with pump systems to draw the beer up from the cellar, cutting time and labour. The invention of the beer engine is widely credited to one Joseph Bramah, a hydraulic engineer and locksmith who invented the hydraulic press, a decent toilet, and a money printing press. In 1797 he patented a manually operated beer pump which he believed would have tremendous advantages for 'the masters of families and publicans'.

Unfortunately Bramah's handpump was rubbish. Whereas handpumps depend on pressure from the beer engine on the bar to create a vacuum that draws the beer up the line from the cask, Bramah's sketches show a system of pistons inside casks, weighted with heavy bags of sand. The piston pushes the beer down inside the cask, through an opening in the bottom, and up the pipe to a simple tap at the bar. It would never have worked, because it failed to take account of both the dimensions of casks, which are bowed, and the height of cellars, which were too low for his pistons. Bramah's idea never poured a single pint. The handpumps that appeared a few years later are often credited to him, but are completely different and were invented by someone else.*

A typical 'beer engine' would have about six handles, and bars were therefore installed on which to mount them, making pot boys redundant. In country inns beer would still be served from jugs, with no bar counter, but by the 1820s, hand pump systems similar to those still seen today were commonplace in urban pubs.

One of the most significant developments in the evolution of the bar itself was the brainchild of our old friend, Isambard

---

* Even though Bramah was crap at beer engines and is credited by history for something he didn't invent, I still love him because he was from my hometown of Barnsley and married a girl from Mapplewell, the village where I grew up. The couple moved south to London – they had to. If you tried being an inventor in Barnsley they'd just laugh at you and say 'Thee and thi fancy hydraulics. Backbreaking labour in the white heat of the world's first industrial revolution, man and machine chained together as one, not good enough for thee and thi posh mates, is it?'

Kingdom Brunel. In 1840 he was faced with a conundrum in Swindon train station.* The first trains had no buffet cars, toilets or heating,† which meant that as soon as they stopped at stations everyone would pile off and into the station facilities.‡ The trains stopped at Swindon for ten minutes, and this was never long enough for everyone to get served. Brunel was an engineer and saw the problem as an equation. The stopping time of the train was fixed, the demand for beer, naturally, tended towards infinity, but the length of the bar was potentially variable. He surmised that the optimal bar shape would be circular, as this would allow staff to serve the maximum number of people in the shortest time. As a result, the central island bar came into being, and is still common today.

As the nineteenth century progressed, urban populations continued to grow, as did the number of pubs looking to make a profit from serving them, and competition became more intense. Added to this, public houses were no longer competing just with other eating and drinking establishments. Glass was becoming more readily available, and the shop window allowed merchants to showcase their wares. High street shops began to look more colourful and attractive, and pubs looked dull in comparison. There would always be a place for the cheap drinking hovel, but in busy areas pub owners started to add a bit of glamour and

---

* Not something you'd wish on many people, but he liked that sort of thing. It appealed to the way his brain worked.
† If you've recently been on a train from London to Norwich, you might ask what's changed.
‡ And here's your answer. Back then stations *had* facilities. Just imagine . . .

aspiration to their premises. The Victorian predilection for clutter led to gas lamps, prints, glass cases, plants and clocks embellishing previously bare alehouses. Landlords slowly realized that their establishments were more than just utilitarian places to get a drink. Frederick Hackwood, in his 1912 book *Inns, Ales and Drinking Customs of Old England*, argued that by the nineteenth century, men didn't go to pubs just to get toped up, but for:

> The cheerfulness, light, and warmth which are invariably offered there, and which too many of the lower class miss at home; by a longing for congenial society, and a desire to be free, if only for a little while, from the pressure of domestic worries and daily cares.

But the biggest change to the places in which we drank wasn't the result of technological development, or a fashion for frippery; it was the consequence of government intervention which tried to make things better for people but got it badly wrong. Again.

Getting out of one's gig

By the 1820s boozing was causing serious headaches for the government. Gin consumption was on the rise again, having doubled between 1807 and 1827, but at the same time, there was concern that the big London brewers were growing too powerful. Additionally, beer was increasingly becoming a recreational drink consumed outside the home rather than a kitchen staple. The licensing system for public houses had been created for a previous age, and no longer reflected the reality of how and where people drank.* There were also wider problems in the economy. An agricultural recession had sent the price of cereal crops plummeting, and the deeply unpopular government saw an opportunity to reverse this by boosting the demand for grain from the brewing industry. Meanwhile, King George IV was on his last legs, and his death would prompt an automatic general election. The Duke of Wellington may have been adored as a war hero after beating Napoleon, but he made a reluctant prime minister in a weak and hated government that needed to do something to try and regain popularity. That something was to be the Beer Act of 1830.

Because of the pressures of the temperance movement and the general attitude of sour-faced disapproval for which the Victorian era is remembered, the Beer Act of 1830 hasn't been much discussed by social historians, and tends not to get mentioned in nineteenth-century history. It was certainly overshadowed by the 1832 Reform Act. But it transformed the nature of pubs – and arguably British society – at a stroke, and set the course for our beer drinking habits for the rest of the century. One historian who could be bothered to study it, W. L. Burn, has suggested that, 'It is quite arguable that this Act was more revolutionary in its immediate social consequences than any other of the reform age.'

Basically the act completely freed up the sale of beer. It was designed to curb the growing power of the big brewers by liberating the market and making life easier for small

---

* This point about licensing may sound familiar. That's because, as Shirley Bassey and the Propellerheads argued so cogently, history keeps repeating itself.

businesses, thereby generating new competition. If it reduced the demand for gin, boosted the price of cereal crops and caused everyone to feel benevolent towards the government as well, that was just dandy.

Since the 1550s, licences for inns, taverns and alehouses had been controlled by magistrates. Even though they were increasingly regarded just as public houses, they were still licensed separately. The 1830 act created a fourth type of outlet – the beer house – outside the jurisdiction of magistrates, and any householder who could afford the licence fee (a mere two pounds) could sell beer, and brew it if he wanted, on his premises. The act also repealed duty on beer, and set permitted opening hours at of 5 a.m. to 10 p.m., apart from Sundays during the hours of religious services.

The day the act was passed the nation celebrated, perhaps unsurprisingly, by getting completely stoated. The Mayor of Arundel, William Holmes, found it intolerable that the masses were suddenly spending the day as idly as he, and complained to a parliamentary select committee that, 'I was obliged to get out of my gig* three times from people coming along, waggoners drunk, when I was returning from shooting on the very day of the operation of the Bill.' Sydney Smith, a Yorkshire clergyman famous for his wit and perceptiveness, had previously spoken out strongly in favour of the liberalization of the drinks industry, calling the control exercised by the big brewers and the magistrates together, 'One of the most enormous and scandalous Tyrannies ever exercised upon any people', but within two weeks of the act being

---

* In those days, a type of carriage rather than a concert by a popular rock combo.

passed he sighed, 'Everybody is drunk. Those who are not singing are sprawling. The sovereign people are in a beastly state.' Twenty years later, you'd think the novelty of unfettered drinking might have worn off, but no. Lord Palmerston quipped, 'The words "licensed to be drunk on the premises" are by the people interpreted as applicable to the customers as well as the liquor.'

The act resulted in cheaper beer and demand rocketed. The number of licensed premises soared. Not only did more householders start to fancy themselves as publicans, but blacksmiths and other craftsmen became licensed so they could serve beer to their waiting customers. But as far as boosting small-scale competition against the big brewers was concerned, it failed utterly. In fact, it had precisely the opposite effect.

Looking back it seems bloody obvious. The big producers were already in a position where they could brew better beer more cheaply than the small brewers. When demand soared and the cost of production fell, the big brewers' economies of scale really kicked in. Ten years after the act came into force, fifty thousand new pubs had opened. Most of these simply could not brew beer cheaper than the big brewers were offering to sell it to them. If they wanted to stay in business they had no choice but to become dependent on their larger competitors for supply. Many beer houses took loans to improve their premises or agreed to favourable supply terms in return for dealing exclusively with one brewer, and so the tied house system was born, where ultimately the brewers controlled the pubs that sold their beer. From this point on, the tied house system increasingly determined what beers were available in a given pub, making it one of the main factors influencing our choice of drink for the next century and a half.

Gin palaces

Those publicans who had a licence to sell spirits as well as beer realized they had another advantage over the proliferating beer shops: their premises tended to be bigger and fancier than the shops, which were often small and unadorned, and some pushed this to its absolute limit. As the century progressed pubs became increasingly gaudy and outrageous. Italian architects and craftsmen who normally built churches were commissioned to embellish these 'gin palaces' with ornately engraved mirrors and windows, carved animals, tiles and mosaics. Outside, on the unlit streets, gin palaces hung huge, gas-lit globes which gleamed in the darkness, calling people to them like moths.

The investment in all this luxury brought pressure for higher returns to pay for it. Publicans began to demand a little more custom from their patrons, and pubs were increasingly configured for maximum revenue. Customers were now always separated from their servers by the bar, and seats were removed so that more people could be squeezed in to stand and drink at the bar. For centuries, publicans had been happy to let customers nurse one drink for the entire evening – even those people who couldn't afford to drink would be given a communal pot to sip from – but now, if people wanted to enjoy all this credit-financed splendour, they had to pay. Hackwood said of the gin palaces, 'The repeated order is the condition of a continued welcome. This attitude of the management is betrayed by the inhospitable seatless bar, specially designed for "perpendicular drinking".'

Different rooms were provided for different classes of customer. There were discreet side entrances where women could enter unobserved, and booths that could be closed off so that business – often business relating to the world's oldest profession – could be conducted in private. 'Snugs', popular with customers because they offered privacy and intimacy, were unpopular with licensing magistrates for precisely the same reason.

It is easy to see why gin palaces became so popular. Utilitarian alehouses may have been a home from home, but the gin palace offered a taste of glamour to people who had always thought that such shininess and brightness was the preserve of the upper classes. As Peter Bailey, a Victorian historian put it, 'The domesticity of the old pub gave way to the commercial glamour of the new people's palaces, gaudy compensations for the meanness of everyday life.' No surprise then that the ruling classes absolutely hated them. The glamour offered by the gin palace may have been only superficial, but class distinctions were being dangerously blurred here. Gin palaces were deeply disapproved of, far more so than drinking in general. Poor people had always got drunk, so that wasn't the main problem. The beef was that they were now doing it in splendid surroundings which they didn't deserve. They simply had no right be in such beautiful spaces. It's not as if they would even *appreciate* them; they were obviously far too uncultured, stupid, docile – just too *poor* – to see the benefit. One description from a book on the Victorian city highlights the strange hostility that some upper-class observers felt towards gin palaces, even as they were drawn to their beauty:

> At one place I saw a revolving light with many burners playing most beautifully over the door of the painted charnel house; at another 50 or 60 jets in one lantern were throwing out their capricious and fitful but brilliant gleams, as if from the branches of a shrub. And over the doors of a third house were no less than three enormous lamps with corresponding lights, illuminating the whole streets to a considerable distance. They were in full glare on this Sunday evening; and through the doors of these infernal dens of drunkenness and mischief, crowds of miserable wretches were pouring in that they might drink and die.

The writer's problem seems not to be that these places are beautiful – he admits that they are – but that 'miserable wretches' are going into them to drink. Of course, he could never actually cross the threshold to verify that the wretched self-destruction of his imaginings is actually taking place.

The attitudes of many within the Victorian Establishment towards the lower classes were at times breathtaking in their hypocrisy. They really did look upon the working class as subhuman and simply not entitled to do the things their rulers took for granted. As the middle and upper classes took their custom away from pubs, they took with them some long-established practices. For example, while it was fine for people with money to go to casinos, it took a big court case in 1854 to determine that the playing of dominoes in ale-houses was not a criminal offence. The well-to-do had objected to alehouses because they were disgusting hovels; now they complained because pubs were colourful and attractive.

Town planning, pub style

London and other industrial cities expanded rapidly in the nineteenth century, swallowing up surrounding villages. Pubs were often the first buildings to be erected on new roads, usually on corners. Predictably, some people were not happy:

> On the pastures lately set out for building you may see a double line of trenches with excavation each side and a tavern of imposing elevation standing quite complete, waiting the approaching row of houses. The propinquity of these places to each other in Camden and Kentish Town is quite ridiculous. At a distance of 200 paces in every direction they glitter in sham splendour.

Building new urban districts was an expensive and risky venture. One way of minimizing the risk and making it less costly was to make sure the pubs were in place to relieve the labourers of their wages as soon as they had been paid, ploughing the profit back in to complete the terraces between the pubs. Pubs became points of reference on the new estates, and this method of urban planning, with pubs on almost every corner, is responsible for the way much of London looks today.

It wasn't like this everywhere though: some landowners and developers had sympathies with the temperance movement, so while Camden and Kentish Town may have been given their shape by pubs, there isn't a single pub in the heart of Bloomsbury, for example. And yet the workmen building Bloomsbury still needed somewhere to get a pint at the end of the day. Consequently, many landowners neighbouring the new development built pubs right on the border. Bloomsbury today is still a large, dry area, hemmed in by pubs on all sides. And then there's Knightsbridge, different again. When this exclusive district of London was developed, the aristocracy recognized that their servants would go to the pub no matter what, and grudgingly accepted that pubs should be built in the neighbourhood to stop the staff straying too far. But all Knightsbridge's pubs are hidden guiltily down back streets, out of sight of the splendid, sweeping terraces.

Many of the new places tried to be a little glitzier than the shabby old drinking dens, borrowing much from the style and nature of the gin palaces. In 1857 The *Building News* complained:

Settled or backed benches, with a plank to each, sufficed in primitive times for the enjoyment of a cup of brown nappy,* with a pipe and a joke; the light of a coal fire, or the glimmer of a tallow fat, illumed satisfactorily the boozy meeting of our ancestral artisans and swashbucklers, tonight it is otherwise – the corner public is radiant of gas, redolent of mahogany, and glittering in mirrors, there are no settles, no stools nor an easy smoking with hard drinking . . . At the bar the dropper in to drink must stand their drink and move on when tired.

---

* 'Brown nappy' is a phrase which has disturbingly different connotations today. Back then nappy was, of course, slang for beer. I know it's childish, but don't tell me you weren't thinking the same thing.

What they lacked in comfort these places made up for in decoration to enchant the punters. Victorian drinking houses pioneered the use of wallpaper and mirrors, and simply couldn't cram in enough stuff. There were shelves full of military paraphernalia, stuffed animals, books and works of art. As Peter Haydon points out in *The English Pub: A History*:

> The Victorian public house, having been reviled for most of the century as the shame of the nation, the fountain-head from whence sprang a national curse and affliction, finished the century as a temple-cum-museum to the endeavours of the age.

The attention given to their design has not been matched since. If the coaching inn was the blueprint for the traditional country pub, the Victorian public house is still the standard in large towns and cities.

The end of unfettered boozing

The 1870s represented the golden age of Victorian beer and pubs. Gradually, we started to drink less beer. Improvements in diet and in the water supply meant it was less important as a source of calories; railways meant transport was less physically demanding, and the growth in business meant that a greater proportion of workers were employed in office as clerks, lawyers and accountants rather than in factories and forges. The continuing rise in personal income, which had for so long benefited the brewers, now led to a diminished role for beer in people's lives. They could afford cheap, ready-made clothing, machine-produced furniture and pack-aged food. The money they had left over for their leisure could be spent on new alternatives to going to the pub. Railway excursions became affordable, music hall was all the rage, and a new game called association football was starting to attract the attention of more and more people.

Faced with tougher business conditions, those brewers who could afford it reduced their costs by buying up their suppliers of malt on the one side, and the public houses that sold their beer on the other. As pubs became dependent on breweries for their supply of beer, the breweries began to gain control over more and more pubs, either by buying them outright or, more frequently, by making loans. Pub leases, especially those in London, were becoming prohibi-tively expensive. Breweries would loan landlords the money for the lease on condition that the pub then only stocked beers produced by that one brewer. The tied house system became the model for the industry.

The brewers could afford to hand out loans after getting into the idea (relatively late in the day compared to other industries) of going public. Big brewers were all run by gen-tlemen, family concerns passed down from father to son. This was one of the reasons why they were so slow adopting busi-ness practices increasingly common in other industries. Then, in 1886, Guinness floated shares on the stock market. The £6 million issue was massively oversubscribed, and brewers realized that there was huge potential for ready cash at their fingertips. The old families retained overall control, but issued large numbers of shares. Four years after Guinness blazed the trail, 200 breweries had gone public, including all the big names such as Ind Coope (1886), Allsopp (1888), Whitbread

(1888) and Courage (1889). With the proceeds, the big brewers bought over 500 pubs a year between 1895 and 1902. In this way they safeguarded their business, but the golden age was over. The number of pubs began to decline in 1877, and continues to do so today. Drinking became increasingly frowned upon. In 1889 Jerome K. Jerome sighed:

> Drinking is one of those subjects with which it is inadvisable to appear too well acquainted. The days are gone by when it was considered manly to go to bed intoxicated every night, and a clear head and a firm hand no longer draw upon their owner the reproach of effeminacy. On the contrary, in these sadly degenerate days, an evil-smelling breath, a blotchy face, a reeling gait and a husky voice are regarded as the hall-marks of the cad rather than of the gentleman.

The pub will never again be the absolute epicentre of our existence that it once was. Nevertheless, it has proven itself the great survivor, the one constant in the evolution of the British community. The village green and duck pond have gone, the church is almost empty, and it looks like the days of the village post office are numbered. Towns have grown and merged. Pubs have changed to reflect developments in the communities they serve, but have, more or less, remained throughout. They are simply too ingrained in our culture to disappear.

Of course, we know this now because the pub is still here. But a hundred years ago, no one knew how things were going to turn out. Nor could anyone have guessed that, having survived so much, British pub culture was about to face its biggest ever threat.

Chapter Six

'The greatest of these deadly foes'

The fight for the right to get tight

I'd like a drink now, please

Picture the scene: you're visiting London for a few days as a special treat. You're excited because you live out in the sticks, and you're always seeing on the telly just how much London prides itself on being one of the most exciting, vibrant cities on the planet, rivaled only by New York.

But it gets better – the main reason you're visiting is that TV funnyman Lee Evans is playing a special one-off show at a West End theatre. You and your partner first fell in love when you discovered a mutual admiration of the great man's work, and somehow you managed to get your hands on a pair of the last few tickets. You've never seen him in the wobbly flesh before – this is going to be a night to cherish for the rest of your lives.

The show is everything you dreamed of. You laugh. You cry. You gasp at the audacious way in which he redefines the very notion of comedy. You marvel at the risks he takes mixing biting satire, searching questions about the meaning of existence and deep insights into the human soul into his rubber-faced antics.

And all too soon the performance is over, the final curtain call taken, and you're back out into the street, the bright lights of the city burning around you. It's 10.40 p.m., and you're buzzing with excitement. Neither of you want the night to end yet, and in this city that never sleeps, surely it doesn't have to. You spy a pub a few doors away, and decide to sit and discuss the spectacle you've just witnessed – nay, the *miracle* – over a drink. The barman glares at you as you enter. You order a beer and a glass of wine, and he hesitates before serving you, finally relenting and muttering 'You'll have to be quick – we close in ten minutes.' You take your drinks to a table, and you've barely started discussing the groundbreaking bit where Evans asked if you'd ever noticed how hard it was to get the cellophane wrappers off new CDs these days and made you laugh so hard that a bit of wee came out when the barman interrupts to say 'I'm going to have to take your glasses now' and moments later you're on the street again. It's 11.15 p.m., and everywhere is closed, every doorway darkened. In the heart of the nation's capital, there's nothing to do except go to bed.

Until licensing laws were relaxed in 2005, this was the reality facing anyone coming out of the theatre or a concert in any town or city in the UK. It's a bit better now that pubs have the flexibility to open later if they wish, and many places near theatres stay open till midnight or 1 a.m. so your night needn't end prematurely.*

---

* Although I went to a gig in Camden recently and discovered that the

There was a sense in the national consciousness that we simply shouldn't be out so late at night, that we needed to have our instincts curbed, and that hasn't gone away. The press is appalled by what it terms 'twenty-four hour drinking', but the reality is that pubs stay open an average of only twenty-seven minutes longer than they used to. Rather than drinking ourselves to death now we are theoretically able, the amount of booze we consume has actually fallen, not increased. We go to pubs less than we used to. Alcohol-related crime and anti-social behaviour have fallen.

If you limit the time people can drink, they actually drink more over a shorter period. Last orders at the bar used to be an unseemly scrum of panic-buying rounds before trying to find a cab or night bus. Without that absolute deadline, we're more relaxed. And this is consistent in licensing law changes around the world – Australian drinking history offers a far more dramatic illustration of the same phenomenon.

During the First World War, the Antipodean temperance movement succeeded in persuading most of Australia and all of New Zealand to institute a 6 p.m. closing time for pubs, on the basis this that was when shops closed, and if you thought about it pubs were just shops that sold beer, so it stood to reason that pubs should close when shops did. The six o'clock swill was born. The Australians, long known for their fondness for the odd pint, normally finished work at 5.00 and now had only an hour's drinking time. They

---

pub across the road from the venue actually closes *early* when there are concerts on, because they don't want the hassle of having to serve a busy throng of thirsty punters so late at night. Some pubs just don't want to stay in business.

rammed the bars to bursting point and for sixty precious minutes focused with astonishing single-mindedness on pouring as much beer down their necks as possible. An hour later the pubs spewed mobs of paralytic, pissed-off blokes into the streets with a whole evening ahead of them and nothing to do.

Pubs had trouble coping with the demand. Anything that stopped people from getting to the bar, such as billiard tables, dartboards, or tables and chairs, was removed. Beer was hosed onto a bar covered with glasses, spillage running onto the floor, the bar staff carefree because the loss was insignificant compared to the sheer volume they could pour down people's necks if only they could serve it quickly enough. Walls and floors were tiled to make it easier to clean up spilt beer and puke.

This suited pub landlords just fine. They were making a full evening's profit for an hour's work, and didn't have to bother shelling out on all that extraneous stuff that makes pubs attractive. And it suited their enemies, the temperance movement, who could point to the drunkards in the street each night at 6.00 and say, 'See? Look at them after just an hour. It's a good job we don't let them drink any longer; where would we be then?'

The fact the system seemed to be in everyone's interest apart from the drinker's meant it stayed in place until the 1960s. Reform was resisted on the grounds that the closing-time riot would merely move to a later hour. But some people could see the insanity of it throughout its history. In 1945 W. H. Woodward, a magistrate and chairman of two licensing committees, said that the policy was the result of 'a battle between greed and fanaticism', and had produced as its outcome:

> A system in which ... citizens drink, jowl by jowl like pigs in a trough, what they are given instead of what they want, and, like pigs, gulp down more than they need of it while they can get it; and, for the privilege of doing so, pay many times the cost of the hogwash they swallow.*

Eventually, common sense did prevail and the law was changed. Unsurprisingly, people began to drink in a more leisurely and controlled fashion. But the regulations introduced during the First World War had remained in place for almost fifty years after it had ended.

But none of this should be that surprising from an English point of view. Because the reason we had such stupid licensing laws of our own until 2005, not to mention the reason British beer is traditionally so much weaker than the 5% ABV common in much of the world, is the safeguarding of arms production in Carlisle to supply the troops fighting the Kaiser's army on the Western Front in 1916. Like the apocryphal old soldiers hiding out on Pacific islands, it took almost ninety years for successive governments to finally accept that the war had ended and to adjust licensing laws accordingly. These laws, and the curious compromise they represented for so long, had a massive effect on shaping our pub culture and attitudes towards drink. They were the

---

* From the tone of his language, I'm guessing that, on balance, he didn't think this state of affairs was a good thing.

outcome of an epic struggle for the soul of the British drinker – a struggle that almost ended in Prohibition and revolution.

Attempting to control the tide

The relationship between government and beer has always been an odd one. Beer has never been illegal in this country, but has always been something of a headache for whoever was trying to run the place. On the one hand, it is a potential threat to ordered society to have workers and soldiers running around pot-valiant and not doing as they are told. On the other, attempts to control the demand for booze by piling on taxes have created a powerful source of revenue which, once tasted, has proven more difficult for any government to give up than a can of Tennent's Super is for the park-bench alky. Governments have long been torn between the desire to do what's best for the people as a whole, their own ulterior motives, and the interests of powerful supporters: namely the temperance movement (especially for the Liberals) and the brewing industry (particularly for the Tories).

The state has historically used two main tools to intervene between the citizen and his pint: taxation and licensing. Conflicts of interest and ill-thought-out use of these tools has meant that controlling measures have rarely had the effects they were intended to produce. Time after time, kings or governments have had an idea, got it wrong, then had another idea to clean up the mess, with the same result. Rarely have they realized when to stop.

The very first recorded attempt at alcohol control is a

typical example. In AD 745 the Archbishop of York ordered, 'No priest go to eat or drink in taverns.'* It didn't work. Not only did large numbers of priests take no notice, those members of the clergy who did agree to refrain from drinking with the masses started brewing in the monasteries, which as we know led to huge leaps forward in the quality of beer.

About two hundred years later, King Edgar of England was the first monarch to attempt to rein in rampant drunkenness among the population at large. He decreed that there should be only one alehouse per village, and followed this up by stating that drinking vessels should be of a standard size and marked with pegs, and that no one should drink further down than one peg in a sitting. The problem was, the pegs were inside the vessel and it was hard to judge how close you were to your peg in mid-gulp. If you went down further than a peg, you had drunk more than you were supposed to. Best drink down to the next peg, get it right this time, and no one will know. Damn, missed again. This time you'll definitely get it right on the peg. At least, that was the excuse. Soon people were using the pegs as markers in drinking races, the handy new standard measures opening up a whole world of competitive drinking. By the twelfth century, the custom of demonstrating your drinking prowess at your neighbour's expense by 'taking him down a peg or two' was seriously exacerbating the problem of drunkenness.

Every time restrictions were introduced people found some way to get round them, or simply ignored them. In the thirteenth century, when brewing supplies were scarce, the Church attempted to control drinking by demanding that

---

*   This being before grammar was invented.

everyone conserved supplies and gave them in for communal brewing at the Church festival. Many people took exception to this. This was the time when Robin Hood allegedly ran riot in the forests, and the truth within the legend is that Britain was far more forested than it is now. People would sneak off into the woods, away from the jurisdiction of the Church, and donate their shares, known as 'scots', to a common pot of their own, and enjoy the fruits of their labours 'scot-free'. Naturally the Church took exception to this, and had scot-ales banned in 1213. And again in 1220. And in 1223, 1230, 1237, 1240, 1255 and 1256.

The first tax on beer was the Saladin tithe, introduced by Henry II in 1188 to raise money for the crusades. Once the crusades were over, nobody quite got around to abolishing it, and some form of tax on beer has been present ever since. Likewise, during the English Civil War five hundred years later, both King and Parliament introduced 'temporary' duty on the sale of beer to help pay for the war effort, which again remained in place when the war ended.

Beer has subsequently been taxed in every way imaginable: the malt was taxed, the liquor was taxed, the hops were taxed, and once we had the hydrometer the specific gravity of beer was taxed. How the tax was calculated may have changed, but the main reason for its imposition never did: in 1900 duty was increased to help pay for the Boer War. So, next time you buy a pint, try if you can to suppress a patriotic gleam in your eye as you hand over your cash, knowing that, with a significant chunk of it, you are commemorating every significant military conflict of the last 900 years.

When it was first introduced, the licensing of drinking

establishments was at least born of a genuine concern for the welfare of the people. In 1329 a proclamation was issued in London, which stated:

> Whereas misdoers, going about by night, have their resort more in taverns than elsewhere, and there seek refuge and watch their hour for misdoing, we forbid that any taverner or brewer keep the door of his tavern open after the hour of curfew.

Concern over the harbouring of misdoers soon spread to a more general interest in ensuring that beer, now officially the second necessity of life after the Assize of Bread and Ale in 1267, was given the care and attention it deserved. As people began to drink it more in alehouses than in their homes, these places had to be regulated to ensure they were kept to a sufficient standard. In 1552, legislation was introduced which forced alehouse keepers to obtain licences from magistrates, and a few years later inns and taverns were included in this. Effectively this was a shift in the attitude of the authorities from punishing the poor punter for excessive drunkenness to 'protecting' them from getting drunk in the first place, by effectively bringing pubs under state control. The licensing system under which pubs still operate today was born.

Putting licensing laws in place was one thing; finding anyone who could be bothered to implement them was another. Punishments such as fines payable to the poor and time in the stocks were always being threatened for people contravening licensing laws, but no one took any notice. Between 1604 and 1627 there were seven acts of Parliament attempting to deal with drunkenness, but nothing actually seems to have happened as a result. A typical act, that of 1606, began:

> Whereas the loathsome and odious sin of drunkenness is of late grown into common use in this realm, being the root and foundation of many other enormous sins, as bloodshed, stabbing, murder, swearing, fornication, adultery, and such like, to the great dishonour of God and our nation . . .

But, for all the bluster, there simply seemed to be little that could be done to prevent the populace from getting mizzled whenever they wished.

Thou shalt not . . .

By the eighteenth century the authorities were getting increasingly pissed off with pissed-up Britain. As we've seen, the problem of heavy drinking was becoming more acute, or at least more visible. In the new industrial towns, pubs would stay open through the night. People would drink all night on Saturdays and crawl out of the gutter on Sunday morning looking for a drink or a fight. The custom of 'Saint Monday' – people adding an unofficial extra day to the weekend to recover – was common. The crown, the clergy and many industrialists decided that things had become intolerable. The morals of the working class needed to be reformed.

But every time the authorities tried to do something to solve the problem they still seemed to end up making it worse. The gin epidemic started when William III deregulated its production and sale, partially to provide what he felt was necessary competition for the brewers. The Gin Act of 1736 taxed gin heavily and led to the mass production of illegal, dangerous moonshine. The 1830 Beer Act was in turn partly designed to wean the masses off gin, but succeeded in encouraging them to drink beer to greater excess than ever before.

By the Victorian era there was a widespread feeling that something fundamental had to be done. Some of this grew from an aversion to all things sensual; food and drink were seen as necessary but not to be enjoyed. Telling your host that you'd enjoyed your food was a sign that you were indulging in base animal pleasures, and many respectable people didn't like to be seen eating and drinking in public, meaning of course that gentlemen never went to pubs. But there was also a growing philanthropism among the middle classes, a genuine concern for the welfare of lesser men. Some wrote of working men spending all their meagre wages on booze, and their families going hungry. Charles Booth, a philanthropist who, along with Joseph Rowntree, published influential studies on the lives of the poor, claimed the heaviest drinking was done by those who could least afford it, and that 'the people drink enough to keep them poor'. These concerns reflected those of factory bosses, who wanted a sober workforce, and the authorities, who cited drunkenness as the single most important cause of crime. In 1891 Lord Chief Justice Coleridge claimed, 'If England could be made sober, three-fourths of her gaols might be closed.'

Temperance meetings were held in church halls up and down the country. As the name suggests, these meetings originally talked about voluntary moderation in the consumption of alcohol, and focused on the obvious damage being done by copious drinking of spirits. At first, the idea of going without alcohol completely was inconceivable to most. But this was soon to change.

The conflict between the temperance movement and the brewers has often been portrayed as an unfair struggle between a disorganized and poorly funded collection of noble pressure groups, and a rich and politically powerful industry. Within this argument is an assumption that the brewers were capable of cooperating in an organized fashion. They weren't. Potentially, their collective power may have been awesome, but the reality was that the big brewers were too busy bickering among themselves to give much support to the trade organizations that could have taken the fight back to the temperance movement. But this hardly mattered. Individually, they had vast amounts of money and power, some of which they spent on sponsoring Tory MPs – those who were not MPs themselves that is.

So the temperance campaigners were the underdogs, albeit with a bark out of all proportion to their bite. They would eventually gain their own powerful supporters in the Establishment, but they would also have to contend with their own divisions. Unlike the brewers, who were so huge that it didn't matter that they couldn't work together, the splits within the temperance movement would eventually prove its undoing.

These splits began in 1832 when a man called James Teare stood up at a meeting in Manchester and claimed that all intoxicating liquor was an enemy to God and to man.* Ten

---

* As this view caught on, it did come into conflict with the very prevalent role of wine in the Bible. One celebrated prohibitionist orator, Frederick

weeks later, seven men signed the first teetotal pledge in Preston, and in 1835 a national society of teetotallers was formed. From this point on, the temperance movement divided into those favouring moderation and those pursuing total abstention. Eventually large sections of the movement favoured total abstention, and regarded beer as a legitimate target. A further split soon occurred within the teetotallers, between those who favoured persuasion and voluntary abstinence, conducting meetings resembling religious rallies and urging people to 'take the pledge', and those who felt that the only way to deal with the problem was to permanently remove the possibility of temptation. This lot believed that heavy drinking was a sin born of moral failure and weakness of character, rather than a reaction to appalling social conditions. Increasingly, hard-line teetotallers demanded a legislative ban on the sale and consumption of alcohol, and spent their energies lobbying politicians rather than working to persuade the people they felt needed saving.

But first blood went to the moderates, who successfully applied pressure for measures to counter the worst excesses of drunkenness without actually trying to prohibit drinking. Acts were passed which forced pubs to close at some point through the night, and in 1869 the thousands of beer houses created by the 1830 Beer Act were brought under the same licensing regulations as other drinking establishments.

Lees, came up with a solution that can only be described kindly as imaginative. His explanation was that in Hebrew wine and unfermented grape juice are represented by the same word. Therefore, it stands to reason that where wine is mentioned in a positive light in the Bible the writer is referring to grape juice, and where it is mentioned negatively they are referring to wine. Simple. He had his Bible re-translated and everything.

Convictions for drunkenness began to fall, and men started to turn up for work on Mondays. Everyone was happy – until the pro-temperance Liberal government tried to push things a little further.

In 1872, a Licensing Act was introduced to force pubs to close from midnight in London, and 11 p.m. elsewhere, until 6 a.m. This would probably have been acceptable, but for one small snag: the restrictions would apply to pubs – where the masses drank – but not to the clubs frequented by the gentry. Landlords deliberately fomented unrest, telling their customers there was one law for the rich and another for the poor. Soon mobs took to the streets chanting, 'Britons never shall be slaves,' and seeking out teetotallers on whom to vent their spleen, until troops were called in to disperse them. The Liberals went on to lose the 1874 general election, and Gladstone reflected, 'We have been borne down on a torrent of gin and beer.'

Gladstone himself was always a reluctant advocate of hard-line legislation against beer. He confessed, 'How can I, who drink . . . bitter beer every day of my life, coolly stand up and advise hard working fellow creatures to take the pledge?' This dilemma was not uncommon. The temperance movement may have been constantly reminding MPs of their duty to protect the populace from themselves, but self-interest among politicians was a persuasive counter-argument. One commentator at the time, Joseph Livesey, wrote,

> Out of 658 Members of Parliament there are probably not a dozen who would claim to be abstainers. These gentle-men have their cellars stocked with liquor, have it daily on their tables, and have it introduced at every social

occasion as a mark of friendship – is it likely that they would pass a Bill to prevent others enjoying the same, according to their means?

Frustrated, the teetotallers looked across the Atlantic for inspiration. America was a new model society, with laws and culture being freshly created. There was no class system and no powerfully entrenched brewing industry, and the temperance movement was doing very well indeed.

Even though prohibition wasn't introduced nationally in the USA until 1920, states were free to implement it on an individual basis. Thirty-three of the then forty-eight states were already dry by the time prohibition became law. This was largely due to a hugely effective public campaign against the evils of the saloon. Alcoholics were portrayed as victims, lured in and broken down. They said that alcohol killed 50,000 people a year. They said that after one taste of alcohol people were hooked and would develop a ruinous habit.* Powerful cartoons appeared, such as the one with the man handcuffed to a giant beer bottle labelled DRINKING HABIT on a saloon bar, while at home his daughter asks, 'Mummy, why doesn't Daddy come home?' And the one called 'Christmas morning in the Drunkard's Home', which shows children in ragged nightclothes weeping at the sight of their empty stockings.

This propaganda advanced unchallenged to the point where prohibition became inevitable. By 1920 drinkers were regarded as such scum that, at the Fifteenth International

---

* Which as we know is bollocks. But doesn't it sound familiar within the context of debates about intoxicating drugs?

Congress Against Alcoholism in Washington, two doctors were able to seriously consider their outright extermination, before pulling back and proposing the more 'humane method' of simply rounding them up into concentration camps and sterilizing them:

> Where you are dealing with a stock that is already defective, a stock which is defective in itself, you can only produce defective stock from it and therefore it is better to destroy the stock entirely ... we must cut off the propagation of these defectives or they will overpower us. In order to do that, I suggest, not to kill the individual or anything of that kind, but the humane method ... the real solution to this problem would be to confine them to farms where they would be treated kindly and mercifully, in a sort of colony where they would be prevented from reproducing.

In a climate where views as abhorrent as these could be aired with respectability, the total prohibition of alcohol was inevitable.

British teetotallers watched and learned. They fought their campaign with meetings, pamphlets and songs, such as this catchy number which demonstrates that 'Just Say No', the rousing chart hit enjoyed by the cast of *Grange Hill* in the late 1980s, was little more than a century-old cover version:

> Dare to say 'No' when you're tempted with drink,
> Pause for a moment, my brave boy and think –
> Think of the wrecks upon life's ocean tossed
> For answering 'Yes' without counting the cost ...
> ... Think of all this as life's journey you go,

And when you're assailed by the tempter
SAY 'NO!'

Hard-line abstainers slowly gained supporters in positions of power, and started to achieve some significant victories. In 1891 Mrs Sharpe, a pub owner in the Lake District, was refused a renewal of her licence without compensation and, she felt, without good reason. She appealed to the House of Lords, who upheld the decision of her local magistrates. *Sharpe v. Wakefield* established in law the right of magistrates to refuse licences on grounds other than the misconduct of the licensee, without compensation of any kind.

For the first time, the brewers started to worry. They felt their industry was being undermined, as a small but growing number of magistrates began to use the power that the Sharpe ruling had given them. Judges who supported the temperance movement followed their beliefs and refused licences regardless of the condition of the pubs. Given that they were men of influence, there were of course many local magistrates who were actually brewers themselves, but they were excluded from licensing sessions on the grounds that they might follow their beliefs rather than coolly appraising the facts of the case. But teetotal magistrates were doing just that, and for the first time the establishment seemed to be favouring the abstainers over the brewers. The wood-panelled walls of gentlemen's clubs across London reverberated with the sound of spluttering indignation.

The brewers fought back, lobbying Parliament for a bill that at least offered compensation to those put out of business on a magistrate's whim. They took comfort from the fact that the arguments in favour of this bill were summed up by no lesser man than the Tory Prime Minister himself, Lord Balfour:

> You will never get rid of the public house from this country and, frankly I admit it, I do not think you ought to get rid of it. What then, should you aim at? Surely at this ideal, that the public house should be kept respectably, should be kept by respectable persons and should be kept in such a manner as will make those who frequent it obey the law and conform to the dictates of morality ... how can you expect the trade which you deliberately intend to make insecure to be filled by men of the character I have just endeavoured to describe?

The Act was passed in 1904, but it pleased nobody. The brewers had won the right to compensation for landlords, but now they complained that this gave magistrates justification to close down pubs whenever they felt like it. Arguably, they were proved right: six hundred on-licences would be removed under the provisions of the act every year between 1904 and 1935. The temperance movement was no happier, referring to the act as the 'Brewer's Endowment Fund'. Outraged that here was yet another prime minister not only caving in to pressure from the brewing lobby, but also openly voicing his support for them, the radical, Nonconformist, teetotal wing of the Liberal party raged that the Tory government was in cahoots with the brewing industry, and took its direction from industry fat cats rather than the people who had elected them.* They were determined more than ever to smash this cosy consensus.

---

* Ha! The very thought.

It's easy when looking at history from a beery perspective to see the temperance movement as a bothersome, cartoonish bunch of interfering, ignorant, bellicose pains in the arse. Most beer writers portray them as such, and I have to admit it's great fun depicting them in this way.* But it's important to see their motivations and achievements in the right context. Many of them were passionately committed to ending the terrible conditions in which the working class lived, and genuinely saw drink as part of the problem. That's why, back then, it was the Liberals who were against beer and the Tories, who have now become outspoken opponents of contemporary equivalents such as drugs, loud music or anything else that young people associate with partying, who were vehemently defending our right to get as wankered as we wished. The core principles of the parties haven't changed, but somewhere between then and now the role and use of alcohol has. In the last hundred years, alcohol has largely ceased to be the bane of the working class.†

In 1906 it was a different matter. That year, there was a general election. Dogged by arguments over the Boer War and protectionism, the Conservatives fell, and the Liberals swept to power with a landslide. Radicalism was in the air. Even with a large majority, the new government keenly felt the influence of the newly formed Labour party. From a standing start, they had taken thirty seats in the election and were

---

* Especially since they ultimately lost and we're all still allowed to get blagged. Oh no, I've given away the ending. Sorry.

† Of course, this is not what you would believe if you picked up any British newspaper in the first decade of the twenty-first century. We'll come on to 'binge drinking' and modern day neoprohibitionism in the final chapter of the book.

making a powerful case for being the voice of the working man. The Liberals had to prove they were the party with the interests of the people at heart, and pursued a vigorous and ambitious policy of social reform. Between 1906 and 1911 they introduced such measures as old-age pensions and the National Insurance system. Within the context of these measures, promoted by a government that was sympathetic to their cause, the temperance movement saw its big chance.

In 1907, a bill was introduced which proposed to cut back the number of public houses by a third. This was bad enough, but the main threat was the further proposal that, after a certain period, all applications for licence renewal would be treated as applications for new licences, vastly increasing the chance they would be refused. In the meantime, compensation to landlords losing their licences was to be slashed, and local vetoes on licence applications were encouraged. The brewers were outraged. They felt they were being hounded, taxed and regulated to a degree unimaginable in any other industry. The young Winston Churchill put this view to Parliament, doing little to discourage accusations that the Tories and the brewing industry were in bed together when he passionately denounced the bill as a 'measure of plunder to satisfy political spite'. Clearly, the brewers were now very scared. Was this the end of centuries of continuous growth, progress and eight-hour lunches? Well . . . no. The proposers of the bill managed to snatch defeat from the jaws of victory when they succeeded in creating a new enemy for themselves, an enemy far more frightening than the gentlemen who ran the big brewers, or even Churchill himself, an enemy who would kill the bill stone dead.

Intoxicated by their momentum, the teetotallers within

the Liberal party wanted to strike as hard as possible while they had the initiative. They hit upon the idea that a key reason lads went into pubs was to ogle the barmaids, and decided that if barmaids could be abolished, this would in itself reduce the temptation to go for a pint. With women just finding their political voice and the suffragette movement starting to gather pace, this wasn't exactly the best timing in the world. Thousands of indignant barmaids flocked to Hyde Park to demonstrate against the measures. Nobody was going to argue with opposition like that. A moment of madness had effectively killed the bill. It just remained for the House of Lords to put it out of its misery.

The Liberals didn't take this defeat lying down. David Lloyd George, a fierce teetotaller and a campaigner for complete prohibition of alcohol in his native Wales since the 1880s, was chancellor of the exchequer. In 1909 he increased duties payable by pubs and brewers by £4 million. These measures were again defeated by the Lords, and the ensuing conflict between the upper house and the government pre-cipitated a general election in 1910. The Liberals won and implemented the measures. Soon the big brewers were paying upwards of 60 per cent of their earnings to the government in tax and duty. At least, they should have been. The brewers had always been inventive when it came to money, and they now successfully argued that the punitive taxation had greatly reduced the value of their pubs, consequently win-ning large reductions in property rates which offset much of the tax. It seemed that even with a sympathetic government in power, the temperance movement could not deliver that final, decisive blow to the brewing industry.

Then war broke out, and everything changed.

World War I: the final conflict

The First World War was always going to be won in factories rather than on battlefields. The generals had a whole new array of toys to play with, including machine guns, tanks, planes and all sorts of shells, which quickly led to stalemate. Trench warfare, with millions of lives lost over a few miles either side of the main trench line, was the result of all this firepower simply cancelling each other out – so long as both sides were still adequately supplied, that is. The historian John Terraine describes it as 'the greatest war of the first industrial revolution':

> The picture is awesome – the production figures of the war; the astronomical mileage of telephone wire and barbed wire; the quantities of sandbags; of pit-props; the diversity and numbers of trench warfare supplies; acreage of cloth for uniforms; horseshoes; tonnages of lint for bandages; the unimaginable totals of weapons; rifles, machine guns, small arms ammunition, artillery of all calibres, shells . . . shells . . . shells.

It would be a war of attrition: the side that could carry on making the most weapons the longest would win. The trouble was, Britain wasn't making enough.

Those all-important shells weren't appearing. The extraordinary enthusiasm with which hundreds of thousands of men enlisted at the beginning of the war led to regiments arriving at the front without sufficient weapons. Stories about munitions shortages were appearing in the papers back home and sapping morale. And the factories simply weren't producing quickly enough.

David Lloyd George blamed the 'lure of drink' for impairing the performance of munitions workers. At the start of the war he was still chancellor, and one of two teetotallers in the five-man war cabinet. He spoke more like a preacher than a politician, and in the early years of the war passionately denounced the evils of alcohol. In 1915 he famously declared:

> We are fighting Germany, Austria and drink; and as far
> as I can see the greatest of these three deadly foes is drink,
> [which is] doing us more damage in the war than all the
> German submarines put together.

Using the very real need to ensure the success of the war effort one temperance leader, Sir Thomas Whittaker, observed that now was the time to strike, 'whilst the overshadowing issues of the war are accustoming the people to restricted liberties'. Lloyd George had spent his whole political life up to this point campaigning against drink with little success, thanks, so he thought, to the lobbying power of 'the brewers ring which seems to govern England'. When war broke out, he had everyone's attention. People felt he had his finger on the problem.

This is partly because Lloyd George did have a point – this wasn't just about revenge against the brewers. Pubs were open continuously from 5.30 a.m. until late at night. The average strength of a pint of beer was 1050° (around 7 per cent ABV), far higher than any mainstream beer today. All-night drinking binges were causing soaring levels of absenteeism from work, and those people who managed to drag themselves in might as well not have bothered for all the use they were in their addled state.

In 1915 the prime minister, Lord Asquith, took the blame for the critical shell shortage and gave way to a coalition government with the Conservatives in which Lloyd George was made minister of munitions. Increasingly, he was seen as the dominant figure in the running of the war. He leapt to his task. The 1914 Defence of the Realm Act (DORA), a piece of legislation which granted the state extensive powers which it was felt were needed to win the war, was repeatedly strengthened at Lloyd George's instigation. DORA implemented a wide range of measures that restricted individual liberty to an extent previously unseen in Britain.

The brewing industry was already suffering from the effects of the war. Before 1914, the USA, India, Australia and Europe had all been lucrative export markets for British brewers. German submarines soon put a stop to that, and also created a shortage of brewing materials at home. But the Germans didn't do as much damage to British drinking as DORA.* Pub opening hours were reduced from nineteen

---

* That's not to suggest that the whole war effort and the legislation that was passed to support it was merely a ruse in order to get at the brewing industry. DORA's main thrust included the introduction of food rationing, conscription, stricter passport controls, deals with the unions to ensure an end to industrial unrest, as well as measures designed to reduce social unrest, including minimum wages and controlled rents. Apparently we were actually fighting for something more important than the control of brewing. However, to read the accounts of this period written by some beer writers, you could be forgiven for thinking that the whole thing, right back to the assassination of Archduke Franz Ferdinand in Sarajevo, was part of a Liberal conspiracy to win greater control over the poor defenceless brewing industry.

hours a day to five and a half: 12.00 until 2.30 at lunch times and 6.00 till 9.00 in the evenings. By 1919, taxes had increased by 430 per cent on beer that had fallen in strength to 1030° (about 3 per cent ABV).

Just in case anyone was still enthusiastic about drinking this vastly overpriced 'near-beer', further measures were added. One was the banning of treating, better known today as the buying of rounds. Anybody who has been to a pub in a group knows that when you are drinking in rounds, unless you are the fastest drinker in the group you inevitably end up drinking faster and in greater quantities than perhaps you would like because, as soon as the first person has finished, you're starting to worry about whether you should be buying, even if you're still only halfway down your own pint. Apart from leading to excessive gatteredness among the regulars, treating was causing bigger problems.* We've already talked about how treating was wrapped up in the business of creating and fulfilling obligation. As the war progressed there was a widespread feeling that, for soldiers returning from the

---

* Let's be honest: among working trades, drinking in groups played a very big role. Apprentices joining a trade were expected to pay a drink fine, and drinking was a way of celebrating anything major that had happened, such as – ooh, one of the lads buying some new clothes, for example. In his *Philosophy of Artificial and Compulsory Drinking Usages*, the Scottish magistrate and early temperance campaigner John Dunlop described some of the things that happened to people who refused to join in the round. Their shoes were nailed to the floor, their tools were hidden, or maybe even stolen and pawned with the proceeds used to buy beer. Miners would pin someone down on top of a coal rake, with its teeth facing upwards, and gently persuade him that, actually, he did quite fancy a pint by placing a crowbar on his chest and forcing him back onto the rake. And I thought my mates were bad.

front, their obligation had been fulfilled in advance. In Lincoln in 1917, one soldier who had been awarded the Victoria Cross got back to his local to find that 120 of the regulars had each bought him a pint, all of which were waiting for him when he arrived. He did his best to accept their kindness and almost died. Although heartening for morale, such behaviour was potentially ruinous for the war effort, and so it was made illegal to buy a drink for anyone other than yourself. Proving that supreme pain-in-the-arse jobsworthiness is another British trait with a long history, the ban on treating resulted in one man in Bristol being fined after buying his wife a drink.

Many other drinking customs and practices were also banned, such as the provision of credit by landlords, the serving of spirit chasers and one that may not sound as familiar to modern drinkers, the long-pull, where landlords would serve a generous over-measure to attract custom.*

In 1915 the Central Control Board was established, a body with sweeping powers over the production, distribution and sale of alcohol. In key areas where munitions plants were located, the government went even further and took direct control. State management schemes were introduced in London, Scotland, and most famously in Carlisle, where there was a large concentration of arms factories. 'The Carlisle experiment' was interesting in that, although temperance sympathisers had the power to do almost whatever they wanted, the state management schemes followed a path of

---

* No, that's not a misprint. Apparently, landlords used to serve more than they were supposed to, not less. Well, they do say the past is a foreign country.

moderation rather than creeping prohibition. The idea was to have fewer but better pubs. Lighter beers were sold, and food, non-alcoholic drinks, games, entertainment and facilities for women were introduced. It was felt that if pubs were places for all the family, this would destroy the culture of single-minded 'perpendicular drinking' among groups of men.

Initially the brewers deplored this interference in their affairs, but the state-run pubs soon became popular among drinkers. For some unfathomable reason, people seemed to like the better facilities, the food and the pleasant environment. Sections of the temperance movement threw up their arms in dismay but turning the pub into a more rounded place with less focus on the dogged pursuit of drunkenness was implemented in the spirit of genuine temperance – drinking in moderation. It proved that, given the right circumstances, people could be trusted with drink and it need not be harmful. This was the last thing the hardliners wanted to happen. Here was a perfect illustration of the paradox at the heart of the temperance movement. Some temperance supporters claimed the Carlisle experiment as a great success, while the rest cried that it was undermining the ultimate goal, total abstinence. The movement was starting to shake itself apart.

Meanwhile, convictions for drunkenness in state-run areas fell by 84 per cent, and Lord d'Abernon, chairman of the Central Control Board, was advocating full nationalization of the brewing industry. Twice the government considered following d'Abernon's advice. Lloyd George was all for it; he wasn't going to be able to introduce total prohibition at a stroke, but if he could wrest control away from the hated fat cat brewers perhaps he could reform the industry and whittle it down.

The first time full nationalization was raised it was proposed by Lloyd George himself. He worked out the probable cost of buying the country's 3,700 brewers and took it to Parliament. He was shot down by both sides. On the one hand, the out-and-out prohibitionists in his own party simply wouldn't tolerate anything which they saw as giving beer a chance to survive. On the other, the Conservative opposition defended the interests of the brewers more blatantly than ever. The alliance was so naked by this time that a prominent brewer by the name of Younger – yes, as in the Scottish beer, William Younger's – was even chairman of the party. Caught in the crossfire the bill died. Understandably, Lloyd George blamed the opposition rather than his own side, muttering acerbically, 'Brewing is a powerful trade, and no-one knows better than my old colleagues and myself what it can do when its interests are menaced.' The issue was raised again in 1917, but by this time the cost of buying the industry as calculated by Lloyd George (£250 million) had mysteriously risen to £350 million. It was out of the question.

But calls for brewing to be squeezed further were still growing, and there was a very real chance that the industry could still be destroyed. The United States began to exert real pressure on the British government. America was now very close to total prohibition and had already entirely ceased producing beer. They were very enthusiastic that Britain should follow suit. American ships were carrying grain to Britain, exposing themselves to the risk of being sunk by German submarines, and the goddamned Limeys were still wasting some of this precious cargo on brewing evil beer rather than on baking wholesome bread. Against the background of a pan-European food shortage, Herbert Hoover, the US food administrator, made veiled threats to the British in 1917 about the difficulty of ensuring an increase in grain supplies unless brewing ceased.

Large sections of the government, including the prime minister, would have been only too happy to oblige. The banning of beer production, even total prohibition, were seriously considered by the cabinet. Production had in fact been capped throughout the war and beer, even in its weakened state, was becoming increasingly scarce. In March 1917, the food controller Lord Davenport attempted to placate the Americans by issuing an order that beer production be reduced still further and capped at a limit of ten million barrels.* That figure was never reached.

The package of measures implemented by the Central Control Board had had their desired effect. Beer consumption had plummeted from thirty-six million barrels in 1913, and would eventually reach a low of thirteen million barrels in 1919. Consumption of spirits had halved. Even taking into account the fact that there were fewer blokes around, and that people had less disposable cash and leisure time, per capita consumption of beer had fallen massively, and the beer that was still being drunk was a shadow of its former self. Significantly, drunk and disorderly convictions fell from 200,000 in the first year of the war to below 30,000 in the last. Death rates from alcohol and cirrhosis of the liver fell through the floor. Arthur Shadwell, the main chronicler of

---

* To put this in context, that's less than the combined volume of Carling, Foster's and Stella Artois today.

drinking habits in the early twentieth century was quick to acknowledge that the measures had been a great success:

> The intemperance we had in 1914 was a very bad thing, a great national weakness and burden, and to have reduced it to one half without any serious drawback is a great gain ... it sets a new standard for a new generation.

Lord d'Abernon of the Central Control Board, added:

> I am convinced that the main cause for the reduction of alcohol consumption is to be found in (a) high taxation, (b) wise limitation and spacing of hours permitted for the sale of drink ... we can congratulate ourselves on a reform, accomplished without social perturbation.

In claiming this victory, Shadwell and d'Abernon were destroying the basis of any arguments for further restrictions, but more importantly let's look at that point about 'social perturbation'. OK, so inebriation was no longer a major problem, but the shortage of beer was becoming increasingly troublesome. A population at war needs its little comforts, and beer in moderation played a significant role in maintaining morale. The German submarines had been so effective that starvation had been a very real possibility, but in this war of attrition beer was, ultimately, as much of a necessity as bread. The point of the anti-alcohol measures had been to ensure maximum production of munitions. Another important plank of this strategy was cooperation with the unions to reduce industrial unrest. In return for a no-strike deal and the acceptance of unskilled men and women into vital skilled jobs, the unions were guaranteed improved wages and conditions, the number of strikes fell from 1,459 in 1913 to 532 in 1916. But the workers were again becoming unruly. In 1917, as the war entered a crucial phase, the number of strikes rose to 730. Communist revolution was tearing through Russia and no one knew where it might spread next, but if Marx was to be believed then it was going to be to an industrial economy with an organized labour force whose interests were being abused. 'Does this sound like anywhere we might know?' hinted the unions.

Judge Parry, investigating the causes of social unrest in Britain, looked at revolutionary Russia a little more closely. In 1891 Tolstoy had written that people drank alcohol:

> not merely for want of something better to do to while away their time, or to raise the spirits, not because of the pleasure they receive, but simply and solely in order to drown the warning voice of conscience.

Russia had prohibited the consumption of vodka in 1914, and after three years the suppressed conscience of the people found its voice in the 1917 October Revolution. Coincidence? Parry didn't think so:

> The two main sources of trouble [in Britain] appeared to arise from the self-sufficiency of bureaucracy and the insufficiency of beer. Bureaucracy in the absence of the anaesthetic of vodka seems to have been the moving cause of Bolshevism in Russia.

In July 1917 the Commission of Enquiry into Industrial Unrest gave its report to the Home Secretary, Sir George Cave, who told the House of Commons:

> The beer shortage is causing considerable unrest, and is interfering with the output of munitions and with the position of the country in this war. There is unrest, discontent, loss of time, loss of work and in some cases even strikes are threatened and indeed caused by the very fact that there is a shortage of beer.

Implemented so enthusiastically, the measures were beginning to cause the very problems they had sought to prevent. Amid a good deal of grumbling, the proposed cap of ten million barrels was abandoned in favour of further reductions in alcoholic strength. Beer could be made continually weaker and smaller, but it just could not be killed outright.

And through it all, although drinkers suffered poorer beer and less freedom to drink it, the people the temperance movement really wanted to hurt were better off than ever. Once again, measures which had been intended to restrict the brewing industry proved enormously profitable for the biggest firms. The huge hikes in duty allowed them to increase prices with abandon, and the brewers were being forced through no fault of their own to turn out weak, characterless beers that, of course, cost less to make. Moreover, faced with the possibilty of nationalization, many family firms who had up to now treated brewing more as a hobby than a serious business decided to sell their breweries to the highest bidder. The number of commercial brewers fell from 4,152 in 1910 to 2,914 in 1920, and the average size of those that remained greatly increased.

The spoils of war?

The remaining large and very profitable brewers rubbed their hands and looked forward to unprecedented riches when, in 1920, wartime restrictions were relaxed and freedom reigned again. Except they weren't, and it didn't. The Central Control Board was wound up, but the draconian duty rates stayed.

There was a new Licensing Act in 1921, which the brewers (and their customers) hoped would restore things to normal. But the restrictive licensing laws were here to stay, particularly the tight controls on opening hours. London pubs could open for nine hours a day, five on Sundays. Outside London, pubs were restricted to eight hours a day during the week. Talk of nationalization or prohibition continued, and the Carlisle scheme would remain in place until the Heath government of the 1970s. But the First World War represented the high point of the temperance movement's influence. Beer had been so emasculated that no one could argue that it was a threat to society or to personal welfare and be taken seriously. Convictions for drunkenness continued to fall throughout the interwar years. Duty, and therefore prices, remained high and demand for beer would never again reach its pre-war peak. In 1924 the calculation of duty on beer was tidied up and related directly to alcoholic strength – the higher the gravity, the greater the duty on the beer. This ensured that beer would never return to the strength to which it had been brewed before the war, and established the standard British ABV of between 3 and 4 per cent, compared to the rest of Europe's 5 per cent. The average British pint would remain relatively weak until real continental-strength lagers rose to prominence in the 1990s, and existing beers crept up in strength to compete. But even now these beers are referred to by most drinkers as 'premium', compared to 'standard' lager and bitter which remain between 3.5 and 4.5 per cent.

The restrictive licensing hours also remained in force until very recently. People eventually forgot that early closing and the ban on all-day drinking had been introduced to promote the efficient production of munitions. As the twentieth century progressed, we just accepted that we had much tighter licensing laws than, for example, most of Continental Europe. Even as we became more familiar with late-night drinking on holiday abroad, we still trudged home at eleven without complaint, apart from those of us who fought and vomited in the streets, just like the Aussies used to do, but five hours later.

So beer came out of its own great war in much the same state as the British empire did from World War I. It had won, but at great cost. Like the empire it had survived, but was greatly weakened, and would never really recover its former glory. And there was more still to come. The after-shocks of the war would continue to change the empire, and the beer at its heart, in the ensuing twenty years of peace.

Chapter Seven

'All the culture that is most truly native'

When people stopped going to the pub

The end of business as usual

Doesn't your heart bleed when someone has been incredibly, undeservedly lucky for a long, long time, and their luck runs out, abruptly and spectacularly?

Around 1920, the big movers in the brewing industry were feeling quite pleased with themselves. The temperance movement, with whom they had been fighting all their lives, whom their fathers and uncles had fought before them, seemed finally to have been defeated. Those breweries that had survived the war had emerged bigger than ever, and now the war was over, an era of peace, prosperity and colossal profits beckoned. Just as soon as things got back to normal.

But social trends and circumstances were about to combine to almost achieve what the temperance movement could not. After two hundred years of success based on technology and progress, the brewing industry was unprepared for the destruction of Victorian certainties that was about to rip their business to shreds. Throughout the 1920s and 1930s pubs emptied, and beer itself became seen almost as a thing of the past.

What the brewers failed to spot was that what passed for normality in 1914 was now gone for ever. Before the war, the country had still been able to kid itself that it was enjoying the golden age of the British empire. By the end of it there were still a lot of pink bits on the world map, but British society and culture were well into a seismic transition. During the Victorian era, those in power had been able to ignore the impact their policies had on the working class because they were insulated from it; they never had to acknowledge the reality of what life was like for the bulk of the population. The war changed all that. Men of all classes fought and died together; lords and miners alike had their limbs blown off and slid into the bottom of shell craters to drown in French mud. At home, women entered the workplace in large numbers for the first time, and 700,000 of their young men never came back to relieve them of their duties. After what they had been through, many were not prepared to resume the roles they had previously been expected to play.

It wasn't just the war itself. Its four years provided a hiatus, a break from the domestic issues of the time. Coming back to these issues after the war, it was suddenly much clearer that social change was on the way. The Labour party was attracting significant support. America had started to demonstrate its economic might and political influence. Women had been granted the vote, and were increasingly able to live life on their own terms rather than in servitude to men. On rare occasions they were even seen in pubs. The employment of domestic servants by the middle classes went into decline. People had to learn to cook for themselves, or go out instead; restaurants proliferated and cocktail parties became fashionable.

It was a confusing time. The 1920s and 30s were characterized by savage economic depression but also by a massive growth in prosperity and comfort for vast swathes of the population. Seemingly contradictory, both developments had one thing in common: unfortunately for the brewers of beer, they stopped people drinking beer.

We can't afford to drink

David Lloyd George had promised that post-war Britain would be 'a fit country for heroes to live in' but a worldwide economic slump meant that by 1922 unemployment had risen to over a million. Money was so scarce that, just when people needed them, the social welfare provisions steadily introduced over the past twenty years were cut. The coal industry fell into such a desperate state that the miners, hardly living in luxury, were faced with pay cuts, precipitating the 1926 General Strike.

But the real damage came with the 1929 Wall Street Crash. By this point the United States was the most powerful economy in the world, and when its stock market collapsed the US government erected trade barriers to protect its stricken industries and recalled foreign loans. This in turn pushed Europe into deep depression. In Britain, the areas worst hit by the depression were those with large industrial workforces. In the mid 1930s unemployment was between

16 and 18 per cent of the workforce in the North of England and Scotland, over 20 per cent in Northern Ireland, and nearly 30 per cent in Wales. Of course, these were the areas where people drank the most beer.

And as beer drinkers lost their jobs, the price of beer soared. Duty was never reduced back to pre-war levels, in fact it was raised after the end of the war. Between 1931 and 1933, taxation on beer increased again by a third. The amount of beer sold consequently fell by the same amount. At the height of the depression in 1933, the total amount of beer consumed in the country fell to under eighteen million barrels, less than half the amount drunk in 1914. The brewers complained bitterly that duty was driving prices up and hitting demand, and yet every time the government increased taxes, the brewers added a little extra and hoped nobody would notice.

In 1933, the government realized that lower tax on a larger volume was perhaps more profitable than a higher rate on bugger all, and decided to reform the system of duty it had originally implemented to try to stop people drinking in the Great War. The new rates of duty were charged according to the strength of the beer. There was minimal duty on a barrel of 1027°, which increased steadily for every 2° of strength. In future, when brewers felt they couldn't put prices up, they saved money by reducing the strength of their beer instead. By 1939, the average original gravity of a pint was 1041°, somewhat higher than it had been by the end of the war, but still far lower than before it. This system ensured that the weakness of British beer relative to that of other countries, the result of a policy designed to help the First World War effort, would continue for the next seventy years.

British beer was in a sorry state. And there couldn't have been a worse time for it to go through a patch of bad form. For the first time, it was getting some competition for the special place it held in the hearts of British men.

We can afford *not* to drink

The depression and society's response to it hit beer drinking hard in the areas where it had been most popular. But the depression was a selective phenomenon, and while a third of people in places like south Wales were unemployed, other areas of the country were enjoying massive prosperity. Unemployment in areas such as south-east England peaked at around 6 per cent, and it wasn't just the well-off who were benefiting in these areas. Working-class people were seeing an unprecedented rise in their standard of living; between the wars, most workers enjoyed a rise in wages of 35 per cent in real terms. The odd thing was, they were still drifting away from beer drinking as a way of life.

Drinking had actually been in steady decline for some time. For centuries, the pub had been pretty much unchallenged as the place to congregate and pass time in, the only amusement outside the home, and for many a place more comfortable than the home itself. But steadily rising wages and living standards were giving people a greater number of options for what to do in their leisure time, and they began to see less of the local. The trend was clear as early as 1905, when Sir Austen Chamberlain gave a Budget speech which acknowledged that tax revenues from drink could no longer be counted on to rise indefinitely:

The fact seems to be that we are witnessing a change in the habits of our people of which we shall have to take account in any consideration of our financial system. I think the mass of our people are beginning to find other ways of expending some portion of the time and money which used previously to be spent in the public house. No change has been more remarkable in the habits of the people than the growing attendance in the last fifteen years at outdoor games and sports and large places of public entertainment like theatres, music halls and so forth which, though not conducted on strictly temperance lines, do not lend themselves to the consumption of drink or offer it as their chief attraction. Again, the extension of cheap railway fares and the enormous growth in cheap excursions absorb a further portion of the money which used formerly to be spent on drink.

In some instances the pub had given birth to the things that were now killing it. Take music hall, the craze of the 1890s. This started life when some pub owners introduced music into their saloons in the 1830s. As the best pubs prospered, they grew and transformed themselves into music halls. The pub that put on music had often been the only entertainment in many working-class areas, but as soon as music hall grew into a separate entity, people left the pub and went there instead.

By the early twentieth century there were an increasing number of alternative leisure pursuits. Technology was racing forward and opening up seemingly countless new options, all of which seemed to have a negative impact on beer culture. In 1896 the first commercial cinema shows appeared in London's Leicester Square, and moving pictures soon captured the public imagination like nothing else before them. Picture houses with magical, exotic names such as Granada and Eldorado* quickly colonized the nation, and by the 1930s 40 per cent of the population were visiting them once a week or more. Cars became increasingly affordable, and whether you got into motoring as a hobby or simply saw them as a new-found means to take the family somewhere nice, they made a massive difference to what we did in our spare time. There were tea shops, coffee bars and ice-cream parlours. There were greyhound races, bingo and football pools to relieve people of any money burning holes in their pockets. And if they could discipline themselves to save some of it, they could afford holidays and even sea cruises.

The brewers simply could not understand. They had always believed that they just had to brew beer and people would drink it, and couldn't work out what was going wrong. Much later, some people in the wine industry just about figured it out. In the mid 1940s Ernest Cockburn, a member of the famous port-shipping family, reflected:

> The 1914–1918 war had left young people with money such as they had never known before, and it seemed to have bred in them an overwhelming desire never to sit down and rest in their own homes. This encouraged them to be everlastingly in search of excitement and amusement, coupled with a desire to dine hurriedly in restaurants.

---

* Once upon a time these were the names of far-off impossibly romantic places, rather than the telly station that makes *Corrie* and the name of a hideous programme that tried to steal its viewers.

This was true, apart from that bit about not wanting to stay at home. As well as the explosion of alternative entertainments outside, the home itself was becoming a more bearable place to spend time. The 1926 Electricity Act established the national grid to provide power across Britain, and by 1940 most urban homes had electricity. Central heating, indoor lavatories and hot running water became increasingly common, and one million council homes were built between 1924 and 1935, making such modern conveniences affordable for working-class people on low incomes. By 1935, 90 per cent of homes had a wireless and many had gramophones and pianos bought on hire purchase. People no longer had to go to the pub for a bit of warmth and cheer. Here was proof that excessive drinking was inextricably tied up with squalid living conditions: with a bit of money and a few creature comforts, people sobered up to a degree the temperance movement had only dreamed of achieving.

More comfortable homes combined with shorter working hours allowed people to take up gardening and other hobbies. Inside pleasant homes, which increasingly they owned themselves, people were able to fill their time with activities that they (and to be honest, perhaps they alone) felt were good ideas. George Orwell elaborated on this particularly English form of personal freedom:

Another English characteristic which is so much a part of us that we barely notice it . . . is the addiction to hobbies and spare-time occupations, the privateness of English life. We are a nation of flower-lovers, but also a nation of stamp-collectors, pigeon-fanciers, amateur carpenters, coupon-snippers, darts-players, crossword-puzzle fans. All the culture that is most truly native centres around things which even when they are communal are not official – the pub, the football match, the back garden, the fireside and the 'nice cup of tea' . . . It is the liberty to have a home of your own, to do what you like in your spare time, to choose your own amusements instead of having them chosen for you from above.

Homes were not just more comfortable, there were a lot more of them. Between 1919 and 1939, 4.5 million new houses were built. Huge suburbs sprawled out from the cities, and unlike during the Victorian building boom, pubs were not the first buildings to be completed. Entire communities lacked a pub within walking distance.*

For those people who could still afford it, beer began to seem very old-fashioned. The great manufacturing industries of the empire were already in decline, and manual work was being replaced by clerical, supervisory and minor professional jobs. The big rise in income among the people who were not unemployed was just one facet of the growth of the middle classes, and going to the pub had of course always been such a working-class habit. Old men still went as they always had done, but their sons were not starting the same life of drinking. In 1935, the *New Survey of London Life and Labour* declared,

The social status of drunkenness has steadily fallen in the eyes of the working class population. Where once frequent drunkenness was half-admired as a sign of virility, it is

---

* That's 'walking distance', not 'staggering distance'. Things really were that bad.

now regarded as, on the whole, rather squalid and ridiculous.

The pub had long been where young men came together and bonded. But even in this primary role, a new activity was emerging which threatened its very relevance.

The beautiful drink versus the beautiful game

Until the later Victorian age there had been a sharp distinction between the upper and lower classes with regard to what you could get up to when you were not at work. Parks were a classic example. What could be better than a large, open space to keep people healthy? Make it beautiful to look at and provide playing fields to run around in and keep fit, and surely people wouldn't even think of going to the pub. Fine, except that large spaces such as Hyde Park and St James's Park in London were reserved for the upper classes. It's not that the parks had bouncers and a door policy. They didn't need them. They were fenced and gated, and charged admission fees beyond the means of the poor. Thus parks remained a place where, if you were rich enough, you promenaded, rode in your carriage, and watched the rest of polite society doing the same while gossiping about them.

But by the twentieth century attitudes had begun to change. Those in power could see that it was useful to keep workers healthy and out of the pub. Public parks, municipal swimming pools, galleries, museums and libraries became increasingly common. In the 1920s and 30s in particular, there was an explosion in such facilities provided by local government and even by employers. People were still often regarded as parts of the machine, but it was appreciated that these parts worked better if they were kept in good condition. Unlike the metal parts of the machine, this meant that they should absolutely not be kept well-oiled.

But ideas for the betterment of the poor didn't always go as planned. Working men were not stupid, and they were able to appropriate and subvert ideas that their well-meaning superiors had developed for them. Nothing demonstrates this fact better than the growth of football.

In the Middle Ages football was a mass-participation sport played between teams of men from rival villages. Sir Thomas Elyot described the game as unfit for gentlemen: 'Foote-balle, wherein is nothing but beastlie furie and extreme violence, whereof proceedeth hurt, and consequently rancor and malice.' But in the nineteenth century, public schools decided to develop codes for the game and civilize it for their own enjoyment. They couldn't agree on one new code of rules, so two rival versions – association football and rugby football – were developed. Association football was intended for the participation and enjoyment of gentlemen, but it found a deep resonance among the working class, and by the 1880s large crowds were turning up to watch games.

Today football and beer are absolutely intertwined; the twin, twisted strands of the British male's cultural DNA. Ironic then really that, when football was first promoted heavily, it was as a way of getting people to stop drinking. Once the upper classes had devised the modern game, it was the Church that had the greatest influence on the formation of football clubs. Having observed the game's mass popularity, a largely pro-temperance clergy realized that this was a great way of prising blokes out of the pub, particularly on a Saturday. People tended to work a half-day on Saturday and had Sundays off, so they would often go to the pub at lunchtime on Saturday and stay there until closing time. Football matches were organized for Saturday afternoons so that people could watch and participate after work, but also to prevent them from drinking the day away.

Workers had scorned many of the leisure ideas previously developed for them but there was something about football. The temperance movement, with a credo of 'healthy body, healthy mind', also appreciated that here was a way of linking their message with an activity of mass appeal. By 1883 a Blackburn publican was complaining that the match was emptying his pub on Saturday afternoons, while Routledge's *Handbook of Football* noted that the popularity of the game meant that, 'The public houses were emptied of their thoughtless occupants, and all the vicious amusements were abandoned.' A similar sentiment was felt in Scotland, where the *Scottish Athletic Journal* commented, 'The football field is one of the strongest temperance agents existing, and during a popular match, the bars are almost entirely deserted. The working population must be amused – is it to be the football field or the dram shop?' Football was becoming a battleground for the hearts and minds of (potential) drinkers.

However, pub landlords were nothing if not businessmen, and they realized quickly that they had a lot to offer the fledgling sport. Church halls aside, pubs were often the only places large enough for clubs to meet, and usually had land adjacent to them ideal for playing the game on. Pubs soon developed close relationships with local teams. These relationships were not always harmonious. Quarrels over rent for changing rooms and playing fields were common, and clubs including Arsenal and Spurs moved grounds according to the deals they could get with publicans. Possibly one of the most significant disputes was when Everton FC fell out with the brewer John Houlding over the rent he was charging them to play on the field adjacent to his Sandon Hotel. He told them that if they didn't want to pay the money they could go and play somewhere else. When they did, he founded Liverpool FC in their place.

As the popularity of the sport exploded the balance of power shifted, and it soon became clear that the pub was more dependent on the game than vice versa. Finally, alarmingly, blokes were doing something other than propping up the bar, and they were doing so *by choice*. Pubs began to use the latest telegraphic technology to provide regular updates on scores as a way of competing for Saturday afternoon custom. They even hired footballers to run pubs in an effort to capitalize on their local fame. In the 1880s six of the Blackburn Rovers team were publicans, and ten years later half the Sunderland side were similarly employed when they weren't on the pitch.

The tug of war for the hearts and minds of fans intensified. In 1888, prominent temperance reformers founded the Football League. This, and the establishment of the FA Cup, saw attendance at games shoot up into the tens of thousands. The brewers took advantage. The fact that temperance campaigners had made the game so popular meant that big new grounds and stands were needed, so the brewers helped build them. Like Liverpool, Manchester United was controlled by a brewer: J. H. Davies, the chairman of Manchester Breweries. In 1909 he provided the £60,000 necessary to move them to

Old Trafford and equip it with facilities that were outstanding for the time. Oldham leased their ground Boundary Park from the brewer J. W. Lees & Co., and Watford was rescued from collapse by Benskin's. But although the brewers were benefactors of the game they did not control it. In 1903, when Manchester City started looking for a bigger ground to replace Hyde Road, the brewery representatives on the club's board fought desperately but in vain against the move because of the impact it would have on their custom, even though it was painfully obvious that the existing ground was now far too small. By 1911, people involved in the brewing industry owned 15 per cent of all shares in football clubs. When brewers today pour millions into sponsorship and TV rights for football, they're merely following a pattern a century old.

Despite all this activity, football was still taking people out of the pub. In 1898, the chief constable for Liverpool commented on the impact that the city's two football clubs had had on its culture, and extended this to sport in general:

> The passion for games and athletics – such as football and bicycling – which has been so remarkably stimulated in the last quarter of a century, has served as a powerful rival to boozing, which at one time was the only excitement open to working men.

In the first few decades of the twentieth century, football succeeded in pulling men out of the pub in their droves, and made a massive contribution to the decline of the beer drinking habit. In the end, however, booze was so much a part of working-class culture that even a new phenomenon on the scale of football could not destroy it, especially not when brewers and pub landlords were working so hard to find any way they could to create associations with the sport. As time went on, attendance at matches inevitably came to be linked with excessive drinking. At the 1909 Scottish Cup Final at Hampden Park the crowd rioted, and drink was blamed.* Surely the fact that tens of thousands of disaffected working-class people who lived and worked in appalling conditions were gathered together in one emotionally charged place shared some of the responsibility for kicking things off in the stands rather than on the pitch? Not to mention the sectarian hostility between the two sides, or the fact that, after a 1–1 draw, the crowd quite reasonably expected extra time to be played until a brusque announcement told them that was it. But the demon drink was an easy target. In the eyes of the Establishment, it would remain a spectre threatening to drag the beautiful game into the gutter, despite any hard evidence that it was a primary cause of violence.†

It took a long time, but in the latter half of the twentieth century the link between football and beer became unbreakable. Thanks to Sunday leagues, big screens to watch the game and even the positioning of the pub as the perfect venue to meet up before and after the match, beer culture

---

* I'd like to rise to the defence of the fans and complain about such predictable stereotyping and the ongoing demonization of alcohol by the pro-temperance establishment. I'd *like* to, but the fact that the rioters made free use of whisky to start fires all over the ground kind of undermines such a defence.
† In 1940 a leaflet distributed at Millwall brilliantly entitled 'Don't do it, chums' warned the fans about their violent behaviour, but made no mention of booze. Not the most significant contribution to the story, but I just wanted to mention the leaflet by name. I was also going to say something sarcastic about Millwall fans. But on reflection, I daren't.

would eventually find a way of not only fighting off, but actually incorporating this threat into itself. But however bizarre it might seem now, the fact remains that in the first few decades of the twentieth century, football was the biggest threat to beer outside the prospect of prohibition.

Drinkers are doing it for themselves

At the same time, and even where beer drinking as a national pursuit still showed signs of life, it was undergoing some big changes from the Victorian pub culture to which the big brewers had become accustomed. In those areas where people were still interested in drinking beer, they were doing it increasingly in working men's clubs.

The relationship between pubs and organized labour stretches back to 1791, when the London Corresponding Society first met in the Bell in Exeter Street, London. Such societies would use rooms in pubs, and the landlord, someone you could generally trust who also owned a strongbox, was often the club's treasurer. But the growth of the working men's club movement as distinct from pubs came later. And when it came, it was an emphatic victory by the lower orders over the Victorian class system.

As licensing laws were tightened in the nineteenth century, Victorian gentlemen with a taste for the good life were concerned that restrictions on the drinks trade to prevent their workers from getting pissed might mean that they themselves would suffer the inconvenience of not being able to get a drink when they so desired. This was easily solved. The licensing laws applied to taverns, alehouses, beer shops and inns exempted clubs. The only clubs around were gentlemen's clubs. Problem solved.

The only thing was, poor people eventually figured out how to form clubs too, with a little help from the more philanthropic of their superiors. Around the 1860s, middle-class clergymen, landowners and businessmen saw the formation of clubs as an alternative not just to the pub but to drinking per se, and helped organize clubs to broaden the horizons of working men. When the Working Men's Club and Institute Union was formed, its objective was to provide 'the Wage-Receiving Classes' with 'inexpensive and comfortable places of resort for their leisure hours'. Key tenets included the provision of 'all the best works in the English Language, in all departments of Literature, History, Philosophy and Politics', the lending of 'Diagrams, Dissolving Views, Maps, Drawings, and Scientific Apparatus for Lectures', and the publishing of 'papers connected with the work of the society – suggestive of various undertakings which may be carried out at these Clubs, for the educational, social, and industrial welfare of the working classes'. But Victorian factory and mine workers were less interested in scientific apparatus for lectures than they were in a space to meet, talk, drink and relax for the short time they had between sleep and work. They politely thanked their benefactors for getting them off the ground, then exploited the rules that had been set up for gentlemen's clubs to gain their own licences and ensure a supply of cheap beer, with fewer restrictions over when they could drink it.

But clubs were not just an excuse for cheaper beer. Entertainment was a key feature, far more than in pubs, and clubs also remained a centre for political debate in an era when the Labour movement was gaining power. From a small number at the time of the First World War, there were over fifteen thousand clubs by 1935. By 1929, four and a half million people were members of working men's clubs.

This new competition was obviously bad news for pub landlords, but initially the breweries themselves were not too concerned – clubs were just alternative places for them to sell beer to – but after the end of the First World War, the cooperative spirit that characterized the club movement led them to brew and distribute their own beer. They couldn't match the quality of the big brewers, but they could beat them on price, and in a recessionary climate this was the deciding factor for many drinkers. In areas such as Yorkshire, Lancashire and south Wales, the big brewers saw a large reduction in demand for their beer. They eventually got much of their trade back, but they had to lower their prices in those areas to do it. Wherever clubs were strong, the price of beer came down across the board.

A future for beer?

Pub life was being attacked from all sides; so much was happening in society, and it seemed that every single development, good or bad, somehow resulted in fewer people going to the pub. In the industrial heartlands people could no longer afford to drink thanks to the depression, and where the depression wasn't hurting, there were countless new things to do instead of settling in for a session at the local. Between 1920 and 1940, the number of brewers in the UK fell by 70 per cent, to a little over five hundred. As always, those that remained benefited from economies of scale, and through the 1920s the biggest brewers weathered the storm, doing little that was new or different in reaction to their declining market. But in the 1930s, when volume really started disappearing, even the self-satisfied big brewers realized they had better start coming up with a few ideas.

It was an astonishing change in fortune. As we've seen, up to this point the brewers hadn't really had to break sweat in order to make money. At every major historical turn, events had somehow conspired to boost the profitability of the biggest players. Now, for the first time in their history, they had to chase people's custom, to persuade them to drink beer rather than simply take drinkers for granted. They were going to have to start *selling* beer rather than merely serving it.

The fightback began in a fairly logical fashion: if people wouldn't come to the pub, the brewers would go to them. In 1935 the Felinfoel Brewery in Wales pioneered beer in cans as a way of opening up the take-home market. The cans had screw tops and were nicknamed 'Brasso cans', after the polish they resembled. Understandably, they didn't really catch on. It would be at least another thirty years before we became convinced that this was a great way to buy beer.*

Bottled beers were a somewhat better idea. The largest breweries could afford to invest in large bottling plants and produce well-conditioned, bright, premium beers on a large scale. Among those still drinking beer this was massively popular, and anyone who wanted to stay in business had to do

---

* Although, when we finally did get into cans, we sure made up for lost time.

it. Bottled beers doubled their share of the market between 1920 and 1939.

The 'improved' public house

But the main change was to the pub itself. By now the big brewers between them owned nearly all the outlets that sold their beer, and the state of these outlets desperately needed to be improved. Pubs looked pretty much as they do today on the outside, but inside they were still quite different. The tap rooms, the dark, narrow bars with their lack of seating, scant food and dearth of basic facilities were unwelcoming. Against its new competitors, the boozer had to relaunch itself as a modern, wholesome leisure pursuit.

Ironically, the pub in its modern guise was devised not by the brewers who needed to find ways of staying in business, but by the government. The Carlisle State Brewery set up in the First World War had continued into peacetime and pursued a policy of building fewer but better pubs. More space and more seating were the order of the day. Antiquated public houses were pulled down and rebuilt with larger rooms and lounges with modern lighting and ventilation in place of the old narrow, congested bars. Novelties such as food and even, God forbid, ladies' toilets were introduced. These new pubs were not just boozing dens for old blokes, they were multipurpose leisure centres for all the family.

There were also reforming pressures from inside the brewing industry. Groups such as the True Temperance Association and the Fellowship of Freedom and Reform tried to take some of the sting out of temperance arguments by reminding everyone that temperance actually meant moderation rather than prohibition, and argued that if pubs were improved and brewers took a more responsible attitude, the problem of excessive drinking could be removed. They experimented with ideas like 'disinterested management', where pub managers were not answerable to the breweries, didn't make any profit from selling beer and therefore had no incentive to pour it down their customers' throats. Not many of these schemes were successful, but they did attract a lot of publicity and encouraged people to think about how pubs could be improved.

The 1931 Royal Commission on Licensing sought to discourage unsavoury habits such as buying beer direct at the bar, then standing up to drink it or disappearing into snugs where you couldn't be seen. The report complained:

> There were still large numbers of houses, particularly in industrial districts, which are poor and cramped in structure, gloomy, often insufficiently ventilated ... the predominating, and very often the exclusive, emphasis is on the sale of intoxicants.

Its proposed solution was:

> To make the public house ... a place where the public can obtain general refreshment, of whatever variety they choose, in decent, pleasant and comfortable surroundings.

There was no bigger fan of the pub than George Orwell, and even he felt the need for change:

> The puritanical nonsense of excluding children and – therefore – to some extent women from pubs has turned

these places into mere boozing shops instead of the family gathering places that they ought to be.

Of course, this is precisely what hard-line teetotallers didn't want. Many abolitionist magistrates argued that better pubs would lead to more drinking. If pubs remained dives the brewers couldn't win sympathy for a more moderate point of view, and the case for outright prohibition would continue to attract support. Ernest Oldmeadow, the editor of the *Tablet*, attended a licensing session in 1929 and described the bizarre proceedings which he saw unfold:

> An innkeeper sought permission to make his house, which lacked light and air, more healthy for his family and customers. The request was fought so fiercely by the local temperance organisations that, as a novice, I asked for an explanation and received the prompt answer, 'We must make drink stink.' I was told that, next to a man lying drunk in the gutter, the best argument for temperance was a squalid public house, and that every attempt by a publican to improve his premises must therefore be resisted to the utmost.

Sidney Nevile, one of the architects of self-improvement within brewing, fought against both this warped temperance logic and the cynicism of his own industry. He pointed out that improved pubs would of course prove profitable. 'A contented, sober, well-catered-for public house population is a sure source of monetary profit as well as a commendable social unit,' he maintained. Besides, if the working class was suffering the effects of economic depression, why not just take pubs away from them and redesign them for those who were prosperous instead? Agreements were reached with magistrates whereby licences for inner city dives where conditions were harsh were surrendered in return for fewer licences for bigger, better pubs in the affluent areas the depression had not hit. The dives were bulldozed, and pubs with gardens, bowling greens and car parks appeared in the new suburbs. The number of pubs declined by more than 4,000 between 1918 and 1938, but as far as brewers, the state and the licensing committees were concerned, they were better pubs.

Change was most visible in country pubs. Inns that had once catered for stagecoach passengers had been all but forgotten when railways spread across the country and made coaches obsolete. A hundred years later, the roads were busy again as motoring became fashionable. Tourism was on the increase, and coach travel in particular meant that charabancs were taking people for a nice day out in the country and looking for places to stop for refreshments. Brewers such as Whitbread in London, Benskins of Watford and Mitchells & Butlers in Birmingham prided themselves on building large, comfortable public houses, featuring play areas, children's rooms and even swimming pools, for the motoring public, and other brewers were forced to keep up.

What you have to remember about these 'improved public houses' is the scale of the egos of those building them. These were the people who a century or two previously had been building beer vats the size of a small town. Now they were focusing their attentions on pubs, and some of the results were interesting, even astonishing.* Pubs were built bigger

---

* Interpret these words any way you like.

with fewer divisions of the internal space. Waitress service and mini-golf courses replaced perpendicular drinking and shove-halfpenny. Some were just vast arenas. Architects were employed, and many somehow decided that mock Tudor would be really cool. Warming to this particular theme, one Barclay Perkins pub on the newly built Downham estate near Bromley staged Shakespearean plays. It was originally the only pub serving a community of 29,000 people, had 35 staff and boasted three dozen toilets. Between 1922 and 1930, £21 million was spent 'improving' pubs in this way. Over 20,000 pubs, a quarter of the UK's total, were rebuilt or refurbished.

The problem with all this was that no one had actually asked drinkers what *their* definition of an improved pub was. Pubs were seldom visited by middle-class people, yet they were designed by architects and town planners who if they did drink certainly didn't do it in the pub, to satisfy licensing magistrates who didn't drink at all. Orwell condemned improved pubs as 'dismal sham-Tudor palaces' which posed a threat to working-class drinking traditions. Real drinkers voted with their feet. In 1937 Watney opened a normal pub half a mile away from the Downham Tavern, without any of the frills. So now there were two pubs serving a community of 29,000 people. Not long after the second one opened, the Downham Tavern was deserted, and had to revert to the traditional pub way of doing things to stay in business.

Some beer historians view the whole improved-public-house idea as yet another despicable crime against beer drinking, a bastardisation of What Pubs Should Be Like, perpetrated by people who didn't have a clue. It wasn't quite that bad. Some of the pubs worked and are still around today in suburbs and on major roads. And you would think that no one could argue with the wisdom of putting in female toilets, serving food and providing a range of non-alcoholic drinks, particularly in pubs that people now had to drive to get to. The real problem was that pubs have always been about that curious mix of being at home and comfortable, and being out. These 'barrack pubs' simply had no atmosphere. Also, people still wanted to go to pubs to drink beer. In these vast palaces with waitress service and their disapproval of drunkenness, you spent half the night trying to order a drink. It could take so long to get a pint that it became a continual process: if you wanted to drink at a slow but steady pace, you had to order your second pint before they'd started pouring your first. Once again, the results of an attempt by the government and the brewers to give the workers what they thought they needed were often unsuccessful. Pubs overall definitely improved, but only at the expense of those trying to do the improving occasionally being made to look foolish.

'Beer. It's lovely!'

There was one technological innovation that the brewers did manage to get the hang of. The period between the wars saw an explosion of mass media, with tabloid newspapers and magazines becoming increasingly common, and the wireless arriving in many homes. The fact that this gave us shared media for the first time and revolutionized communications within society was all very nice, but the most important impact as far as the brewers were concerned was the fact that they could now reach an awful lot of people through advertising.

Until the 1930s beer advertising had consisted of promoting the brewer's name as prominently as possible on the fronts of pubs, on mirrors inside, and on the sides of buildings. When cheap mass media coincided with the growth of bottled beers, this began to change. The first ad campaign comparable to anything we know today came from Guinness. At the turn of the century, the stout specialist had rejected the tied-house strategy of the other big brewers and was starting to feel pretty vulnerable. What Guinness did have was a singular beer with a strong reputation. The company's future was in building this reputation through the new media, and so the first modern beer advertising campaign was born. In 1928 the London ad agency S. H. Benson came up with 'Guinness is good for you', a line which reflected the reasons many older drinkers were devoted to it. Doctors were successfully canvassed for their support of the idea. The first press ad declared, 'Guinness builds strong muscles. It feeds exhausted nerves. It enriches the blood. Doctors affirm that Guinness is a valuable restorative after influenza and other weakening illnesses.'

The 'Guinness is good for you' ads, with the John Gilroy-illustrated zookeeper and animals, were so enduring that the line is still readily recalled decades after it last ran. By 1953, the campaign was so well established and liked that the company was able to produce a special commemorative ad for the coronation that featured no reference to Guinness by name or illustration of the product, but which was still instantly recognizable as a Guinness ad. Plates and prints of the advertisements themselves do a roaring trade in fashion-able antique markets and tourist tat shops alike. They are part of our national heritage.

But all brewers were now trying to think about why people might want to drink their beer, and suggest possible drinking occasions. One ad by Whitbread in 1934 suggested solitary drinking for women. Under the headline, 'A Whit-bread and a Sandwich in the Middle of the Day', complete with a picture of a woman sitting in the garden supping her beer, the copy reads:

> When you 'haven't the time' or 'can't be bothered' or 'hate to sit down by yourself' – how glad you will be that you ordered a dozen of Whitbread's Pale Ale! A glass of this clear light beer and a sandwich is light, just right in the middle of the day. The goodness of malt, the flavour of hops. Who wants to cook, just for one! Whitbread's superb Pale Ale. Have it delivered at home.*

Pub signs began to promote the name of the brewer more heavily, and advertising inside the pub was also stepped up. In 1920 Watney's came up with the bright idea of supplying their customers with mats on which to rest their pints, wood-pulp affairs a quarter of an inch thick, with the names of their pale ale and Reid Stout colourfully emblazoned across them. The practice soon caught on more widely.†

---

* The strategy of trying to sell your product to women as a surrogate companion for when you're on your own may not have proved an enduring one for beer. But the same idea applied to chocolate, for some reason, has been going down a storm for decades.

† Although I can't help thinking it was a waste of money – once people were inside the pub they had no choice but to drink the beers you served,

But a few individual advertising campaigns were not enough to stop the widespread decline in drinking. The Brewers' Society, the professional body for the industry, had been lobbying the government for lower duty, and in 1933 they got it. There was just one condition. Beer was now so weak that the problem of excessive drunkenness was well down the list of issues facing the government. The state of the economy was far more pressing, and one area that was causing particular worries was farming. Lower duty was granted on condition the brewing industry reduced prices to the consumer and did something significant to boost its own output, creating a bigger demand for barley, thereby helping out the farms. The Brewers' Society agreed. They decided that what was needed was a joint, generic campaign for beer itself. Because beer was now seen as a drink for old men, they produced ads that showed young family groups drinking it, emphasizing the wholesomeness of the ingredients, the link between beer and sport, and the social role of the public house. In a speech to the trade, Sir Edgar Sanders of the Brewers' Society underlined the scale of the task, in words that must have chilled the temperance movement: 'We want to get the beer-drinking habit instilled into thousands, almost millions, of young men who do not at present know the taste of beer.' The campaign had to raise the status of the product, so it was important that 'drawings of family groups should not depict a lower social status than that of a middle class family'. The ads were signed off with the line 'Beer is Best'. But surely the best posters, the ones that said everything that

---

and were probably there because they already wanted to. Still, it gave birth to a whole host of pub games, for which we will always be grateful.

ever needed to be said, were those that ran with a different three-word slogan of genius: 'Beer. It's lovely!'*

The temperance movement decried the initiative as a 'sinister campaign to enslave youth to the drink habit', and countered with their own campaign, waspishly replying that 'Beer is Best – Left Alone'. But against ads on posters, newspapers, buses and trams, and even a song, a cinema film and a travelling revue,† their protest was drowned out. Coincidentally, and with no intention of creating PR spin whatsoever, the ads first ran the same week that prohibition finally ended in the United States, in December 1933. Demand began to rise steadily, and the collective advertising of beer was deemed a success, remaining in place until 1970.‡

Concentrated into two decades, an enormous number of things had happened that would for ever change the way

---

*   There's just no way of arguing with it. However, there is one three-word slogan that's even better. Collective advertising campaigns had also been developed for tea planters, fruit and milk producers. Also, the fishing industry was running a campaign with the appeal to 'Eat more fish'. This is advertising genius, so good it had to be copied. On the nation's motorways, dotted about the place, there are still lorries belonging to potato growers which are emblazoned with the slogan 'Eat more chips'. What's so great about this is that if it just said 'Eat chips' your reaction would be, 'Yeah, yeah, I already do,' but there's a massive power to 'Eat more chips' that's impossible to resist. Like it's your national duty to do so, but also the most delightful thing you could ever do. Or is it just me?

†   I could speculate on what this all entailed, but I think that on this occasion it would be more amusing left to your imagination.

‡   One of the last TV campaigns featured cricketers Tom Graveney and Freddie Truman, boxer Billy Walker and footballers Denis Law and Bobby Moore, not to mention the entire Liverpool football team, underlining just how important a few pints could be for the performance of our top athletes.

we spent our free time. Going to the pub to get trolleyed, which for so long had been the only option many people had available to them, was now joined by a whole host of competing alternatives. Beer drinking would never fully recover but it wasn't finished yet. The brewers and their pubs had been shaken and had had to change the entire way they approached the selling of beer. But change they finally did, eventually finding ways for beer to become part of the new leisure landscape both in and outside the home. From a low of 17.9 million barrels in 1933, consumption crawled back up to 24.6 million barrels in 1939. Of course, this was the year that war broke out again. After a period of massive societal change following the last one, the cycle of upheaval started all over again.

Chapter Eight

'Keep the bar open, we'll be down in twenty minutes'

The home front in World War II

Beer goes to war

When war was declared against Germany in 1939 no one really had any idea what to expect. Memories of the horrors of the First World War were still fresh in the minds of most adults, but there had been twenty years of social and technological progress that would clearly change things. But how? Unable to anticipate what might happen, some simply rebuilt old battle lines. The French remembered how the First World War had been dominated by trench warfare in defensive lines, and had prepared by building the Maginot Line, an impenetrable network of trench and bunker defences to stop the Germans in their tracks. Just like a scissors-paper-stone game, the Germans responded by making war highly mobile, launching the blitzkrieg or 'Lightning War'. Their Panzers simply drove around these impenetrable defences, and conquered France in weeks. The rules had changed, fundamentally.

In the fight for the right to get a drink (or the fight against the demon drink if you were on the other side), the rules had changed in a similar fashion. As the French military dug in on the Maginot Line, the adversaries on both sides in the Battle of the Booze drew themselves up in their old, familiar battle lines, failing to appreciate how different things would be this time around. Beer was about to undergo a remarkable transition. No longer a threat on a par with Germany itself, beer and the pubs that served it would become national heroes, playing a major role in winning the real war against Nazi Germany.

The phoney war

Before these beery heroics could happen, there was an old score waiting to be settled. The temperance movement was still powerful, with around three million active members. They had scented victory in the First World War. The brewing industry had been on its knees, saved in the end only because faint-hearted government ministers had prioritized issues such as industrial unrest, winning the war against Germany and preventing communist revolution ahead of the evils of a pint of 3 per cent ale. They had almost done it. Now they were back, and this time they were going to finish the job.

Almost before the real war had started, the National Temperance Federation issued a manifesto called 'Alcohol – A Foe to Britain', which urged its membership to give 'earnest and unceasing national service in the conflict with alcohol'. They described a dark and frightened country, with families uprooted and men sent off to war, and were convinced that the last thing needed in this situation was the welcoming cheer of the pub:

> In such a situation public houses packed nightly to suffocation are a blot on the nation's honour. We therefore proclaim that it is the duty of every good citizen to confront drink, the enemy of the country, with the example of his own self-discipline and determination to abstain while the war lasts. It is equally the duty of the Government to see that Britain's strength is not wasted nor her cause endangered by the lure of drink.

This must have sounded somewhat forced even to their own ears. They quickly followed this initial salvo with a more considered plan of attack. A food shortage was developing rapidly, thanks largely to the threat posed to shipping by German U-boats, which had brought Britain to the brink of starvation in 1917 and were already busy destroying Allied supply convoys. In 1940 alone, two thousand merchant ships would be sunk. Not only were imports of grain severely limited, but the overall scale of international trade was drastically reduced, meaning that Britain was simply less wealthy and there was a narrower range of goods available. Remembering the support they had received from America in the First World War, temperance campaigners leapt on the issue of scarce food supplies: there wasn't going to be enough of anything to go round, so how could we even consider using barley for brewing beer when it could be used for bread or cattle feed?

In response, the *Brewer's Journal* vigorously – some might say a little hysterically – promoted the nutritional benefits of beer, claiming one barrel of beer had the cumulative food value of: ten pounds of beef, eight pounds of mutton, four pounds of cheese, twenty pounds of potatoes, one pound of rump steak, three pounds of rabbit, three pounds of plaice, eight pounds of bread, three pounds of butter and six pounds of chicken. Oh, and nineteen eggs. What else did we need? Well, on top of its nutritional value, the brewers pointed out that alcohol acted as an aid to digestion, and that the antiseptic properties of hops could prove vital in wartime. There was also protein from the malt, energy from the sugar, the 'cleansing' abilities of yeast and mineral salts essential for strong bones. Echoing the advertising campaign of the time, the article proudly concluded,

> On all counts, therefore, as a war time drink 'Beer is Best', and the nation must see to it that it has a plentiful supply ... The public should be told in war time of the food value of beer and, moreover, of the enormous importance to the country of the by-products of beer.

That's right. Not only was beer literally the best thing since sliced bread, but the by-product brewers' yeast produced things like Marmite, rich in iron and vitamin B. And you say that's not enough? You say what about cattle feed? Well how about the fact that spent grains from the brewing process, once all this goodness had been extracted, could still make a tasty treat for cows?

It was an impressive argument. The only problem was, nobody was listening. But then nobody was listening to the temperance lot either. The only people arguing about the danger or the benefits of beer to the war effort were Temperance campaigners and the brewers who opposed them. What neither side had fully appreciated was how different the booze battlefield in 1939 was compared to 1914. At the outbreak of the First World War the average working man was spending a great deal of his time in the pub, consuming copious quantities of beer that was about 7 per cent ABV in strength. But by the late 1930s opening times had been reduced, the strength of beer was much lower and people were drinking much less of it. Drunkenness had been in sharp decline for years, and was simply not an issue of national concern any more. Very few people were genuinely concerned with the danger posed to the war effort by rampaging bands of mashed-up monsters.

It began to dawn on Temperance supporters that they were losing the argument, but the clearer this became, the louder they raged:

Alcohol we should regard as a fifth column, the enemy within our gates, sabotaging armament output, sapping morale and responsible for physical unfitness by inflaming passions.

And how about this one?

People are talking about invasion, but we should not trouble about that. No great empire has ever fallen because of an attack from outside. History has proved that. Countries only went down because they became decadent, morally corrupt, and their strength was sapped by drink, and all the other evils that came in its train.

There was no evidence anywhere to support their view, only evidence that directly contradicted it. The more they foamed at the mouth, the more they were ignored. Lady

Astor alleged that a pint was more scary and life-threatening than a whole division of German Panzers,* and asked a minister whether he realized how many women were terrified of sending their sons to army camp not because there was a very good chance they were going to get blown to bits but because – horror! – such camps might have pubs nearby. When Churchill decreed that soldiers fighting at the front should be ensured a ration of beer of four pints a week 'before any of the parties in the rear get a drop', temperance campaigners argued that drink might prove a threat to security. Arseholed on just over a half-pint of weak beer a day, troops might start giving away vital military secrets and totally undermine Allied strategy. In reply Major General Sir John Kennedy sighed drily, 'The British soldier can always be trusted to take his glass of beer without any risk of giving away the small knowledge about the war in his possession.'

In the view of the majority, the temperance movement was more likely to hinder the war effort than help it. The campaign was recognized for what it was: a cynical attempt by the movement to use the war to further its own, irrelevant agenda. People were dying every night thanks to the bombs that rained down into their streets and homes, so to be told

---

* She showed the same admirable sense of perspective when she famously declared, 'I would rather commit adultery than drink a glass of beer.' Not that there was much chance of either. Lady Astor was the woman Churchill enjoyed verbally abusing over dinner, and was the other party in this famous and often-quoted, alleged exchange:

Astor: 'Sir, if you were my husband, I would poison your drink.'

Churchill: 'Madam, if you were my wife, I would drink it.'

Astor: 'Sir, you're drunk!'

Churchill: 'Yes, Madam, and you're ugly. But in the morning, I will be sober.'

to stay off the booze to preserve your health was either ridiculous or downright offensive, depending on your point of view. Finally the temperance campaigners were told to just shut up and go away. The minister of agriculture stood up in the House of Commons and denounced their propaganda methods as 'most discreditable'. Quentin Hogg MP told his constituency teetotallers in no uncertain terms:

> You must clearly understand that the national emergency is not a moment to introduce temperance propaganda under the cloak of national necessity. Beer is the innocent pleasure of many millions, especially those who bear the brunt today.

This wasn't just a defeat; it was a comprehensive rout.

The backbone of the country

Unlike the First World War, this war had a home front thanks to the ever-present threat of German bombers. It would be fought in towns and cities throughout the country rather than solely on some foreign field, which meant that the morale and fighting spirit of the men, women and children who were about to get blown to pieces at home was just as important as that of fighting servicemen. The government was quick to recognize this, and was also quick to spot the importance of the great British pint in keeping up the country's spirits. So ministers ignored the temperance movement's claims that beer was wasting vital foodstuffs, but equally they didn't pay too much attention to the brewers' protestations that beer was the best food ever invented. They simply decided that if the British didn't get their pint, they would get really upset and wouldn't be quite as ready and willing to give Jerry a good hiding. Beer was seen as being so important that unlike almost every other important food-stuff it was never rationed at any point during the war. J. R. Clynes MP, a former food controller and home secretary, summed it up:

> I know the need of the man engaged in heavy war industries for his occasional glass of beer; and he does not want to get his ration book out every time. To men in heavy industries beer is food, and necessary food at that ... To the working man beer is food, drink and recreation ... To keep our factories humming and their workmen contented and healthy, it will be of the first importance to avoid creating a grievance among men who are working today harder than ever before.

Far from being a social problem, the pint was now a patriotic right.

Moral (and morale) issues aside, the government had another huge interest in keeping the beer flowing, which they didn't talk about quite as publicly. In the first year of the war, tax on beer was increased three times, from twenty-four shillings a barrel in September 1939 to eighty-one shillings in July 1940. Beer was now taxed at a rate twenty-two times higher than it had been in 1914, and no wartime government was going to lose that kind of revenue. In the first year of the war, revenue from beer duty topped £150 million. The brewers expected the resultant price hikes to slaughter demand, but it actually increased. The government realized they were on to a good thing, and piled on more tax. By the end of the war the basic rate on a barrel had shot up to 140 shillings – over seven times higher than it had been at the outbreak of hostilities. Not all the rise was passed on to the punter, but a pint of mild still more than doubled in price. And yet demand just kept increasing – beer consumption actually rose by 25 per cent between 1938 and 1945. Those scooping up all this money simply couldn't believe their luck.

Behind the healthy demand for beer lay the fact that the war was having some perversely beneficial effects on business. Just a few years after the appalling hardships of the depression, suddenly everybody had a job. The vast numbers of men conscripted into the forces and the need for the wartime economy to supply them with everything from bullets to clean pants, meant that everyone had to work, and many were paid handsomely. Yet although people had more money, there was very little to spend it on thanks to wartime restrictions on virtually everything of value. The only place to spend it was in the pub, and once you got in there, the choice available at the bar had been severely reduced. Not that we were ever a nation of wine connoisseurs, but supplies of wine and spirits were virtually wiped out by wartime trading conditions and whisky was diverted abroad as a valuable source of trade revenue. This meant that even a pint that cost double the price it used to was suddenly much more attractive and affordable for everyone.

The fighting local

From 7 September 1940, London was bombed by wave after wave of planes for seventy-six nights in a row. More sporadic bombing carried on after that for a further six months. Over thirteen thousand Londoners were killed and another eighteen thousand were injured. In the face of this appalling onslaught and the gloom of the blackout that it precipitated, the role of the pub in the community was transformed. With most other leisure pursuits out of action, it was once more the focus of local life. And yet drunkenness was almost unknown. The pub was now a social centre providing food, drink, shelter and comradeship. People who wouldn't have been seen dead in a common pub before the war were becoming regulars. Even women became fixtures at the bar, with one brilliantly condescending brewer's spokesman commenting on the 'pint-pot girls': 'Possibly because women are earning more money and cannot spend so much on clothes, they have taken to buying drinks.'

The beer itself was almost incidental. It was the camaraderie associated with the pub, the symbolism of it, that was most important. Senior figures from all walks of life queued up to eulogize the pub as a focal point for resistance, the very kennel, if you will, of the bulldog spirit. A. P. Herbert MP commented early in the war:

> In these days, it seems to me, the British pub, the people's club, has justified its existence as perhaps it never did before. For it has been the one human corner, a centre not of beer but of bonhomie; the one place where after dark the collective heart of the nation could be seen and felt, beating resolute and strong.

Even the clergy, for so long associated as a body with the temperance movement, agreed. The Reverend Edgar Rogers of Essex even went so far as to claim, 'After the church, the public house ought to be the most sacred spot in town or village; and after the public house, the school.'

The *Brewers' Journal* noticed that this change in attitude was reflected even in the way people referred to the pub:

The licensed house has been given a different appellation, varying with the times and with public feeling towards it. The turn of the century found it often termed the 'drink shop' or the 'gin palace'; in 1910 the cold term 'public house' was most usually employed. With the 'reformed house' period that followed in 1920 onwards the 'inn' came into vogue. The 1930s found the 'pub', written just like that, in common parlance ... Now it is 'the local' – a neighbourly, part-of-us phrase that today finds increasing use on the wireless and in the press.

Apart from its tangible benefits, just knowing that beer was there was to prove vital. The point was not that we could physically crush the Nazis while standing at the bar, but that beer and pubs were a potent symbol of everyday British life. If the pubs were still open, it meant the bastards weren't grinding us down. Normal life was carrying on without too much disruption. Lord Woolton commented:

If we are to keep up anything like approaching the normal life of the country, beer should continue to be in supply, even though it may be beer of a rather weaker variety than the connoisseurs would like. It is the business of the Government not only to maintain the life but the morale of the country.

This symbolism was well understood by the brewers and the authorities. When Canterbury was heavily bombed in

1942, Mackeson delivered to pubs first thing the following day, even though it was not the normal day for deliveries. They were the only brewery to make deliveries to Canterbury that day, and the police wrote to them in gratitude for the image of normality they provided in the midst of adversity: 'It was much appreciated by all the populace. The heartening sight of seeing a brewer's drayman making normal deliveries was most cheering.'

The pub was part of the very essence of the Blitz, and of people's resistance. On the one hand its cellars were a refuge during bombing raids, and afterwards the landlord would bring refreshments out into the wrecked streets to those clearing up. On the other, the prominent corner locations of many pubs meant thousands were damaged or destroyed. A condition of being given a licence was that you had to open your pub when you said you were going to, come what may, so it wasn't uncommon in the East End to see bombed-out pubs rigging up a plank on top of two battered barrels and declaring themselves open for business. To modern eyes it might almost look stupid if it wasn't so brave, so goddamned *cool*. One photograph in the Courage brewery's archive shows the landlady of the Elephant & Castle pub proudly scrubbing her front step while yards away workmen start to deal with a massive bomb crater that has completely wrecked the road. Whitbread's in-house magazine commented a few years after the war that:

> To many thousands of bombed and nerve-worn London-ers, the public house offered a welcome respite from the pandemonium outside and overhead. It was one of the few remaining sources of comfort and encouragement on which they could always depend.

Restored to the centre of the community, the pub helped bring down class barriers. In the 1940s most pubs still had a public bar and a saloon bar. The public bars were basic spit-and-sawdust affairs, whereas the saloons had carpets and comfy seats. Even though the same beer would be served from the same pumps to both bars, it cost more to drink in the saloon. As beer prices rocketed, the posher drinker went next door to the public bar, adding further to the spirit of comradeship in the face of hardship.

The pub helped win the war in practical as well as symbolic ways. Not content with all that tax revenue from beer, the government figured the happy drinker was good for a few bob more. Pubs had a history of savings clubs and loan clubs, particularly through the depression, and this idea was now revived to help pay for tanks and Spitfires. The brewing industry launched the Tank'ard Fund with the intention of paying for a whole battalion of tanks. Pubs were given a poster which showed Hitler cowering in a tankard beneath the slogan 'Stamp the blighter'. Customers bought stamps to stick over his face until he was obliterated.

Beer for our boys

The succour of a decent pint was at least as important for those fighting as it was for the civilian population. Air Vice-Marshall Sir Cecil Bouchier recalled how important beer was to RAF aircrew:

> I remember how the chaps used to flock up to the mess at the end of each day's fighting, flop down on the hall

floor, just as they were, straight from their aircraft, and call for their beer.

This was their one great relaxation, the beer they had dreamt about all day. No-one drank anything but draught beer and mighty good stuff it was, food and drink to the tired and thirsty. Often a leader bringing his squadron home, fearful of being late, would radio from halfway across the Channel – 'Keep the bar open, we'll be down in twenty minutes.'

As well as being a refuge for civilians the pub was a gathering place for members of the forces before dangerous missions, and the first port of call for those lucky enough to come back. Soldiers were even billeted in pubs, which would have been unthinkable in 1914.

There were one or two headaches though, such as the burning strategic question of whether it was acceptable for officers and other ranks to drink together in the same bar. Although the class system was taking as sound a beating as the Nazis, it was proving just as resilient. The minister of war gave long, hard consideration to the issue, and eventually decided that it would be acceptable. Of course it was, you might say, until you take into account the fact that before the new guidelines were issued, landlords had actually been expected to refuse to serve the riff-raff if an officer happened to be in the pub. Now this new centre of the community, this new focal point of what defined the British nation in the face of adversity, was not allowed to show any kind of class or rank favouritism, neither by the public nor the government. The working man's haunt had become the refuge of the whole nation, and within its doors everyone was equal.

One particular account of the relationship the fighting man had with the pub gives such a good flavour of everyday life in the war that it really has to be quoted in full. Jack Showers, the literary landlord of the Stanhope in Yorkshire, wrote of how one bomber crew was adopted by his pub:

I interviewed the whole crew in front of the mike and I can still sense the hush, even as I write, as the packed house heard them tell first hand of how they had run into an electrical storm while over Germany and had the horror of seeing the 'kite' immediately in front of them struck; it exploded with the full bomb load on board. This novel news caught the imagination of the newspapers who featured it in their early morning editions the next day.

Naturally they were lionised that night, and I could see that it would be quite out of the question for them to return to base before morning, so we accommodated the eight of them. From that night on our place became the 'Target for Tonight' with these happy-minded heroes who visited us with regularity every 48 hours: in fact we adopted them as our pet bomber crew, for they all loved my wife who was a real mother to them. Many a happy night did those boys spend with us, and many a grey dawn saw them depart, perhaps never to return; and we would silently watch and wonder.

The thing we had dreaded for so long did come to pass, for one dark night the door opened and only one of that crew came in. Breathlessly we watched and waited, fearing the worst, for they had always followed one another in quickly. The story however, was clearly written in the poor boy's eyes and, with a break in his voice, he told us that he had been sick and had not gone on the last flight . . .

British beer and the camaraderie that surrounded its drinking was becoming a symbol charged with ever greater and more profound meaning. Brian Glover, in his book *Brewing for Victory*, describes a startling government propaganda film that was shown in cinemas during the war:

> Under the title 'Free House', a Ministry of Information film showed several sailors from different nations drinking in the bar of a pub. Each man tells why he left his own country to fight the Nazis. Beer flows freely. A British sailor enters and says that after the war they must share the wealth of the world, like they are sharing this barrel of beer. The glasses are refilled and everyone drinks to the future.

This is a measure of how much things had changed. The specific wartime message of international fellowship against a common enemy is clear and fair enough, but put that aside and you have government propaganda using beer as a metaphor for the common good. And the near-Marxist suggestion of shared ownership of wealth (of the barrel of beer), starts to explain why the end of the war precipitated a general election Labour landslide that was very different from those that came at the end of the twentieth century and the start of the twenty-first, in that it was based on a firm promise to implement socialist policies. The particular relationship that men have when sharing a pint together was to be a model for a brave new world.

This beery international fellowship came to include many

nationalities but, in terms of sheer numbers, no group was as prominent as the Americans. This could have been dangerous. Britain was a scary foreign country, and nowhere was scarier than the pub. Every man who came here was given a book telling him how to behave, which included the following passage:

> The British have theatres and movies – which they call cinemas – as we do; but the great place of recreation is the tavern. The usual drink is beer, which is not an imitation of German beer as ours is, but ale (but they usually call it beer or bitter). The British are beer drinkers and can 'hold it'. Beer is now below peace-time strength but can still make a man's tongue wag at both ends. You will be welcome in British taverns as long as you remember one thing – the inn or tavern is the poor man's club or gathering place where men have come to see their friends not strangers.

But the British generally welcomed their American allies with reciprocal gracious acceptance and understanding. In an article sensitively entitled 'The Yanks are coming; they are here' in 1942, the *Brewers' Journal* advised:

> The mine hosts of our hostelries should be on the lookout for United States servicemen and give them the welcome they deserve ... all of them are far from home and kindly, unostentatious concern for their welfare will not be misunderstood.

It turned out to be a beautiful friendship. General Patton stayed at the Bells of Peover in Cheshire, where he would regularly enjoy a pint with Eisenhower and other generals to wind down after a hard day's strategizing. One pub in particular, the George in Huntingdon, went to great lengths to make our overseas cousins feel welcome, building an American doughnut bakery in the courtyard.

On the front line

As the war progressed, more and more of those nice Americans kept appearing down the local. Something major was going on, namely the huge build-up in preparation for the invasion of France. The D-Day landings in June 1944 represented the biggest single movement of men and military hardware in history. Several armies and everything they needed to live and fight had to be shipped across the Channel as quickly as possible. When our boys got there, after clawing their way up the beaches through barbed wire and a hail of bullets to grab a precarious fingertip hold on France, it was felt that they deserved a beer. And none of that foreign shit neither. Blissfully unaware that their children would be throwing the stuff down their necks with abandon in thirty years' time, the British army would not tolerate lager, despite optimistic overtures from the local brewers of *bières blondes*.

No doubt they would have drunk it quite happily if nothing else had been available, but fortunately this wasn't the case. The British soldier had to have his ration of good, old-fashioned, nut-brown British beer, no matter where he was. Churchill had said so. Beer was already army issue in places such as North Africa, supplied in cans painted dull olive green like any other standard military item. But D-Day was a special occasion. You want one potent symbol of how important beer was to the war effort? On the very day of the invasion itself, Spitfires flew into France with barrels of beer strapped under their wings. The planes that had won the Battle of Britain, those expensive, precious fighting machines guzzling scarce supplies of petrol, spent the most crucial day of the war so far making deliveries for breweries.

The Spitfire was the most potent icon of British resistance and fighting spirit in the Second World War. Strap a barrel of beer under each wing, and it was an image powerful enough to propel a soldier straight into the heart of Berlin. Some squadrons perhaps felt that if the German defenders saw these planes ferrying their precious cargo in such an overt manner, they would have thought, '*Mein Gott*! They've brought their beer with them! We'll never defeat them if they get through! We must stop them at all costs!' So to make themselves less of a target, they converted their spare long-range fuel tanks to carry the beer. Presumably an enemy warplane that looked like it was actually going to attack you was felt to be less of a threat than one taking in a few pints for the troops. But the other reason for this subterfuge was even more incredible. Many of these flights were not actually authorized: pilots carried them out unofficially, and they did not want to be rumbled by their superiors. To fool the admin guys, when they were filling out the report of what ordnance they were carrying, they would refer to their cargo as 'XXX Depth Charge'.

By hook or by crook one brewer shipped over 2,000 barrels of beer into Normandy in June 1944. Each one carried a label which read, 'A gift to our fighting forces from Mitchells and Butlers Limited, Birmingham. Best of luck. If this cask is returned we will refill it and send back to you.

Replace cork.' Almost scarily, in the midst of the fury and desperation of the landings, this promise was so compelling that the barrels were somehow returned.

If you think all this sounds like hard work, spare a thought for those charged with supplying our boys fighting in the Far East. At first the troops made do with beer brewed in India, but as they pushed forward supply lines became stretched. Word reached Churchill that the lads were down to a ration of three bottles a month. Again, he intervened and demanded that something be done. The idea of a floating brewery was mooted, and a Royal Navy ship was actually turned into one, complete with mash tuns, coppers, the lot. It would distil sea water and brew in the middle of the ocean. It was christened Davy Jones' brewery, and represented such a remarkable feat of ingenuity that we should probably overlook the fact that it took so long to get right that it didn't actually start brewing beer until several months after the war had ended.

Keeping it flowing

At no other time in British history had an intoxicating drug enjoyed so much symbolic importance. The brewers must have been unable to believe their luck. The war against the temperance movement had been won, pubs were full, demand was rocketing, and beer's place in the heart of the community seemed assured. The only problem was ensuring that the phenomenal demand could actually be met.

The most immediate threat to beer production was from the air. This was obvious to everyone except the rump of the temperance lobby who, gamely keeping up their increasingly absurd rhetoric, claimed that brewers had nothing to fear from the Luftwaffe because, in the words of the Reverend J. Norton, 'Hitler knows that if Britons go on drinking at the present rate we shall lose the war,' and had therefore given his pilots the location of every brewery in Britain and told them to leave them intact. However, we can only assume that the Fuhrer then decided that waiting for the British to die of liver cirrhosis perhaps wasn't the strategy to win him the war as quickly as he might have liked. In London and other key cities such as Liverpool, Newcastle, Portsmouth and Coventry, pubs and breweries were hit as hard as anything else. By 1944 it was estimated that a total of three thousand pubs had been destroyed outright as a result of enemy activity, with thousands more severely damaged.

Through the bombing, the beer had to flow. Old rivalries were put aside and brewers supplied each other's pubs in times of particular adversity. There was even a scheme whereby brewers temporarily exchanged the ownership of pubs to tighten the areas their estates covered, and so reduce transport costs. Even breweries flattened by the Blitz still found ways to carry on. Keith Groves of Manchester brewer Groves and Whitnall recalled:

> For several months in bitter weather, the men and girls of the bottling works carried on their task of producing the firm's bottled goods under the most severe conditions. About one-third of them worked totally in the open air, with their only comfort the doubtful warmth of coke braziers; the remainder in roofless and windowless buildings.

In some cases a beer was entirely, irreplaceably, destroyed. Remember how the isolated single-cell yeast strains give a particular beer its unique character? Some of these strains were lost, which meant several popular pre-war beers could never be reproduced.

Brewers had an additional challenge in that many still used horse-drawn drays. Throughout the 1930s these had been joined by motor lorries, but many had been retained for symbolic purposes and had become much more important again now fuel was scarce. So, on top of everything else, brewers in the middle of target cities were worried that when the bombing raids started the horses would panic. In the tense weeks of anticipation before the Blitz began, Watney's tried an interesting experiment at their Stag Brewery in London. Someone who was obviously keen to impress had heard from his mate's brother girlfriend's cousin that goats were a calming influence on horses. No word of a lie. A goat was duly placed in the stables, but on the first bombing raid the terrified animal was found cowering in a corner shaking, while the horses were chilled, seemingly unaware that anything was wrong. This was a crap goat. So crap in fact, that the employees of the brewery could have been forgiven for suspecting that it was actually a German spy. As one man reminisced:

It was never known what he'd do next; he disappeared for some days, until he was found by a gateman in the wastepaper store having a good feed of old cheques and accounts. Then again he wandered to the engineer's department and removed and ate the time cards . . .

When the bombs weren't falling, the brewers could concentrate on worrying about the chronic shortage of brewing materials. The problems with shipping and the huge demands of the armed forces led to rationing across the board. In addition, labour shortages caused by conscription into the forces and full employment in the factories meant that farmers struggled to meet the required harvests at home. The beer had to flow freely, this much had been made abundantly clear. But while the government supported the brewing industry and regarded beer as vital for the war effort, they were looking for quantity rather than quality. Reductions in the strength of beer were demanded soon after the outbreak of hostilities, to make fermentable materials go further. By the end of the war the average gravity of a pint had fallen from 1041° to 1034.6°. Strong ales disappeared altogether from the bar, to be replaced by weaker beers indistinguishable from one other. Early in the war there were even rumours that the government was planning to introduce 'pool beer', a single national brand each of bitter and mild. But if there was anything guaranteed to scare the nation more than the threat of life under the jackboot it was the idea of beer brewed by the government, and this thankfully never came to pass.

Lord Woolton looked on the bright side, presenting the situation to the House of Lords in May 1942 like this:

Some 25 years ago many people begged and prayed for a light drink which the working people might have, and which would give them pleasure and satisfaction without the evils of excessive drinking. We have that beer now;

people are enjoying it and it is doing them very little harm. I believe that this policy has met with the approval of the country.

The *Brewers' Journal* argued that it depended on how old you were. They conceded that the younger generation, which included the bulk of the armed forces, saw beer mainly as a thirst quencher and the drinking of it as a social act, but they grumbled under their breath that:

There is a section of the public comprising mainly the older generation of men who deplore the lack of strength in the national beverage as it reaches them today.

As the war dragged on the supply situation worsened, and further steps had to be taken. The situation became critical in 1943, and brewers were asked to cut back their use of barley by 10 per cent. The government was also happy to 'suggest' that beer be made with increasingly bizarre alternative materials. First oats were proposed. Some brewers did the best they could. It wasn't that oats didn't *work* exactly, more that most brewers would have hesitated to serve the resultant brew to Hitler, let alone their brave and defiant countrymen. Then, briefly, potatoes were suggested. This was the last straw for many brewers who, war or no war, felt this was taking the piss out of them and their carefully crafted brews. Guinness had a go with dried potato flakes and found it made their prized stout taste of – you'll never guess – potatoes. Greene King of Suffolk also gave it a go, but reported that beer made from potatoes precipitated vicious attacks of farting among their customers.

The supply of hops was another problem as farmland was

being given over to more essential supplies such as wheat and grazing for cattle. Moreover, the main hop fields were in Kent. Traditionally, East End families would spend their summers havesting the hops, but as Hitler's invasion force gathered on the other side of the Channel, there was a sudden unwillingness to go any nearer the likely landing zones. This particular problem did ease thanks to the Blitz. Caught between the threat of German troops in the fields and the certainty of German bombers over their homes, the East Enders flocked back to the hop fields.

Brewing was hit far worse than many other industries by staff shortages. The problem was that dabbling in running breweries was a very popular pastime among retired army majors and colonels. When war was declared they bristled their handlebar moustaches and urged the men in their employ to do their bit, to enlist and fight for king and country. They did such a good job of it that virtually entire workforces did as they had been told and marched off, leaving the breweries deserted. Drastic measures were called for. Who was going to make the beer? The ex-colonels sat around, scratched their heads, then thought of an idea so brave, so bold, that it could only have been conceived in wartime and during a dire national emergency. They would employ *women*. Guinness, either unaware or forgetful of the fact that women had until recently been in charge of brewing for centuries, avoided this for as long as possible. Ireland was neutral in the war, and they managed for a while by importing Irishmen, but they eventually had to succumb to the inevitable. Amazingly, it turned out that women were actually capable of brewing beer. One Guinness historian was really tickled by the fact:

Soon only visitors from St James's Gate [Guinness's Dublin brewery] were surprised to see blonde heads bobbing over the sides of skimmers, manicured hands ramming huge pockets of hops into coppers and trim figures deftly manoeuvring casks about the bank.

Through all these various trials, the nation's breweries pulled off the miraculous feat of maintaining production at pre-war volumes. The problem was that with pubs full to bursting with people with cash in their pockets, demand for beer was far outstripping these levels.

Even when they had supplies of beer, pubs had headaches serving it. Everything was in short supply, and people were nicking glasses from pubs on a scale that would shame even the most enterprising student today. In one Mitchells and Butlers pub there were 325 glasses at the beginning of one evening and eleven at the end. Some brewers started to charge deposits on glasses, and in Feltham in Middlesex one man was sentenced to three months in prison for taking a half-pint glass. Bottles were scarce so, after a decade of heavy promotion of bottled beer, people were encouraged to drink draught again. If Brewers were lucky enough to get their hands on some bottles they still had to worry about bottle tops thanks to the metal shortage, and labels thanks to the paper shortage. The value of everything was appreciated anew.

Eventually, pubs began to close on certain days of the week, or close early. Notices appeared asking everyone to drink a bit less so we could all have a share. Some landlords encouraged people to drink shandy. Brewers and licensees in Manchester came up with a plan to divide their stock into nine, selling two ninths each on Friday and Saturday and one ninth every other day of the week, which meant at least they could open the pubs every day. The government was concerned. The home intelligence committee of the Ministry of Information wrote of pub closures in a secret report:

> In Rugby three out of four pubs are said to close one night a week. This shortage appears to have more effect upon the factory workers than any naval disaster; they interpret this shortage to mean that we are in a worse position than is being disclosed.

When pubs started closing and people got nervous, as soon as the pubs opened again they would descend on them and drink them dry, exacerbating the problem even further. The problem grew steadily worse as the war progressed.

As VE Day approached, there were rumours that pubs were so low on stocks they might not be able to open. The *Brewers' Journal* spluttered indignantly:

> It would be unthinkable that this centre of social life, where men and women foregathered in the dark days of the war for mutual courage and encouragement, and to arm themselves for the trials of tomorrow, should close its doors on the day of liberation from the direst peril that has ever beset this land.

So that was us told.

Beer wins the war

When it finally arrived, VE Day was a riotous celebration the like of which those of us who weren't yet born will never see and can scarcely imagine. But afterwards the pubs stayed shut for two days, landlords and bar staff as drained and empty as their casks. Just as in the First World War, beer had fought and won a battle comparable to that of the country at large. Both had won a glorious victory, but both had been left hugely weakened. Those pubs that hadn't been bombed out hadn't been refurbished for years, and most wouldn't see a lick of paint for years to come. The quality of beer was, by normal standards, dire, and its supply got even worse in the first, faltering years of peace, as a shattered and exhausted country, waking up to the task of rebuilding itself, faced even greater shortages of materials than during the war itself.

Drinking habits had changed, and had been defined for the future. Women were in pubs, beer was lighter, and drinking it was much more of a social experience. The range of types of beer available before the war – mild ale, golden ale, nut-brown ale – had also been severely reduced and many would never return. The young generation of post-war drinkers favoured bitter over mild, and would increasingly favour nationally advertised bottled beers.

In addition, the war had finally defeated the old enemy, the temperance movement. The *Brewing Trade Review* wrote:

The war has broken up many old prejudices and dispelled many deep-rooted illusions. None, perhaps, has been more completely shattered than the idea that the devil lurks at the bottom of every glass of beer.

The pub had completed its transition from a murky hole where men – just men – stood at the bar and purposefully downed pint after pint until they could no longer stand into the beating heart of the community. Beer had demonstrated that it was so much more than a drink: it was a ritual symbolising everyday life, normality, decency and comradeship as well as being a powerful symbol of national identity.

No one guessed that the triumph wouldn't last; that this was a high-water mark in the fortunes of the pub and in the first twenty-five years of peace things were going to change all over again. For now, there was no question of its importance. As the *Daily Sketch* newspaper put it:

> Here, with talk and song and good comradeship, with darts and shove-ha'penny and devil-among-the-tailors,* the spirit has been maintained which makes our people go into war as friends who know and trust one another. Waterloo was not only won on the playing fields of Eton. The tap room of the Red Cow had a good deal to do with it as well.

---

* No, sorry – I've no idea either.

Chapter Nine

'You will be crushed whether you like it or not'

How Carling transformed the business of brewing and drinking

Just when you thought the war was over . . .

It's a story close to the heart of any patriotic Brit. A dark, moonless night somewhere in Nazi Germany, 1942. A lone German guard steps out of his hut, adjusts the rifle on his shoulder, sniffs the night air and lights a cigarette. A low drone emerges from the darkness. The guard looks up to the hills and sees Our Boys, a squadron of Lancaster bombers, hugging the ground to avoid being detected by radar. As they fly in we see they're over a dam. The unfortunate German guard is about to witness the famous Dambusters in action – or so we think.

As the first bouncing bomb hits the water and skims towards him, the soldier drops his rifle, shrugs off his tunic and assumes a goalkeeper's stance. He catches the bomb, as big as a spacehopper and flying with considerable force. He staggers back under the impact, but remains heroically firm and saves the dam. More bombs follow, coming quicker now, and he stops every one of them in a series of ever more acrobatic saves. Inside the aircraft, the pilot shrugs, takes off his oxygen mask and says, 'I bet he drinks Carling Black Label.'*

Six years later (or fifty, depending on how you look at it) the Carling Brits get their revenge. In one of the last 'I bet he drinks' commercials, the way things work out was switched again, this time in our favour. In a typical modern-day Mediterranean resort, British holidaymakers use skill and ingenuity to recreate bouncing bomb technology, artfully landing their towels on the hotel sun loungers before the German tourists get there. The dramatic, slow-motion photography and rousing Dambusters theme remind us who really won that particular conflict.

Carling was there at every significant moment in the Briton's life, and in his history. It didn't just hate the Krauts, it hated the Frogs as well. It wasn't just there in the Second World War, it was also the favoured drink of King Arthur: in one ad Carling produces a glorious synchronized swimming display as Excalibur is thrown into the lake.

Like all the great lager ad campaigns, 'I bet he drinks' eventually ran out of steam. But instead of following its advertising into obscurity, Carling pulled off a master stroke, ensuring that its place in the heart of the English male would be safe for a generation longer than its waning peers by

---

* It's an interesting, although perhaps unforgivably pedantic, point that this version of events is in some ways closer to the truth of the Dambusters story than the idea we have from wartime legend. The Dambusters raid wasn't that successful – they damaged a few dams but missed destroying most of their key strategic targets, and those they did flood were quickly repaired. The famous bouncing bombs were never used a second time.

securing the sponsorship of football's Premier League. In the 1990s Carling was synonymous with football, and as football enjoyed unprecedented glamour and widespread popularity, Carling's fortunes went the opposite way to many other 'standard' lagers.* As virtually everyone else's sales started falling in the face of new competition from premium-strength Continental lagers, Carling's increased. By the late 1990s it had an unassailable lead as the biggest-selling beer (in volume terms) in the country, with three million pints a day consumed. The story of Carling is the story of *the* brand that defines what it is to be an English lad. For a long time it even had the Union Jack on the can.

Ironic then that it's not an English beer at all.

When you think about it, how could it be? The English have never brewed lager. Lager is *German* for God's sake! The English brew mild, bitter, stout and porter. They're famous for it. Lager has always been imported, or has at least pretended to be. No, Carling came from a place that, as far as the English lad is concerned, is cold and dull and not worth bothering with. The only thing he knows about it is that he's got a second cousin who lives there somewhere who sends a Christmas card every year, who came to visit when he was about eleven and had to share his bedroom and was a bit odd. Yes, you know where I'm talking about. Carling came from Canada.

---

* Standard lagers are those with less than 5 per cent ABV – most of them are between 3.5 and 4.5 per cent – and are more affectionately known as 'cooking' lagers, or a variety of less flattering names.

The man who bought the world

Initially, the man responsible for introducing Carling Black Label (as it was known until recently) to Britain wasn't even that bothered about the beer itself. He had bigger things on his mind, like building up the biggest national brewery group in the UK and thereby transforming the entire shape and nature of British brewing. And that was only in his spare time. What he did in Britain was little more than a hobby for the greatest entrepreneur in Canada's history, not to mention one of the most successful racehorse owners who ever lived. His legacy to us is a mixed one, but nevertheless every lager drinker should raise a pint to the memory of one man who, more than anyone else, is responsible for what we drink today and who we buy it from. I am, of course, talking about Edward Plunket Taylor.

Eddie Taylor was always going to be huge. He knew this from the start, and it took him little more than the first twenty years of his life to make it very clear to everyone else.

Taylor was born in 1901 to a successful but not overly rich middle-class family in Ottawa. As often happens when someone becomes rich beyond most people's wildest imaginings, there have always been jealous rumours that Taylor was born with a silver spoon in his mouth. The truth in Taylor's case is not so much that the family didn't *have* a silver spoon, more that the silver spoon belonged to Grandpa, who kept it locked up in a drawer and wouldn't let anyone near it, not even to stick in the mouth of the new baby as he emerged. Charles Magee was a rich man who had succeeded through his own efforts. He felt that the greatest gift he could bestow on his family was to allow them to do the same, and not hamper their endeavours by thoughtlessly sharing his wealth with them, thereby cruelly blunting their ambitious instincts. Magee wouldn't give permission for his beloved daughter to marry Taylor's dad until the poor sod had proved his worth by getting £1,000 in the bank by his own labour, and this was a lot of money in those days. The couple ended up marrying late in life.

They did, however, get together in time for children still to be an option, and Charles Magee seemed to have a lot more time for his grandson Eddie when he finally appeared on the scene. He still refused to go near the lad with a spoon of any description, but he did teach him about business. Moreover, Eddie Taylor began with an unusual degree of natural intelligence, ingenuity,* and personal charm. His grandfather helped add to this ferocious ambition, entrepreneurial spirit, an almost mystical knack of reading the truth in a company's balance sheet, and a merciless killer instinct that would have put the pinstripe-and-red-braces corporate raiders of the 1980s to shame. E. P. Taylor was to become the proto-yuppie.

By his and the century's mid twenties, Taylor had already started up and profitably sold off a couple of his own businesses, and had built a very successful career as a bond salesman. Granddad Charles Magee didn't live to see the flowering of his protégé. He died in 1918, finally, reluctantly, giving up his wealth. He left interests in a vast array of companies, which were divided up among the family. One

---

* He invented the double-sided electric toaster when he was eighteen years old. No, seriously. He did.

such company was Brading Breweries. Taylor's Dad still didn't get a cut of the money, but he was made company president. In 1923 Uncle Delamere Magee, who had inherited a share of the company, decided it would be a good move to appoint young Eddie to the board of Brading. This was his big chance. Eddie got the books out, took a good look at the market, and drew up his plans.

At the time North America was in the grip of prohibition. Canada wasn't quite as dry as the United States, but was still suffering. In Ontario the production of beer was legal but its consumption was not, so Brading was exporting to neighbouring Quebec which, being French, didn't see what all the fuss was about and never banned booze. It wasn't a great state of affairs. Brading and thirteen or so nearby small breweries were all operating at less than capacity and were bottling soft drinks to help make ends meet. This made them all vulnerable targets for takeover, should anyone want to buy them. Taylor did, because he rightly guessed that prohibition couldn't last. He worked out a way of approaching these breweries and taking control of them by trading shares for some of Brading's own. He would work out a deal and take it to the board of Brading for approval, and was paid for his time, effort and vision in shares of the new company that was the result of each merger. Starting out with no shares, as the mergers piled up, so did Taylor's ownership.

In this way Taylor had acquired a number of small breweries by 1929, and was already looking like a player when the stock market crash hit. On top of prohibition, the great depression which followed meant brewery shares were next to worthless. It was an audacious gamble, but Taylor managed to keep his programme of acquisition going through this period. In fact, he stepped up his efforts. In 1930 he acquired virtually every significant brewery in Ontario, including Carling, which had been enjoying relative success, particularly with its new Black Label product launched in 1927. Almost overnight, the newly christened Brewing Corporation of Canada,* a conglomerate with Brading at its core, had become one of the handful of key players in the Canadian brewing industry, with Taylor its architect and subsequent chairman. He became a household name throughout the country, the young Richard Branson of his generation.

But Eddie soon found out that taking over companies was the easy part. His new corporation was a mess. He had bought a load of moribund old breweries and stuck them together, and they were collectively losing money in the middle of a hideous depression. From 1931 to 1935 he kept the company afloat, raising cash to pay day-to-day running costs by ingenuity and sheer personal charm. Then in 1935, due in no small part to Taylor's own efforts, the new Liberal premier of Ontario relaxed the laws governing alcohol, allowing it to be sold and consumed in public places. Finally the brewery turned in a profit, and Taylor could now really start getting to work. In 1930 Taylor had fifteen breweries which between them had fifty brands and an (admittedly largely unused) annual production capacity of close to a million barrels. By 1937 the company, now known by the snappier

---

* Just the first in a history of corporate names which demonstrate that, whatever other talents the man may have had, Taylor believed in calling a spade a bit of wood with a kind of flat, sharpish metal blade on the end for digging the ground up with.

but no more creative title of Canadian Breweries Limited, consisted of six breweries producing twenty-seven brands, with almost 35 per cent of the Ontario beer market. The rationalization continued until in 1954 the remaining four subsidiaries produced a mere eight brands.

By the mid 1950s Taylor's ambitions in Canada were becoming frustrated. His business interests had expanded well beyond brewing, and his holding company, the Argus Corporation, was exerting a more powerful influence on industrial, corporate and general business activities than any firm had ever done before in Canada. You don't get to be that big without making enemies and, rightly or wrongly, Taylor was increasingly getting into trouble with people attempting to sue him for creating a 'quasi-monopoly situation'. If he wanted to grow further (and there was no doubt that he did – he had 'a duty to the stockholders') he had to look abroad.*

Throughout his life Taylor maintained that the motivation for his slash-and-burn tactics was that bigger companies had advantages for the consumer, such as higher and more consistent product quality. But even a mild cynic could argue that Taylor's actions had as much to do with getting rid of potentially troublesome competitors. There's no one more cynical than the British, so when Taylor turned up in the UK he was greeted as though he were carrying the plague.

---

* See, he was being altruistic, not greedy! What do you mean, 'But surely he was the biggest stockholder?'

The economist and the gentlemen

If the 1920s and 1930s had knocked some complacency out of the brewing industry for the first time in its history, World War II put it back. Once again the big brewers felt they could do what they wanted, demand would keep on coming, and no one could do anything to rattle their cosy existence. They were slow to respond to events, which meant that sharp outsiders like Taylor could take what he wanted while they were still choosing which Burgundy to have with the main course. Things were still run in a very polite and decent fashion. In the face of falling demand some consolidation among breweries had already happened, but any sales that did take place were voluntary and above all gentlemanly. Brewing was regionally based; each player had its own patch, so there was no need for things to get nasty.

But things were starting to change. Professor John Vaizey of Cambridge University caused a stir with his book *The Brewing Industry 1886–1951*, in which he analysed the industry and urged it to change. Vaizey was an economist and was writing in the middle of the century when economists truly believed they were able to reduce the complex behaviour of markets to simple formulae and to read and predict them scientifically. He wasn't an evil man, he just visualized the world in the one-dimensional way that economists can, seeing equations and functions where the rest of us see people, buildings and cash. And in brewing, he saw an industry going badly wrong.

Vaizey felt that brewing had once been ahead of the field. Along with coal, steel and textiles, it had been one of the first industries to be listed on the stock exchange, but because of complacency it was now verging on the anachronistic. The big families still held the majority of shares, provided most of the board members and took an active role in management. As a result they were not as aggressive as they should be, not as single-minded in the pursuit of pure profit. They were distracted by other things which Vaizey referred to as 'professional and social camaraderies', loyalties engendered by their way of doing things which meant that the industry 'was not as technically progressive as prosperous enterprises might usually be expected to be'. By looking after their employees and taking long lunches instead of slaving away themselves, they were letting the side down:

> Because members of these families, educated at the older universities or at Sandhurst are still on the Board, there are some restraints on commercial pushfulness and an emphasis on dealing 'properly' with employees and the public.

If the big brewers wanted to survive as businesses, argued Vaizey, they'd better start behaving in a more businesslike fashion, placing emphasis on good, modern, scientific economics rather than heritage and tradition. They needed to rationalize the number of beers they produced, close down old-fashioned breweries and seek economies of scale from up-to-date, more efficient units placed near the new motorways, minimizing distribution costs.

Vaizey's work was a turning point in the way the industry regarded itself. His intervention is still seen by serious beer lovers as cataclysmic. He was advocating the destruction of everything they held dear: eclectic brews, endless variety and quaint, old-fashioned breweries. In the eyes of traditional beer lovers, the bastard was Pol Pot with a doctorate.

Some changes were already taking place. A new breed of publican was appearing as the brewers replaced tenant land-lords with appointed managers, in an attempt to take more control of how their beer was sold. The problem was that these people were often relatively inexperienced and didn't have much of a clue about how to keep beer properly. The quality of draught beer was increasingly poor as a result, and there was a substantial switch to bottled beer which, although pasteurized and artificially carbonated, was at least reliable. Bottles meant that beers could be sold on a country-wide basis, and some national brands did start to appear. But these innovations weren't being driven with any real sense of urgency. The market still consisted mainly of draught ale and stout, products that did not travel particularly well no matter how they were kept. Most brewers saw no need to establish themselves on a national basis, and carried on as they were.

But both the population and the economy were growing, so there were more people spending more money. And they were increasingly likely to want to spend it in pubs. The war's transformation of the pub into a place where anyone could go proved more than a passing fad. Middle-class people and women in general started to frequent pubs again for the first time in nearly two centuries, and they seemed happy to drink beer while they were there. In addition, the post-war baby boom meant that, by the early 1960s, there were far more young people reaching drinking age with money in their pockets than there had ever been before. From a low point of 24.6 million barrels per year in 1958 beer consumption began to rise, and would carry on doing so until 1979, when it would peak 71 per cent higher at 42.1 million barrels. And yet the brewers were still carrying on in their same old complacent rut.

The big British concerns' most crucial error was that they still saw themselves very much as brewers of beer. Pub real estate was chronically undervalued, figuratively and literally, by all the breweries. Property re-evaluations were rare. One study in 1962 showed that of twelve companies in which Whitbread had an interest eight had not calculated the value of their properties for at least fifteen years. Even those pubs which hadn't been bombed twenty years before were showing signs of neglect. Any brewer with big enough cash reserves to improve its pubs had been prevented from doing so by the ongoing post-war rationing of building labour and materials, and when restrictions were lifted they were slow to react. This meant the accounts of brewers often drastically under-estimated the true value of what they owned. If someone predatory were to come along with a bag full of money, he could therefore acquire them for much less than they were worth before anyone realized what was going on. Taylor had just sewn up a market that faced much bigger problems than this. He must have been rubbing his hands with glee.

Edward Plunket Taylor comes to town

Taylor had been in love with Britain since he spent time here during the Second World War. Like the American army, he too had enjoyed a few pints down the local, when he visited as an intermediary between the British government and Canadian arms manufacturers.* Ironically, the opportunity to enter the British beer market initially presented itself back to front. Taylor was approached by Thomas Carter of the Hope & Anchor brewery in Sheffield, who was looking for a partner to brew and sell his Jubilee Stout in Canada. In 1953 the two men signed a deal whereby Taylor would look after Jubilee in Canada in return for Hope & Anchor introducing Carling to Britain.

Carling got off to a pretty good start. Because most pubs in the UK were tied to breweries, the brand had immediate distribution to Hope & Anchor's 200 outlets. The same wasn't true in Canada, and Jubilee Stout wasn't performing as well there as Thomas Carter would have liked. He felt he was giving more than he was getting, and so asked Taylor to help drive his business in the UK as well as push his brand in Canada. Taylor readily agreed.

The tied-house system was proving as much a frustration as it had been a boon. Two hundred pubs were not enough for what was now Taylor's number-one brand. Taylor and Carter signed a further declaration that stated their intent to create a national brewery group in Britain.

Whether Taylor's opponents realized it or not, it was a good time to be doing business. The reaction to post-war austerity developed into a full-blown culture of hedonism as the 1960s got into full swing and the economy boomed. On top of that, there were changes in the law helping things along. In 1961 and 1964 the first serious licensing acts in over

---

* Judging by Taylor's love of British beer and pubs, we can safely assume his particular local never experimented with the idea of potato beer.

forty years were passed. A new type of licence was created for hotels and restaurants to encourage the sale of alcohol with food, and grocery stores were permitted to hold off-licences. This measure just happened to coincide with the arrival of supermarkets in the UK. There were less than 250 supermarkets and superstores in the UK in 1959. By 1979 there would be 7,500, and most of these, along with corner shops and convenience stores, would stock alcohol. The total number of off-licences, which had been static for years, shot up from 26,000 in 1959 to 41,000 by 1979. The off-licence explosion prompted a huge growth in canned and bottled beer. Those people who were still a bit nervous about going to the pub could now drink at home. The take-home trade started to rise as a percentage of the beer we drank, as it continues to do today. The nation was drinking freely and happily, as it hadn't done since the Victorian era. And not only was there a higher demand for beer, but unlike most other countries very little of this was imported. The big European lager brewers were making few inroads into a market where people were fanatically loyal to their local brews and very set in their ways.

Taylor took his stake in the Hope & Anchor and went at it like no one had ever seen. He began his now-familiar programme of acquisitions, mergers and consolidations by buying a Scottish brewery, John Jeffrey & Co., in 1959. By the end of the following year he had formed United Breweries, a group with over 2,800 pubs in Yorkshire, Scotland and the south of England. The conservative brewing industry, indeed the whole British financial scene, was reeling.

Every aspect of Taylor's approach was a clear statement of intent. He instructed his broker to buy the minimum amount of equity (£25) in every single publicly quoted brewing company in the country. He did this so that, as a shareholder, he would be sent automatically a copy of each brewer's full financial information. This information was freely available and there were far less confrontational ways of acquiring it. The brewers were outraged; you simply didn't buy shares in each other's companies.

Taylor's style was a curious and compelling mix. Apparently, you couldn't help but like the guy face-to-face, but he was brash and upfront, gauche in the eyes of an industry which could look down its nose at this upstart outsider but was powerless to stop him. Anthony Avis, a former director of one brewery that eventually became part of Taylor's empire, splutters indignantly in his memoirs:

> [Taylor] had been driving round the United Kingdom and bursting in upon startled directors . . . with only the slimmest of introductions, suggesting mergers with the eloquence of a carbon paper salesman.

Looking back to that period, Arthur Elliott, a lawyer who had been part of the first deal with Hope & Anchor, described the general reaction to Taylor:

> I don't think he was ever described as dishonest or a sharp operator, but rather as a steamroller, or a harvesting machine who will just gather you in. You'll be part of the flock whether you like it or not and you will be crushed whether you like it or not.

The *Stock Exchange Gazette* concurred, remarking that there seemed to be 'little to prevent Mr E. P. Taylor from obtaining ultimate success'.

The birth of the 'Big Six'

Finally, the industry started to fight back. It was becoming clear that in order to prosper you simply had to be part of a huge corporation, but a lot of people were damned if they were going to be part of a huge corporation that belonged to a bloody Canadian. It was a matter of principle. Taylor's attempts to build a national brewing chain meant that he inadvertently prompted everyone else to do the same, creating trading blocks that were too big for him to take over – or so they thought.

This was all happening in the midst of a general consolidation of British industry. Because of its localized nature, brewing was starting from the back of the grid, but this just made the pace of the mergers and acquisitions to come all the more breathtaking. Ind Coope Ltd, Tetley Walker Ltd and Ansell's Brewery Ltd became Allied Breweries, a group of fourteen breweries with 8,575 pubs, 125 hotels and 1,780 off-licences. The famous London firm Courage merged with several other big brewers to escape Taylor's clutches, forming the fourth-largest brewer in the UK with 4,800 pubs. Watney Mann, a large but localized London brewer, was created in 1958 by the merger of Watney, Combe Reid and Mann, Crossman and Paulin. They thought they were safe, until they were almost bought a year later by another aggressive entrepreneur, Taylor's nearest rival, Charles Clore.

Clore was another outsider, a non-brewer, which, again, probably explains why he was able to see what was happening when no one inside the industry could. He was a working-class Jewish boy from the East End of London who had made a fortune with his company Sears Holdings, a 'shoes, hosiery machinery and shipbuilding conglomerate'. From this base he went into retail and property, and eventually bought Selfridges department store. He was a proud Londoner who saw the potential of pubs. Watney Mann was at the time the biggest pub operator in London, so he decided he wanted to buy it. People were somewhat doubtful of Clore's passion for brewing heritage, and the fright caused by his near-successful bid rippled through the industry. Clore soon moved on to other markets and everyone breathed a sigh of relief. Then in walked Eddie Taylor.

After their narrow escape with Clore, Watney Mann took one look at Taylor and decided to buy breweries and pubs all over the country, becoming a national operation with around 6,000 pubs by the mid 1960s. The rest of the big brewers now knew that if they too didn't build themselves up into bigger combines pursuing ever-greater economies of scale, someone from the outside would come in and do it for them. At a Brewers' Society meeting to discuss the issue, Colonel Bill Whitbread exclaimed, 'Our only hope for the industry is to integrate, or else disintegrate.' In 1960, Scottish Brewers and Newcastle Breweries came together as Scottish & Newcastle. Whitbread, which had up to now relied on reciprocal agreements rather than outright acquisitions, changed its policy and swallowed up as many of the breweries with which it had relationships as it could.

The 1960s became a race to buy, buy, buy, with Taylor at the front. In 1962, after a long, hard fight, he succeeded in merging with Charrington to create the third-largest brewer in the UK, with over 5,000 pubs and a market value of £78 million. In Charrington United he had his national brewery, but this was no longer enough; now he wanted to be the biggest. But the market was closing up and serious competitors starting to emerge. In 1966 Charrington United pursued eighteen different firms and succeeded in acquiring only one. Eventually, Taylor persuaded Bass to talk to him. In July 1967 he met the chairman for lunch and, strolling round St James's Park afterwards, the two men hammered out a deal which created Bass Charrington, the UK's largest brewer with over 11,000 outlets and an unprecedented 19 per cent share of the British beer market.

The supply of the nation's beer had been transformed beyond all recognition. Along with his direct creation of Bass Charrington, Taylor had had a significant indirect influence in creating the other five of what were now the UK's 'Big Six' breweries: Allied, Courage, Scottish & Newcastle, Watney Mann & Truman, and Whitbread. By 1972, these six brewers produced 72 per cent of the country's beer.

A life's work

Finally satisfied with his achievements and entering his seventies, Eddie Taylor called it a day. He removed himself from the board of Canadian Breweries back home, and eventually resigned from the board of Bass Charrington in 1972. He sold the mansion in Surrey and retired, more or less, to the Bahamas, to spend more time with his wife and horses, leaving the British drinker to contemplate his legacy.

The effects of consolidation were immediate. Between 1958 and 1970 the Big Six closed fifty-four of the 122 breweries they owned between them. Brewing undoubtedly became more efficient as a result – productivity increased massively in the remaining breweries – but countless local brands were lost, and across the country beer drinkers were angry. If you didn't want the brewery, they grumbled, then why the hell did you buy it in the first place? The answer was that companies had to be big to survive. If you were not big and profitable, you would be bought by someone who was. 'Inefficient' breweries could be bought and closed down and their output moved to big new breweries, which could produce more and were therefore more profitable. Or that was the theory. And in some cases the brewers didn't want the smaller breweries they were buying anyway. What they did want were the pubs attached to those breweries, pubs which they now recognized as retail outlets and sources of profit rather than community centres and homely hostels. But the harsh economics of modern corporate life meant little to the legions of men sitting wondering where their beloved milds and bitters had gone, and precisely what they were supposed to do with the pints of Watney's Red Barrel provided in their place. From their position, it just looked like pure avarice.

Throughout his life, Taylor protested that he was not driven by greed. Despite the huge rationalizations that followed his mergers (within two years of the final merger, Bass Charrington alone had closed six breweries, nine bottling plants, twenty depots and a distillery) he saw himself as a creative kind of guy, preferring to emphasize that he was building large firms rather than destroying small ones. In Britain he had created a modern brewing industry and had begun the transformation of the habits and preferences of the British beer-drinking public, but to beer historians he is something of an Antichrist. Even in Canada he was regarded as the ultimate capitalist ogre. But he was charming and likeable, and undoubtedly ferociously intelligent. When you look at everything else he did when he wasn't buying breweries, it seems that above all he was driven by an insatiable lust for life. Oh, and he did a lot of work for charity as well.

The creation of Bass Charrington made Carling Black Label the first national lager in the UK, with huge distribution. In 1965 it was launched on draught in thousands of pubs. Whether you like the beer or not, you have to admit it was an awesome achievement. But as far as transforming the beer market was concerned, distribution was only the start of it. The real task facing big lager breweries like Bass Charrington now was getting people to drink the damn stuff. That may seem hard to believe now, but for a long time we really, really didn't want to drink lager at all. And to unravel that particular story, we need to follow the Dambusters all the way back to Germany, where it all started.

Chapter Ten

Saccharomyces carlsbergensis

How lager (eventually) conquered Britain

Liquid gold

For the most part, lager receives short shrift from serious beer enthusiasts. It is often regarded as a cheap, inferior, faux-beer, as uncultured and base as they imagine the people who drink it to be. Sure, most of the lager we drink in Britain doesn't have the character and complexity of real ale, but you have to ask yourself: if it's that bad, how come it is over-whelmingly the most popular style of beer in the world? Are we all just stupid?

The fact is, for the majority of men today, there are few images that resonate so profoundly, that are more alluring, more moving, than a chilled, freshly poured pint of lager on a summer's day. If you are religious you might be moved to argue that lager is incontrovertible proof that God exists, and that, despite all the floods, plagues, famines and boy bands he inflicts upon us, at the end of the day he likes us. Which is curious really, because the origins of lager actually do lie within the Church. Remember who discovered the preservative and balancing properties of the hop, creating the basic recipe for beer as it is still brewed today? And who made a huge contribution to the development of pubs with the establishment of inns for weary pilgrims? That's right. Not yet content with their services to beer drinking, the monks decided to create the basis for modern drinking culture across the globe, and went and invented lager.

The mystery of bottom fermentation

In the fifteenth century some Bavarian monks were wrestling with a problem. They had figured out that there was something invisible – call it yeast, godisgoode or whatever you like – that caused beer to ferment. This reaction always happened in the top of the brewing vessel, with the surface of the liquid foaming and bubbling away, and leaving a thick head that had to be skimmed off before the beer was barrelled.* Brewers knew enough about how fermentation worked to keep some of this stuff back and put it into the next brew, thereby getting some degree of consistency between batches. The headache was that, as fermentation happened on the top of the vessel, it was exposed to the elements. It was open house for any microscopic organism passing by that felt like gatecrashing the party. Natural airborne yeasts, the smelly

---

* The head of fermenting yeast is traditionally referred to as barm. If you wanted to accuse someone of being daft, a colourful metaphor might be to suggest that their head was full of nothing but bubbling foam – that is, that they were barmy. So now you know.

and slightly unnerving cousins of the more cultivated yeast families, would often pile in and ruin the delicately balanced brewing process.

The Bavarian monks studied the situation. They realized that they had a bigger problem with spoiled beer in the warm summer months, and guessed that temperature might have something to do with it. They experimented with keeping the beer cooler during fermentation by storing it in caves, and packing the vessels with ice, when they could get it. The fermentation process took longer, yeast being more sluggish in cooler temperatures.

What interested the monks was that some of the yeast would sink to the bottom of the vessel and ferment there instead. It didn't form a thick head on the surface, and was more stable. Gradually, by trial and error, the monks managed to isolate and cultivate the yeasts that preferred to ferment at the bottom. Two different types of beer then emerged: the traditional top-fermenting bitters, ales and stouts, and the new bottom-fermenting beer that took longer to make. The process for making this beer was called lagering, after the German word for 'to store', so beers brewed in this way became known as lager beers. In Britain we don't know that the lager bit refers to the production method, and we just call the beers lager. In much of the world lager is often simply referred to as beer because it's the generic, the only type readily available. Alternatively, it might be referred to as pilsner – but we'll come back to that in a minute.

Of course, if you could only brew a beer in low temperatures it was always going to be difficult to brew consistently on a large scale. For centuries lager remained a seasonal beer available only in winter. But beer drinkers in central Europe really liked it. It tended to be lighter than bitter as a drink, and the process went particularly well with the local hops. By the middle of the fifteenth century lager was massively popular in cities like Munich, and grew to dominate beer tastes in areas such as Bavaria and Bohemia, places which would eventually become parts of Germany and the Czech Republic.

Now I know this next bit might sound like it's wilfully reinforcing an unfair national stereotype, but it has to be said: the Germans took their lager brewing very, very seriously. We've already seen how possessive King Wenceslas was about his hops in neighbouring Bohemia. In Germany they decided that lager brewing was an exact science. There was to be no experimentation, no deviation. One style of beer and that was it. Of course it was a particularly nice style of beer, but they did take it a bit far. In 1516 Duke Wilhelm of Bavaria devised what legendary beer writer Michael Jackson (no relation) referred to as 'the world's best known purity law'.* The *Reinheitsgebot* decreed that a proper beer must contain four, and only four, ingredients: barley, water, hops and later, when we knew a bit more about it, yeast.

This was good in that it prevented brewers from adulterating their beer – a common problem when ingredients were scarce. As a result, Germany has been considered the ultimate authority on lager brewing for centuries, but it has also meant that Germany has acquired a reputation for consistency and uniformity rather than bold, exciting

---

* Not that there are that many purity laws most of us could name, but you know what he means.

beers.* The EU recently declared the *Reinheitsgebot* invalid under the terms of European trading standards. Xenophobic British beer fans must have wondered whether to laugh or cry. The Germans, the people who are so into Europe, having one of their strongest traditions undone by the union they are so keen to create. Most German beers are still brewed according to the *Reinheitsgebot* even though technically they no longer have to be. It's a centuries-old tradition, finely honed, turning out high-quality but similar lagers. If they were feeling a bit racy they could always try different hops or experiment with a new yeast strain, but that was it. That kind of experimentation does, however, bring us on to the next development in lager's story.

The dawn of the golden age

All the time we've been talking about lager, you've probably been picturing in your mind a pint of golden liquid with drops of condensation trickling seductively down the side of the glass. But you're wrong. Most lager was nothing like that until the mid-nineteenth century. Although the brewing process and the yeast strains were different, lager used the same malts as other beers and therefore looked very similar to everything else, dark brown with a foamy head.

This changed when the burghers of Pilsen, a small town in Bohemia, agreed that they desperately needed to improve

---

* This is not entirely fair – there are a few weird and wonderful German beers, such as ice beers and smoked beers. But they've only got themselves to blame.

the quality of their beer and poached a lager brewer from neighbouring Bavaria. Josef Groll brought with him pale malting techniques that Bavarian brewers had stolen from English pale ale brewers, and smuggled in precious Bavarian lager yeast. Putting these together with Moravian barley (Moravia along with Bohemia now make up the Czech Republic), the local soft water and the Saaz hops so beloved of King Wenceslas, he created a new pale, golden beer that delighted the town. Thanks to the growth of railways across Europe and political unification in Germany, the popularity of pilsner lager spread so quickly across the continent that there were countless imitation pilsners before the inventors had time to patent either the process or the term. You can still find dark lagers in specialist beer shops today, but pilsner caught the imagination of the beer-drinking world. If you think of lager today, you're thinking of pilsner, which is why the occasional pedant will still attempt to correct you if you refer to a decent continental pale beer as lager.

The fact that the Bohemians (Czechs) and the Germans had between them created the world's most desired beer was all very well, but it was a bugger to get hold of. For a time, pilsner's popularity was a source of frustration to its brewers. They realized they could be making a mint, but it was impossible to brew the beer economically. To make a decent pilsner it had to be stored at a consistent temperature of 7–9°C, ideally for around four weeks. Refrigeration had not yet been invented, so ice would be 'harvested' in winter from lakes and rivers and stored in caves and cellars. Ice could be bought commercially but it couldn't be manufactured, so it was expensive. Louis Pasteur who, as we know, found it hard to resist thinking about beer when, really, he had better things to do, worked out that every pint of lager required more than a pound of ice to see it through the lagering period, which made it very expensive to produce. This further contributed to making pilsner the most treasured of beers. In the nineteenth century, lager really was reassuringly expensive.

Although it probably seemed like a long wait at the time, pilsner fans did actually see this problem solved relatively quickly after the beer was created. It would be ludicrous of me to suggest that the scientists of the day dropped everything they were doing to focus on making commercial pilsner brewing viable,* but progress was pretty rapid. In 1850 James Harrison, a Scottish emigrant to Australia (which just happened to be desperate for cold beer and which features more strongly in our story later on) invented the first practical ice-making machine, a clumsy contraption that used liquid ether. Ten years later a French engineer called Carre developed a better version, using compressed ammonia gas, and commercial ice-making machines began to appear in European breweries. As well as allowing lager brewing all year round, refrigeration helped produce lager of a more consistent quality, and enabled it to be transported, kept and served at the necessary low temperature. Lager may take longer to brew, but it is more stable and travels much better than ale. The stage was almost set for it to conquer the world.

---

* So I won't. I'll just let it hang in the air while I lay out the facts for anti-lager conspiracy theorists to stitch together.

Star yeasts: the next generation

There was just one major headache remaining. Like any other beer, lager was still unpredictable. Bottom-fermenting yeasts might have been more stable, but they were still yeasts: complex cultures, forever mingling and interbreeding whenever they got the chance. Despite the best efforts of mid-nineteenth-century brewing science, each generation of yeasts was slightly different from the last, so no matter how tightly controlled the process was, there was always an element of the unknown.

The hero of the hour was that man with the microscope again. Louis Pasteur was still obsessed with two things: unlocking the mystery of yeasts, and pissing off the Germans given any opportunity. He'd done great work with the British to understand brewing, but German-style pilsner was spreading rapidly not only across Europe, but also to the New World. Lager was fast becoming the dominant beer style across the globe, and Louis didn't like this. The British were not that interested in lager, so he resolved to find someone else who was.

Pasteur didn't have to look far for disciples prepared to take his work further. Jacob Christian Jacobsen, the owner of the Danish Carlsberg brewery, had a very simple aim for his business. He wanted to produce the best possible lager beer, and would do anything to help make that happen. That's why, in 1845, he travelled from Denmark to Munich to bring back two quarts of Bavarian yeast, acknowledged as the best in the world. With no refrigerated transport, he had to stop the coach constantly to cool off the yeast in water to prevent it from going off. He eventually got it back home safely and his brewing laboratory got to work analysing and experimenting with it. Emil Hansen, one of Jacobsen's scientists, using methods Pasteur had taught him, examined yeast from a bad brew and established that it contained competing strains. In 1883 he succeeded in isolating single yeast strains for the first time, and found one that suited pilsner perfectly, going with the hops and the lightly roasted malt to give a light, fresh taste. Because yeast reproduces by cell division, once a single strain had been isolated it could effectively be cloned. By keeping the yeast strain isolated in laboratory conditions and carefully cultivating it, Carlsberg could guarantee that its beer would always ferment and that, for the first time ever, it would taste the same, batch after batch. In honour of those who had made this breakthrough, the yeast was named *Saccharomyces carlsbergensis*. It was brewing's version of splitting the atom.

Of course, Carlsberg were not the only acolytes of Louis Pasteur. Before long they had stiff competition from a certain Gerard Adriaan Heineken, a Dutchman who, funnily enough, also wanted to produce the world's finest pilsner. He bought the Haystack brewery in Amsterdam in 1863 on a clear mission to save the good burghers of the town from the peril of crap beer. He visited Germany, hired a German master brewer, and established the world's first proper private brewing laboratory in order to perfect a recipe and brewing process. In 1886 Dr Elion, another pupil of Pasteur, isolated a yeast cell of superior quality from which he was able to culture a pure strain: the Heineken A-yeast.

The yeast strains used today in beers such as Carlsberg and Heineken are the direct descendants of those discovered over a century ago, cultivated and painstakingly preserved. Heineken's A-yeast is still grown in Amsterdam and exported to their other breweries around the world. It is the foundation of the entire company and the most valuable asset it holds. There are even rumours of the yeast culture having been kidnapped and held to ransom, and it is now guarded very closely.

Heineken and Carlsberg were way ahead of everyone else, and soon reaped the benefits. Yeast has an enormous influence on the taste of a beer, and after isolating their single strains, the two companies could reproduce quality beer time after time, and with refrigeration send these beers to compete with others anywhere in the world. Germany and Bohemia carried on brewing pilsners that most beer aficionados still regard more highly, but Holland and Denmark produced the names that were to dominate the beer-drinking world. At the time of Hansen's discovery in 1883, ale and lager were enjoyed in roughly equal measures. Lager now accounts for 90 per cent of the beer drunk in the world. Everywhere that people drank beer and could afford refrigeration, pilsner lagers boomed. Everywhere, that is, apart from Britain.

Not today, thank you

British brewers watched the development of pilsner lager very closely. When Prince Albert returned from one of his regular visits to a German spa expressing great enthusiasm for pilsner, there was naturally a bit of a buzz around it. Small volumes were imported, and domestic brewers started to experiment with lager in the 1880s. But British drinkers just didn't want to know. The big pilsner brewers were aghast that such a big beer-drinking nation – and a fashion-conscious one at that – was utterly uninterested in the trendiest thing to hit brewing since the hop, and they struggled to understand why.

Brewing historians have been trying to explain it ever since. Perhaps it was all to do with climate. Refrigeration made a world of difference in places where freezing cold winters and very hot summers created problems for brewing. But in Britain, the summers weren't particularly hot nor the winters that cold. Certainly British brewers baulked at the investment in refrigeration that their counterparts around the world were going for.

A second possibility is that we remained unaware of how lager was sweeping the rest of the world. But this doesn't wash, even though we have always been somewhat parochial in our tastes. When lager finally took off in the 1970s, a hundred years later than everywhere else, the rise of package holidays was cited as one of the main causes, as we finally started to see, smell and taste what the rest of the world was up to after decades of ignorance. But it's not that simple. The British empire covered a huge chunk of the globe back then, and London was full of treasures and toys brought back from foreign lands. Tourism among the upper classes was well established over a century before the first charter flew into Majorca. Thomas Cook ran his first railway tour (a temperance one) in 1841, and it was common for the well-to-do to go on a European tour after leaving university. In 1896 the *Journal of Brewing* noted 'the introduction of light German beers into this country':

Owing to the enormously increased facilities offered during recent years by various railway and steamship companies, much larger numbers than formerly of our countrymen have visited Germany, Belgium and the United States.

We were perfectly aware of what lager was, where it came from and who was drinking it. We just weren't that bothered about it.

No, there had to be something more than that behind lager's failure. And of course there was. Europe may have been going mad for a light, sparkling beer that looked great served in new, fashionable glassware, but we already had one of our own. Burton pale ale was well established in Britain by the time lager came calling, and it played the same role here that lager did everywhere else, catering for the taste for something lighter. The Burton brewers in the late nineteenth century were ahead of their time when it came to marketing, and responded to the threat from lager by heavily promoting their light, carbonated bottled beers. British brewers took their lessons from Pasteur before the continental lager experts, but they carried on brewing the same beers they always had.

When you think about it, another large part of the problem has to have been that lager just wasn't British. And it wasn't just foreign, it was *European*. We've always wanted to distance ourselves from that lot across the Channel, and things were no different in the Victorian era. We might have dallied with the occasional foreign fashion craze, but this was *beer* for God's sake! Beer had made us what we were; the Prince Regent had said so. We had an empire on which the sun would never set! European beer in the heart of this Empire would have been like the Queen marrying a German, or in our own times, like James Bond driving a BMW.* We had an empire won and run by people fuelled by beer, and that beer just had to be British.

There was one exception, and there are no prizes for guessing who that was. Scotland began importing pilsner-style beers from Continental Europe in the 1870s, and sales grew five-fold between 1880 and 1895. Tennent's spotted the trend and started to brew their own lager in 1888. They were successful, and opened a custom-built lager brewery in Glasgow in 1906. Other brewers soon cottoned on, and Scotland developed the taste for lager, which it still has, a full sixty or seventy years before the English caught up. To be fair, Scottish beer was already a lot more like lager than English beer; it was less hopped, lighter, less bitter, without the big frothy head typical of traditional English ale. On top of that, in 1896 the *Brewers' Guardian* suggested that the taste for lager had been brought home by Scots travelling in Europe and North America. At the time, one of the country's main exports was people looking for work. Whatever the reason, I suppose the most surprising thing is that there was more to lager's success north of the border than simply a wish to be contrary towards the English.

As Queen Victoria died and the empire began to crumble, our resistance to lager remained as solid as ever. In the 1920s, the situation facing foreign lager brewers interested in the British market was made even more miserable when duty on

---

* OK, maybe those are bad examples. But since when has nationalistic prejudice been rational and consistent?

beer was related directly to alcoholic strength. Pilsners were all brewed to around 5 per cent ABV at a time when British brewers were turning out products at around 3.5 per cent. Added to the cost of physically importing them, lagers could only be sold at a massive price premium over domestically produced beers. OK, so fifty years later this would prove to be one of the main features of popular lager brands, but back then style over substance was an unknown concept in beer. There was a small and gradually increasing demand for imported bottled lagers, but they remained a tiny proportion of the beer market as a whole.

Then there was the issue of temperature. We all know that lager really has to be drunk cold to be enjoyed. By the 1920s, household refrigerators were common across the United States, but they didn't take off here until after World War II. In the pub, draught beer is temperature controlled and kept in cool cellars, but lager was sold only in bottles until the 1960s. There are still pubs today which don't have fridges behind the counter, just those dusty, odd wooden shelves which always seem to have Sweetheart Stout and a single can of Coke that looks like it's been there since the 1970s. This was entirely normal until relatively recently. Even when we finally got fridges at home, they still didn't appear in pubs. If lager was only ever served warm, it was never going to get anywhere.

After the Second World War it looked like things might start to pick up a little. Now I know that when we looked at the war we talked about how important it was to get good old British beer to the front in Europe, and how lagers weren't good enough for Our Boys. But once they'd drunk their weekly ration of the good stuff they did bravely sample a pint or two of foreign muck, and gradually they acquired a bit of a taste for it. Not as good as British ale obviously, but it was drinkable under such desperate circumstances. This was nothing new: throughout history conquering armies have often adopted the tastes of the lands they occupied and brought those tastes back home with them. In the late 1940s and early 50s Britain started to get a bit more of an appetite for French wine and cooking, and Continental lager enjoyed a small amount of growth.

The end of the war also meant that the big pilsner brewers could start thinking about exporting again. By this time Carlsberg and Heineken were selling as much beer in their respective home countries as their populations could physically drink, and they had to look to foreign markets in order to continue growing. Heineken in particular pursued a vigorous policy of foreign expansion, the result of which is that today it can be found in nearly three hundred countries worldwide, with 85 per cent of its sales outside its home country. By 1950, both Heineken and Carlsberg had resumed exports to Britain, but thanks to their products' high ABV and concomitant high duty, they sold tiny amounts. In 1951, Heineken sold just 2,500 pints. In desperation, they launched a weaker beer more suited to British tastes, but there was still nothing doing.

Now. Heineken as a company takes itself very seriously indeed. It is still family owned and remains committed to the principles of its founder, who wished simply to sell the world's best beer, across the world. They are obsessed with quality and consistency. In nearly three hundred countries, Heineken stands for the best beer you can buy. The officially sanctioned story of Heineken simply seethes with indignation when it discusses Heineken's attempts to crack the British market. We'd forced them to sell out on their principles and launch an 'inferior' product, and we still weren't interested. And if that wasn't bad enough, the few of us who did give it a try had the audacity to experiment and – gasp – *meddle* with the flavour!

> The British tradition of drinking pilsner with a shot of lime turned the quality message emanated by Heineken 1040* into a farce. 'Since the lime juice destroys any beer taste, a sales argument based on the gravity of the beer resulting in better taste does not impress the British lager buyer, and certainly makes no impression on the retailers' was the conclusion given in a travel report of 30 September 1957.

Even when we condescended to drink this nectar, seemingly we couldn't drink it properly.

And Heineken still faced the problem of getting distribution in tied houses. Carling's sales at this time may not have been spectacular, but Eddie Taylor's frantic acquisition strategy at least put his brand in front of drinkers so they could choose to ignore it. Heineken realized that to really break into the British market they would have to deal with one of the big breweries. In 1961 they entered into a cooperative agreement with Whitbread, which gave the brand access to tens of thousands of pubs. At the end of that year though,

---

* Heineken 1040 was actually quite a bit weaker than their normal, high-quality beer, which was 1048 degrees (about 5 per cent ABV), so it's a bit rich of them to talk about its quality the same way they would their normal beer.

lager's share of the total beer market remained at a paltry 3 per cent.

You'd think the lager producers would have got the message. Around the world, lager immediately captivated the imagination of anyone who came across it. It represented beer's coming of age, the combined result of centuries of brewing expertise and several massive leaps forward in terms of scientific discovery and innovation. No one who drank could resist it. Except us. Even as the world started to shrink and become more open, allowing lager to dominate the beer market in just about every country where drinking was legal, the UK stuck resolutely to good old-fashioned bitter. This was the drink that had made us what we were. It had built an Empire and won a world war. Nothing was going to displace it in our affections. The only things that might change this would be some kind of social revolution, or a seismic shift in the way we thought about beer. And in conservative, fashion-obsessed Britain, neither of these things could possibly happen . . . could they?

The box

On 2 June 1953 over twenty million people in Britain watched the coronation of Queen Elizabeth II on television. Many of the sets were so new they were barely out of the packaging before people were crowding round them to watch the spectacular event. Three years previously the *Daily Mirror* had warned, 'If you let a TV set through your front door, life can never be the same.' After a slow start, the coronation proved that it never would. By 1959, 60 per cent of British adults were tuning in for anything up to five hours a day. The home became the primary focus of the leisure time of the nation.

Predictably, people started to write obituaries for the pub once more. We were going to stop leaving the house altogether, and in an era where there wasn't yet a take-home drinks market to speak of, this in turn surely meant television was going to kill off beer drinking on any significant scale. The analysts and commentators were of course right in predicting that television would change our relationship with beer. But as for the nature of that change, they got it hopelessly wrong. Television was an unparalleled opportunity to reach vast numbers of people via the newest, most exciting advertising medium yet known. All those beer drinkers sitting staring into the corner of the living room instead of being in the pub were a captive audience. For those brewers big enough to afford it, the box presented an opportunity as well as a threat. And for lager in particular, it was to prove a turning point.

The dawn of the branded age

The brewers had been using advertising for many years. But, Guinness aside, they had promoted themselves as corporations selling a range of products. There was also still the industry's collective advertising. All the big brewers paid into a central pot and ads with lines like 'Good Wholesome Beer' and 'Beer – The Best Long Drink in the World' appeared in the press and, through the late 1950s and 1960s, on posters.

But Heineken and Carlsberg were different. They were not

promoting themselves as breweries; they were selling their beers as individual brands. As supermarkets appeared and off-sales started to grow, people were not just going into a bar and asking for 'a pint' or 'the usual', but were instead going into shops and having to choose beers by name. Collective advertising faded into the background as budgets were massively increased and concentrated on fewer brands. Apart from the fact that Heineken and Carslberg had only one product, and so in a sense the brewery *was* the individual beer, this approach made a lot of sense for lager. Even the most devout lager fan has to admit that, whatever its manifold strengths, the golden liquid doesn't have the same level of character and complexity as a good ale. If you're trying to sell the stuff there's really not that much to say about it. But it wasn't enough simply to say, 'Hello, we're a big brewer and here's the lager in our range.' There had to be more of a *story* about it, something individual. Heineken and Carlsberg had stories; they were foreign and exotic. Slowly, sales began to creep up.

The British brewers could see that the bloody Continentals were not going to go away. They therefore decided that they needed to launch their own lager brands. Eddie Taylor's company, on the way to becoming Bass Charrington, stepped up promotional support behind Carling Black Label once it had national distribution. In 1961 Ind Coope launched Skol with a heavy advertising campaign. Guinness, Courage, Bass and Scottish & Newcastle formed a joint venture to brew and market Harp. We might not have been drinking it yet, but lager began to seep into the national consciousness.

Saying the right thing to the right people

When television advertising first appeared, there were worries that it was so potent that it could brainwash people into buying whatever was dangled in front of them. Thankfully, it proved less straightforward than that. Lager brands spent massively on advertising, out of all proportion to how sales of lager were actually growing. The problem was, no campaign was going to make any difference if it was talking to the wrong people, and saying things that they were not interested in hearing.

After trying in vain for decades to persuade blokes in pubs to swap a pint of mild for a fancy new lager, brewers were looking for someone else who might be interested in what they had to say. Early lager ads were therefore targeted at women. By the 1960s it was normal to find them in pubs, and lager was seen as the perfect drink for them: it was alcoholic, but lighter than bitter and easier to drink. In bottles, and served in small, ladylike glasses, it looked just right, and the birds probably liked all that poncey European nonsense. Skol ran adverts with lines like 'A blonde for a blonde', and seemed to think they were being sophisticated rather than condescending. It didn't work. Beer has always been seen as a manly drink. If it was for women it couldn't be proper beer, simple as that.*

---

* Every now and again some brewer will have another punt at a beer targeted at women. They never work. It's not that women don't drink beer, of course they do. It's just that a beer that goes out of its way to say that it's especially for women just makes everyone suspicious. Women drink beer but it's masculine, and they're fine with that. A beer that says it's just

Back to square one. The brewers looked for someone else to bother. And finally, they figured it out.

It's an accepted fact in beer drinking that young men going into pubs at the start of their drinking careers tend to want something different from what their dads drank. It's another step in the journey of self-definition, creating your own identity. Of course you don't actually think of it in those terms when you're experimenting with Woodpecker cider or Banana Bols, but looking back on it in later years you know it's true. The young generation of the 1960s, more than any before it, was growing up noisily. They had money in their pockets, and were increasingly keen to spend it down the boozer. The newly merged brewers had finally started spending to improve the state of their pubs, and their growing attraction to moneyed young people was intended to be the return on that investment. Quoted in an article in the *Financial Times* in 1968, the marketing director of Allied Breweries said,

> Young people in their twenties and their girlfriends* are increasingly using pubs as a social place . . . This class of new beer drinker is less price-conscious and moving towards the well-branded products rather than the plain mild or bitter. Against this is another discernible trend, not unusual in times of tight money, of a swing into lighter and cheaper beers.

---

for girls is like one of those creepy blokes without any mates of his own sex.

* That's 'Young *people* and their girlfriends'. This being pre-women's lib, chicks had clearly not yet acquired the status of fully paid-up people.

These young people – and their girlfriends – were creating their own culture, and it was pointedly at odds with the Establishment. They were rebellious and increasingly questioning of authority and their elders. They used pubs in a different way, and looked for symbols of status and independence wherever they went. OK, so ordering a fizzier pint isn't quite in the same league as laying siege to the American embassy, but it came from the same place. It simply stood to reason that these young men would want to drink lager. If it had been scorned by their parents, it sounded like just the thing. If only the brewers hadn't been telling them for years that it was what chicks drank, it would have been simple.

The first step the brewers took was to make lager look a bit more like a man's drink. If lager was going to be sold in significant volumes, it needed to be on draught. Get it served in a pint glass, and maybe, just maybe, your mates wouldn't take the piss. Harp launched on draught in 1964, and Carling followed in 1965. The campaign to get women to drink lager had consumed vast amounts of money. With the draught pint in place, the brewery would now go out and spend fortunes claiming emphatically that lager was a man's drink, had never been a woman's drink, had always been a man's drink and always would be.

There was just one small snag. In line with the British way of regulating alcohol in a manner that was restrictive, without quite condemning it altogether, the Independent Broadcasting Authority ruled that brewers were allowed to advertise beer, but not to refer to the fact that it gets you drunk, or to being drunk in any way. In other words, the brewers were quite at liberty to advertise their beers, as long as they didn't talk about the benefits of drinking those beers.

They were still able to talk about things like taste, but they wouldn't have wanted to. Advertisers are not actually allowed to tell barefaced lies, no matter what you might think. The standard lagers and keg bitters of the 1960s and early 1970s were of very dodgy quality taste-wise, and the lagers all pretty much of a standard – undifferentiated in terms of taste, strength and brewing quality. All you could really count on was that eventually they got you lashed, and the brewers weren't allowed to say so. So what could they talk about? Well, they could *position* their brands, portraying the kind of people who drank them, or at least the people who the brewers wanted you to think drank them. Oh yes, and they could show cleavage.

Nearly all the campaigns were the same. There would be three blokes in a pub. Not one, because then he would be sad. Not two, because that might mean they were gay. Three blokes. They'd be young, cool, having a good time, messing about under the watchful but indulgent eye of the landlord. Two of them would probably take the piss out of the third, perhaps playing a joke on him, then they'd all drink the brand in question. And every single commercial seemed to have a barmaid with big tits squeezed into a low-cut top, giving them the eye. The final frame of the ad would inevitably be a pint on the bar next to the pump, with the barmaid's cleavage providing the backdrop. It wasn't subtle. Lager drinkers were men, absolutely no fucking doubt about that whatsoever mate, geddit? Millions of pounds of TV advertising expenditure said so.

This laddish formula became so successful that everyone jumped on it. Soon, all beer advertising was starting to look the same. The tool supposed to differentiate brands from each other was reinforcing the perception that they were identical. But once lager began to be accepted by men, brewers tried to differentiate it from bitter. Lager was more expensive, so it needed a more premium image. The particular type of laddishness in lager ads gradually became a little cooler. Lager drinkers were just a bit sharper than bitter drinkers, the humour slightly more clever (although we are talking small degrees here) than the cheerful, old-fashioned blokeishness of bitter ads. Double Diamond 'worked wonders' and its drinkers were 'only here for the beer', but lager drinkers were here to be a bit smarter than that, and grab the girl as the bitter drinker descended into his cups. Harp combined product promise with emotional benefit when it claimed to 'stay sharp to the bottom of the glass'. The lager drinker was one step ahead.

It worked. Lager took off among young people to the point where concern began to mount that heavy TV promotion of beer was leading them to overindulge. In 1975, the IBA introduced a new code of practice for alcohol advertising, making it even stricter in 1978. Anything targeted too overtly at blokes under the age of twenty-five was prohibited, and advertisers were barred from suggesting that alcohol consumption helped you out with sexual prowess, social success or physical strength.* Moreover, lager was still growing quite slowly despite the weight of marketing investment behind it, and it was getting harder to find anything interesting to say.

---

* You might well think that alcohol does help with these things. You might even believe you have proof of it, in the form of a snog on the dance floor to 'Careless Whisper', a relationship, or a hazy memory of how funny you were. But however much you believe it, the IBA weren't going to let any brewer even hint that this kind of thing went on after a few jars.

After all this effort and ingenuity, it still looked like lager was doomed to remain a niche product.

Policemen's feet and two-way mirrors

The boys at Heineken had come so far, and were not going to give up without a fight. They were going to make us drink lager, no matter what it took. In 1969 they entered into a licensing agreement with Whitbread to brew the low-strength Heineken 1032 in the UK. Licensing agreements like this compelled the local brewer to put heavy support behind the brand, and in 1974 Whitbread went to Collett Dickenson Pearce, the ad agency that had created 'Happiness is a cigar called Hamlet', to see if they could work the same magic with Heineken. The agency recognized that the difference between lager and bitter was that lager, being lighter and served colder, was more refreshing. There was a danger that talking about this product benefit contravened the IBA regulations, so they wrote some commercials that talked about refreshment in a metaphorical way, arguing that people wouldn't take them seriously, that nobody would believe the beer was literally having the effect claimed in the ads. The launch commercials showed Heineken refreshing policemen's tired feet under laboratory conditions, and refreshing a piano tuner's tired ears, and finished with 'Heineken refreshes the parts other beers cannot reach.' The IBA bought the argument that the ads weren't really claiming what they seemed to be claiming, and approved the campaign.

Even so, the ads still almost failed to run. They were quite revolutionary for the time, requiring people to 'get' the construct rather than simply sit and watch passively. It was a risk, and Whitbread decided that the ads should be researched. There are two broad types of research: quantitative, when you survey a large number of people to produce statistically significant data; and qualitative, when a few people are asked their opinions in much greater depth. The most common way of conducting the latter is over beer and sandwiches, in focus groups, in a nice little room with a two-way mirror behind which the advertisers can sit and watch the discussion without intruding. That's what Whitbread decided to do with their new Heineken campaign. The results are worth a look not only because they illustrate how wrong market research can be, but also because the verbatim quotes from beer drinkers almost forty years ago provide a rare and interesting insight into what our drinking lives were like back then.

It was April 1974. The thirty blokes who attended the focus groups all felt that traditional keg bitter had significantly declined in quality over recent years. In contrast, lager was felt to be of much better quality. Given that we're talking about weak, standard 'cooking' lager, it gives you some idea of how poor bitter was at the time. This promise of higher quality came at a higher price. Lager wasn't stuff you just bought to get bevvied. It was bought to savour, and was drunk for its refreshing properties. It was never going to be consumed in large quantities by louts. Oh no. The researcher illustrated this point in his report, using a quote that reminds you that this was a time when racism was still considered a legitimate topic for sitcoms:

Lager does not seem to compete strongly with beer as a way of getting drunk, partly because of the cost and partly because of beer's traditional occupation of this role. ('Irish navvies will always drink beer.')

The researcher was also quite concerned about whether lager was seen as a proper man's drink yet. 'There was no evidence that drinking lager on its own has any significant connotations of effeminacy,' he reported, but lager and lime, which was quite popular, was a different matter. 'Women were said to prefer it this way' and some of the younger lads drank it, but one straight lager drinker summed up his opinion thus: 'Queer little fellows drink lager and lime. Halves of course. The plastic set.'

The problems with the advertisements themselves started with the fact that everyone seems to have taken them very, very literally:

The 'piano tuner' himself was recognised by a few respondents as an actor in the TV series *Are You Being Served?* For some this reduced the 'finest piano tuner in Europe' claim, made at the beginning of the commercial, to a 'blatant untruth'.

If the ads had been done seriously, if they had been for a soap powder or fabric conditioner, no one would have batted an eyelid at this kind of product demonstration, but this sending up of advertising conventions was seemingly lost on the target audience; apparently the joke passed them by. Many of these punters had already said that they preferred lager to bitter because it was more refreshing, but seeing this played back to them in an exaggerated manner was unacceptable:

> The mental image they obtained appeared to carry almost *medical* overtones. Heineken came across as a great 'restorative', but the commercial ignored the equally important sheer *enjoyment* that respondents expected to gain from a lager. One respondent maintained that the [policemen] commercial would be more effective as a Lucozade ad.

The endline, the common thread between the ads, the summation of the idea, was just rubbish:

> The slogan 'Refreshes the parts other beers cannot reach' was seen as appropriate to the rest of each commercial but not on its own. Respondents had great difficulty recalling it verbatim or approximately verbatim. ('On its own it doesn't stick. No rhythm about it.')

The agency managed to persuade Whitbread that the research was wrong, and the Heineken commercials aired. Luckily, in 1975 and 1976 we experienced the hottest summers anyone could remember. All lagers were refreshing but Heineken was the brand actively talking about refreshment. Heineken sales shot up from 460,000 barrels in 1973 to a peak of 1.7 million barrels in 1989. But it wasn't just the heat that sold the beer; once the commercials were on air they were talked about and loved, and 'Refreshes the parts . . .', supposedly so unmemorable, entered the vernacular and, in 1998, the *Oxford Dictionary of Quotations*.

The ads versus the programmes

Heineken became the best-known brand in the country, but all lagers benefited. Lager exploded, and within two years of the Heineken campaign launching accounted for a quarter of all beer volume. After seeing Heineken's success, the other brewers were quick to follow. Lager advertising became creative, irreverent and very funny.

There was Carling Black Label which, like Heineken, adopted hyperbole and showed people performing superhuman feats, such as the window cleaner doing the outside of a plane in mid-flight from the Costa del Sol. Some ads were self-referential, ripping each other off, like the one where the Old Spice aftershave surfer is doing the business and then suddenly crashes into the pub on a tidal wave, all under the calm gaze of the two Carling blokes who sit in the corner and say, 'I bet he drinks Carling Black Label.'

There was Hofmeister with George the Bear, who apparently represented the drinker we all wanted to be. It's true. When the campaign was researched someone actually said, 'He's the sort of bloke I'd like to be.' A dodgy cockney in a bear suit wearing a bright yellow nylon jacket and a tiny pork pie hat; that's what we aspired to. 'If you want great lager, follow the bear.' Many of us did and Hofmeister sales rocketed, until it emerged that George was one of the most popular television characters among children. The campaign was banned on the grounds that it might encourage kids to follow the bear into their local and try to get served.

And then there was Kestrel. For a while, the number-two

brand in the market, with ads that featured kestrels flying about. Don't ask.

The late 1970s and early 1980s was a barren time for English comedy. It was after Monty Python and before *The Young Ones*, and lager ads satisfied the ever-present need for catchphrases to recite in offices and school playgrounds. Whether kids wanted to drink the beer or not, whether the ads were targeted at them or not, they ran around imitating figures from ads such as the camp, lisping Roman from Heineken's slave galley who, after the slaves on one side of the boat have been given Heineken and those on the other have been given 'another leading lager', charges in and yells, 'Stop! Stop! We're going round in *circles*!' Lager accounted for 34 per cent of beer sales by 1980, and 51 per cent by 1990.

Self-definition . . . with a pint

Lager is now as universally British as chicken tikka massala. This is something that perplexes serious beer writers. Most lagers, as least the ones we've had in Britain, are fairly characterless, and look and taste virtually identical. Any differences there might be in taste are further obscured by the fact that they are served at such low temperatures. So why did we go for lager in such a big way?

Partly because the brewers put so much money behind it, but if it was simply a matter of brewers forcing change on us to suit their own best interests, it wouldn't have worked. They'd been trying to force us to drink it for years. Then suddenly it took off. People still went into pubs that sold bitter as well as lager, but in ever-increasing numbers they chose the latter of their own free will. Even in off-licences, where the quality of canned or bottled bitter was more consistent and reliable, we still chose lager. Against the dodgy image and reputation of keg bitter, lager was new, fresh, exciting and cool.

It wasn't just the advertising that was responsible; those long hot summers certainly helped along the way. Lager volumes are still heavily affected by how nice the weather is, and brewers pay close attention to long-range weather forecasts, adjusting their volumes accordingly. Also, there was the growth of foreign travel, with eighteen- to thirty-four-year-old potential lager drinkers finding themselves awash with the stuff on package holidays. Even back home we were starting to get more adventurous with what we ate and drank. As Andrew Barr comments in *Drink: A Social History*:

> It is inconceivable that the explosion of Indian restaurants in Britain should not have affected taste in drink. They have made eating out a much less formal experience in which it is permissible to consume lower-class lager rather than higher-class wine. People who would have considered going into a pub and ordering a pint of lager to be inappropriate to their self-image have thought it perfectly acceptable to drink lager in an Indian restaurant. Doubtless it is as a result of drinking lager in Indian restaurants that many people have become lager-drinkers at all.

But whatever other factors came into play, the dramatic growth in lager started with the Heineken advertising campaign. More than anything else, lager grew because the choice between it and bitter had an image dimension. Image and lifestyle were becoming more important in society from the 1960s onwards, particularly for the young people who were emerging as the most attractive market to the brewers. The brewers were not simply selling beer with all this advertising; they were creating brands. Brands create emotional reasons for choosing between different products as well as, or even instead of, tangible product differences. Over the last forty years, this emotional aspect of brands has been expressed more overtly through advertising in Britain than it has anywhere else. We have a funny attitude to brands and marketing. We don't like the direct sell because, if we're honest, we find raw commerce a little vulgar. Advertisers realized, when trying to sell something to your typical Brit, that you had to dress it up with a bit of entertainment, probably with a splash of wry, self-effacing humour, to make the selling bit a little more palatable. When lager brands were restricted in what they could say, they stumbled across just how powerful the image dimension and the use of humour could be. Today, brands in every market play on our heart strings. The most successful do this by making us laugh, by exaggerating, by taking the piss, by letting us in on the joke and not patronizing us, by requiring us to become involved in the story and watch it a bit more closely in order to get it. Heineken didn't just break the mould of beer marketing; it redefined the whole of British advertising, and changed the way we think about what we buy. Naomi Klein must hate it.

Chapter Eleven

'A diet of Pot Noodles, Mother's Pride and Harp lager'

Kegs, casks and the decline of bitter

Progress is our friend

There's an old episode of *Blue Peter* from the late 1960s that was shown recently on one of the BBC's increasingly common self-referential nostalgia fests. John Noakes is guiding us through the Kitchen of the Future. All the food in this kitchen comes in packages with little compartments, measured and pre-prepared. All the plates are made from disposable paper. They come out of a handy dispenser with PLATES written on it, next to the plastic cups dispenser which has CUPS on it. When they are finished with, the plates get thrown into the PAPER bin. All the cutlery is plastic and comes in little cellophane packets and gets thrown in the PLASTICS bin. Everything is systematized. Everything that could conceivably be made out of plastic is made out of plastic, and Noakes pronounces the word with relish, repeatedly smacking his lips around plastic. Plastic is the point of the whole piece.

At some point, I'm sure he talks about how we will be doing things in the year 2000 – it felt like everyone did in the 1960s and 70s – hanging on to the concept of the millennium like it was the official arrival of the future. The entire kitchen and everything that goes through it is cheap and disposable, a triumph of modernist progression for progression's sake with no thought given to aesthetics, taste or sentimentality, all of which you may now think are pretty important when it comes to any aspect of the home, and the kitchen in particular. Which is probably why, when the year 2000 finally lumbered around, we didn't have kitchens like that.

But back in the 1960s this reverence for all things processed and synthetic was par for the course. Plastic was brilliant. People simply could not imagine that it would very quickly come to be regarded as cheap and inferior to boring old-fashioned ceramics and stainless steel, because at the time it was just so damn *modern*. Disposability was the ultimate symbol of how far we had come. Throwing everything away as soon as it had been used wasn't even a hedonistic thing, it was simply efficient. Just as in the Industrial Revolution, progress was being made at a phenomenal rate and it was *good*. In town centres, stripped-down, functional blocks were replacing all that unnecessarily frilly Victorian architecture. In the kitchen cupboard Cadbury's Smash was supplanting tiresome old potatoes. And in the pub, keg bitter was ousting traditional, cask-conditioned ale. The drink that had defined us for so long, the drink that had 'made us what we are', was under threat from the god of *progress*.

Bad beer

Cask-conditioned ale is a complex liquid. It is still 'alive' when delivered to the pub, meaning that the yeast is carrying on a slow, secondary fermentation while the beer lies in the barrel, adding an extra layer of aroma and complexity of flavour, and producing a natural sparkle in the glass. Contrary to popular myth, cask ale shouldn't be warm. It should be kept at cellar temperature rather than room temperature – cool, but not so cold that it kills the flavour. And with the yeast still working in the barrel, it needs to be kept stable, and ideally should be left to settle for a couple of days after delivery to the pub. At beer festivals and in pubs where they take their ale *really* seriously, the cask will be lying on its side directly behind the bar, but in most pubs the cask is kept in the cellar and the beer is drawn up via a hand pump, or beer engine. When the handle is pulled a vacuum is created which sucks the beer up the pipe from the cellar and into the lovingly held glass.

Keg bitter is much more straightforward. It is filtered, pasteurized and chilled, then sealed in a container and pumped with carbon dioxide to make it more stable and consistent, and to prolong its life, so it stays in drinkable condition for months rather than days. Rather than yeast, it is the added carbon dioxide that gives the beer its sparkle, the same as in fizzy pop or carbonated water. The keg is pressurized, and gas is pumped into it to force the beer up the pipes. Keg bitter is, essentially, no different from a supermarket four-pack save for the size of the can.

The history of keg bitter actually stretches back to the 1930s, when it was originally developed for overseas sale. The problem with cask ale is that it is notoriously difficult to maintain in peak condition. It's like milk – once you've opened the container it goes off very quickly unless it's kept in the right conditions, and even when treated well it has a limited shelf life. Many pubs have trouble getting it from the cellar to the bar without ruining the taste even today, so getting it across the Channel was always going to be extremely difficult. The export market required something much more stable. In the 1930s, Watney began experimenting with filtering and pasteurizing their beer instead of running it live into casks to mature, and pumping the kegs with carbon dioxide to lend artificial life to the brew. It may not have tasted quite as nice as a well kept beer, but it was a hell of a lot nicer than one that had gone off, and was much easier to keep and to transport over long distances.

At first it was never intended to sell keg bitter in Blighty, where good old cask ale in reasonable nick was readily available. I mean, who would buy it? Well, the East Sheen Tennis Club, for one. In 1936 they complained to Watney that because they sold virtually no beer during the week, it was staying in the pipes for a long time, and would more often than not be dead and foul by the time it was served to the customer. Watney decided to give the club the new beer they had been experimenting with, which they called Red Barrel. But this was regarded as a one-off. Most pubs didn't suffer from this problem; with regular custom the progression of beer through the pipes was generally quick, and opened casks would rarely end up unsold long enough for beer to go off. Whitbread did consider replacing their celebrated pale ale with a carbonated beer, but were given short shrift by one ardent beer fan at the time:

> It is inconceivable that anyone who drinks beer thoughtfully could really prefer artificially conditioned beer. The difference is that between freshly made tea and tea made with tepid water. It is the difference between butter and margarine. It is the difference between the clear reasoning of H. G. Wells and the diatribe of an angry woman. It is the difference between real beer and sham beer ... It is impossible to consider anything except naturally matured beer.

But after World War II things changed. The war had claimed pub landlords among its victims just like it had claimed everyone else, and a lot of expertise had been lost; many pubs had been bombed, and for a long time there was very little money to repair them. Whatever it had really been like before the war, the quality of beer could only suffer afterwards.

By now most pubs were owned by the handful of big breweries that supplied them, who were replacing the departed jolly landlords with managers less skilled in keeping beer. As a result bottled beers, which were more resilient to the bumblings and negligence of the new breed, were thriving by the 1950s. Keg bitter (as opposed to cask) was essentially the same thing on a larger scale. Its stability meant that it was long-lasting and profitable enough for the breweries to build nationally distributed brands and profit from economies of scale. Over the course of the 1960s and early 1970s, keg bitter went from nowhere to accounting for nearly half the volume of beer sold in pubs. OK, so maybe the pasteurization process meant that, compared to the rounded taste of cask ale, it tasted a little of burnt sugar, but so what? It was far more efficient. It was progress. It was more scientific, more modern, so it had to be better. Keg bitters such as Worthington E (Bass), Double Diamond (Allied), Courage Tavern and Whitbread Tankard ranked alongside Watney's Red Barrel as the biggest-selling beers in the country. As if to emphasize its modernity, your typical keg bitter did away with the tall handle of the beer pump and announced itself with a little box on the bar with a light inside, made of – yep, you guessed – plastic.

These developments worried those who were seriously into their beer. The Big Six brewers made lots of reassuring noises about how everything they were doing was obviously in the long-term interests of their customers. Come on lads, this was modernisation! It must be good! There would be increased efficiency and lower costs. The price of beer would *plummet*, honest guv. But the benefits failed to materialize. Anxious to demonstrate that it was not their fault, a flock of economists gathered to scrutinize the newly merged industry in the early 1970s to find out what had gone wrong and generally to try to look like they were of some use. They demonstrated that the large combines were not as profitable as had been hoped.*

The embarrassing thing was, the smaller breweries that had escaped the merger frenzy, such as Boddington's in Manchester, Wolverhampton & Dudley in the Midlands and

---

* Maybe we'd have guessed that, but they used longer words, and probably a few equations, to say it.

Greene King in the south, were actually delivering better returns than the big combines such as Allied, Bass and Whitbread. In the mad scramble, many of the units that now constituted the big brewers had been bought for far more than they were worth. On top of that, they had been family-run concerns for generations; they didn't like all this modern corporate nonsense and it was proving difficult to blend them into seamless, streamlined wholes. And then there was the fact that all this modern equipment and technology that was supposed to deliver these massive cost savings didn't come cheap.

From the outside, all drinkers saw was that the price of beer was going up, not down as had been promised. National brands were sold at a premium, and local ones were getting harder to find – the merger and consolidation activity meant that the number of different beers on sale in the UK halved from 3,000 in 1966 to less than 1,500 a decade later. Of course, fiddly cask beers were the ones that disappeared, making way for the national, heavily promoted keg bitters. And if you wanted to take your custom elsewhere, it was getting increasingly difficult to find a pub that wasn't owned by the Big Six.

The alcoholic strength of beer was another point of contention. Strange as it now seems, brewers were under no obligation to tell you how strong your pint of beer actually was. The Consumers' Association did a survey of the leading brands in 1972, calculating the original gravity of beers and comparing it with a previous survey. They found that, while the price of beer was steadily increasing, the brewers were cutting alcoholic strength. And, surprise surprise, the keg bitters tested were consistently weaker than the cask ales. By the time the *Which?* report was completed, several of the biggest British beer brands allegedly were so weak they could have been sold legally in America during prohibition.

It was a dismal state of affairs. We were being given less choice, between weaker beers that were tasting worse, and we were paying more for it. So much for progress and efficiency. God knows what John Noakes must have thought.

The drinker strikes back

Consumer grumbles over the state of beer grew more audible. Some operators responded by resorting to outright deception. In his 1973 book *The Death of the English Pub*, Christopher Hutt describes a pub in the City of London that had wooden barrels displayed behind the bar with pipes leading into them from the beer pumps. Any but the most paranoid drinker would assume that the beer they were being served was cask ale from the barrel. The truth was that the barrels were empty. The pipes went straight through them and down into the cellar, into metal kegs of dead, artificially fizzy bitter.

The earliest organized attempt to mobilize the general feeling that This Wasn't Good Enough and Something Had To Be Done was the Campaign for the Preservation of Beers from the Wood, which was formed in 1963. The reasoning was that, if you wanted to be purist about it, cask ale was only *really* cask ale if it was matured in a wooden cask. The very same beer run into metal casks was bad. Aluminium barrels had been introduced in the 1950s and were increasingly used for 'cask' ale as well as keg bitter. Metal casks were modern, so how could anything that was kept in them be traditional? The society's president was a retired City banker. They had a special club tie featuring wooden casks on a black background, 'implying mourning for the passing of real beer'. They didn't actively recruit members; people had to find out about them, as anyone who really appreciated proper beer somehow would. Membership was then determined as follows:

> Prospective members are asked to name their local, which has to be approved by the Society. They are also asked to sign two pledges – firstly, 'to stimulate the brewing and to encourage the drinking of beers drawn from the wood'; secondly 'to denigrate the manufacture and sale of beer in "sealed dustbins" (keg beer) and to discourage its consumption'.

As a consumer rights movement they didn't achieve much. But then, to be fair, they probably didn't regard themselves as a consumer rights movement. This was more like the Secret Seven than an organization with serious intent to actually achieve anything, merely a forum for like-minded people to gather and grumble. From the way they operated, you almost get the feeling they would have been quite happy for cask ale to disappear altogether so they could write angry letters to the *Telegraph* about it.

But protest against the changes in beer had started to take root and grow. In 1972 four angry young beer drinkers from Manchester formed the Campaign for the Revitalisation of Ale (CAMRA). This was a more militant, more action-oriented organization. One of the founder members, Graham Lees, declared that CAMRA:

was born in an era of unfettered big business whizzkids whose ultimate strategy was a drinking Britain controlled by perhaps only three super breweries, owning all of the country's 60,000 pubs and each churning out a similar insipid bastardised beer.

From where they were sitting it looked as though cask ale was about to be bumped off entirely and permanently, as small breweries continued to close and keg bitter became weaker, nastier and more pervasive. The founders belonged to the generation that had grown up protesting against everything from war to straight clothes. And three of the four were journalists. They knew how to get their point across to a broad range of people. From the start, their tactics were aggressive, belligerent and designed to gain maximum publicity.

The brewers were not expecting organized resistance on any significant scale, and CAMRA hit them hard. They staged mock funerals for closing breweries and gathered petitions of protest. Being journalists, they launched *What's Brewing*, a monthly newsletter that drew their members' attention to what the Big Six were planning to foist on us next, as well as to what was happening with cask ales. In 1974 the annual *Good Beer Guide* was launched, and later the same year the first beer festival took place in Cambridge. The idea caught on, and before long festivals were happening in every region of the country. In 1975 a huge national event took place in London, and The Great British Beer Festival became the biggest annual fixture in the beer fan's calendar.

It's ironic that one of CAMRA's beefs has always been that the big brewers brainwash us with sophisticated marketing, making us drink stuff we don't really want to, because in its early days CAMRA itself displayed the occasional stroke of marketing genius. For example, they coined the term 'real ale' for cask-conditioned and bottle-conditioned beers to emphasize their superiority over keg bitter. The other stuff was ersatz beer, 'near beer', not beer or ale at all. The term did not exist before CAMRA began campaigning with it.* They quietly changed their name to the snappier Campaign for Real Ale, and even succeeded in getting the term into the *Oxford English Dictionary*. It's a clear indication of the success of the movement that everyone – the brewing industry included – now refers to the cask-conditioned stuff as real ale, a feat of repositioning comparable with Tony Blair's success in getting even the Conservatives to refer to his party as New Labour, forcing them to redefine the argument on his terms.

CAMRA's message got through. Regular drinkers who had been increasingly unhappy now knew they were not alone, and began to grumble about the state of their beer, realizing that they need not just swallow it and keep quiet. By 1973 CAMRA had five thousand members, by 1976 thirty thousand. The Big Six recognized that they needed to do something to placate these people, and started to dust off the old

---

* Or so I thought. On a trip to India, I discovered in a copy of the *Calcutta Gazette* dated April 13 1809, an ad with the headline 'REAL ALE', which went on to announce a 'Public Auction By Williams and Hohler At their Auction-room on MONDAY next, the 17th April 1809, ONE Hundred and Forty-three Dozen of excellent REAL ALE, warranted good, the property of an Up-Country Trader, leaving of business.' Given that brewers sending beer to colonial India did their best to get as much yeast out of the beer as possible, they used the term in a different way. But it just goes to show.

hand pumps and put cask ales back on the bar, even launching new beers. Those in the brewing industry who had most sympathy with CAMRA felt confident enough to leave their corporate employers and start up small craft breweries of their own. Cask-conditioned ale, which had been in danger of dying altogether, was off the life-support machine.

The monopolistic behaviour of the Big Six was called into question. Talk of further mergers and rationalization in the brewing industry became increasingly unpopular, and in 1977 the Price Commission investigated the brewers after several steep price rises. Their report attacked the tied-house system as anti-competitive and, commenting on the heavy spending since the big mergers of the 1960s, it asked:

> To what degree has the customer benefited from this massive expenditure by the large brewers, most of which, after all, he has paid for in higher prices for his beer? So far as brewing and wholesaling is concerned we have found that large brewers have derived no apparent advantage from larger scale, more concentrated operations. Their costs and prices are higher and their percentage profit margins lower ... The coincidence of higher prices and lower profit margins gives rise to fundamental questions about the trade and its organisation.

CAMRA had received official endorsement of its views, and the state of our beer was now an issue of national debate. The organization itself was described by Michael (later Lord) Young, then chairman of the National Consumer Council, as 'the most successful consumer movement in Europe'.

The story of CAMRA is fantastic stuff for anybody who enjoys a decent pint. Britain still has a unique beer culture in the world. People joke about pints of 'Old Scruttock's Rusty Bollockbiter' being brewed with bits of wood and the landlord's toenail clippings, but in pure product terms real ale is a fantastic drink, with at least as much depth, complexity and variety as wine.

The main difference compared to lager is that a decent ale is so much more *rounded*. There's so much variety and complexity. You could start off with a decent, classic bitter like London Pride, with hints of nuttiness and caramel in a dry, refreshing balance, or perhaps one of its northern cousins, a Yorkshire bitter such as that made by the Acorn brewery in Barnsley, darker and chewier with a hint of licorice. Fancy something lighter? Then why not try a golden ale like Wye Valley's Hereford Pale Ale or the revered Timothy Taylor Landlord, where a shift towards lighter, more delicate malt allows the citrus and earthy tones of hops to come to the fore? And if you get an appetite for those hops, why not go the whole hog and quaff a full-strength, traditional IPA such as the tropical fruit explosion that is the awesome Jaipur from Thornbridge? Or perhaps you'd like to marvel at how Mild manages to pack so much mocha and chicory flavour into such a low alcohol beverage? There are ales enhanced by other ingredients such as the magical Badger Golden Champion, delicately tinged with Elderflower to create a slightly perfumed character that dances just above your tongue, the essence of a summer's evening and the best barbecue beer ever created. At the other end of the seasonal cycle, hearty winter warmers and Christmas ales explode like something from *Charlie and the Chocolate Factory* with jammy red fruit and spices, one sip containing all the flavours of a Christmas pudding. If you think Guinness seems to have lost some of its character these days, you'll love the dark coffee grounds and chocolate delights of a traditional porter or stout. And if you're looking for the perfect way to round off this psychedelic assault on your taste buds, finish the evening with a barley wine or old ale, two or three times the alcohol weight of a traditional beer, with winey, sherry and Madeira notes coming through the alcoholic warmth.*

British real ale culture continues to flourish and develop as one of the most extraordinary and satisfying epicurean banquets on the planet, revered by beer fans around the world. That it exists today is thanks in no small part to CAMRA's efforts. So this all just begs one question: why – in an age of unparalleled culinary sophistication and experimentation in the UK – do half of the UK population claim never to have even tried a single real ale in their entire lives? Why – if you're one of that 50 per cent – are you sitting there now thinking, 'But I just thought it was flat and warm and drunk by old men and geeks in beards and sandals?'

The trouble with image

Since the mid-1970s, the biggest event in the real ale calendar has been the Great British Beer Festival. For years it was held in the vast exhibition hangar of Olympia in London, and recently moved to Earl's Court. I started going in

---

*   I've just realized this paragraph should probably carry a health warning: remember everyone, always drink responsibly. Never drink more than one of these beers in any one year, otherwise your head will fall off.

the late nineties, when I began to fall seriously in love with flavourful, crafted beer. Every year I went, and every year I hated it.

Given that I love fresh, tasty beer, I should have loved the festival: literally hundreds of different ales from all around the country, plus a little *bieres san frontieres* stall in recognition of the fact that countries like Belgium, Germany and the USA could brew a decent drop. The cavernous space was hung with advertising banners that made you appreciate anew the incredible extent and diversity of Britain's brewing culture.

But the problems started before you even got in the building. There was a separate queue for CAMRA members, and brightly bibbed stewards wandered the length of the main queue shouting that CAMRA members could jump the queue and get in cheaper. Did they want the rest of us to be here or not?

Once through the door, the answer became clearer. The festival was staffed by unpaid volunteers, which was admirable in itself. Many of them took a week's holiday from work to be there. But to judge from the manner in which they related to paying customers, you could only assume that they were usually employed as tube train drivers, prison wardens, or customer care representatives for Hackney Council, Virgin Media or British Gas. Either that, or they were angry, sad, frustrated, downtrodden and bullied, and this was their one chance to wield power over the general bastards of the public who normally made their lives so miserable. One year, as soon as you entered you were confronted by a bank of people wearing T-shirts bearing the slogan 'Not for lager boys', sending the message, intentionally or otherwise, that if you were not already a real ale aficionado, you could turn the fuck around and fuck the fuck off.

Another year, I managed to persuade my wife to go along. She was into blonde, summer ales at the time, and went up to a volunteer-run bar to ask if they had any. 'We've got this one that's strong and gets you pissed quickly, and this one that's weaker and gets you pissed more slowly. Now which do you want, I'm busy,' came the reply. It was six years before I could persuade her to visit the festival again.

She's lucky I didn't take her to the Battersea Beer Festival, where I was once physically assaulted by a harassed volunteer, clearly way out of his depth and incapable of dealing with crowds, because I was unwittingly standing in his way.

Back at Olympia, once you'd negotiated your way past the door you were on your own. Beers were put forward to the festival by CAMRA branches, which have a regional, federal structure, so the festival space was organized along those lines. If you went there thinking, 'You know what? I really fancy trying a beer from the North West of England,' you were fine. But if you wanted to focus on a particular style of beer, or just wanted to try something interesting, it was random guesswork. There was a programme, which also listed beers in alphabetical order by brewer – again, fine if you already knew what you were looking for. It had tasting notes too, but 'Good nose, with delicate mouthfeel' (Daleside Blonde) or 'Mellow, bitter, dry-hopped with Styrian Golding to produce a crafted session beer' (Highgate Fox's Nob) were of no use whatsoever unless you were already a fully paid-up member of the real ale club. On the occasion of real ale's highest visibility to the world at large, there was no effort whatsoever to get new people into decent beer.

This apparent hostility towards 'lager boys' went beyond the beer festival. In serious beer writing no one ever deviated from the point of view that CAMRA saved the world, while lager drinkers were portrayed as brainless morons who knew no better.

The most industrious and influential British beer writer in the CAMRA vein is Roger Protz. Roger has always written passionately about his love of real ale, and remains equally vociferous in his disdain for big multinational brewers. He reserves special disgust for mass-marketed lager:

Promotions suggest that unless you drink lager you are in some way odd, not a proper paid-up member of your peer group. If you want to be 'streetwise' and have credibility with the opposite sex then you must consume lager. It is a remarkable victory for marketing power, for here is a drink largely without a definable taste or character that within two decades has come from nowhere to challenge the supremacy of mild, bitter and stout.

He sees this as part of a wider trend which we are powerless to resist. Writing in 1987, he claimed:

Lager is also part of a general and peculiar trend towards blandness in foodstuffs. Light white wines, homogenised and dosed with sulphur dioxide, are preferred to the robust palates of rich red wines. Instant coffee finds favour because of its lack of 'offensive' coffee taste. White bread with the texture of damp tissue paper is in far greater demand than chewy wholemeal. The logic of the modernists is that we should exist on a diet of Pot Noodles, Mother's Pride and Harp lager.

According to Roger, CAMRA just managed to save us from this dictatorship of tat.

> The concern for healthy living and better quality food has been made possible by a climate that CAMRA helped produce.

It's not quite as simple as that. The failure of the big brewers to get us to drink lager for so long demonstrates, if any demonstration is needed, that they can't just make us do what they want. As we'll see in the next chapter, even when they eventually got us to drink lager, we didn't put up with it for long before we started rejecting the ersatz versions we were being served and seeking out the proper European brews.

The sorry tale of the most reviled brand of the keg era is a perfect illustration of this point. In 1970 Watney took the trend towards 'slick marketing' to what must have been, in their eyes, its logical conclusion. Red Barrel lost the barrel from both its name and its bar presence, as the little plastic red barrel was replaced by a big red plastic keg, standing proud, heralding the 'Red Revolution'. I suppose they must have been trying to cash in on the revolutionary sentiments of the late 1960s. The doors of pubs were painted red. Sales reps wore red socks. There were posters featuring lookalikes of Chairman Mao and Fidel Castro with pints of Watney's Red in their hands, with the strapline 'You've only got to taste it. Watney's Red'.

Most people who did as they were told and tasted it didn't like it. Monty Python based one of their most famous sketches around an extended rant which had 'Watney's Red Barrel' (sic) as its coda. The beer was reviled to the point

295

where a clearly hurt Grand Metropolitan (Watney's parent company) chairman grumbled in the company's annual report about 'a virulent word-of-mouth campaign' against the brand. After spending £2 million advertising Red between 1971 and 1974, spending was abruptly pulled from the brand the following year. They quietly killed it off altogether in 1979.

The point of this is that Watney's Red was clearly a ridiculous proposition. Look, I was only eleven when it disappeared for ever so I never drank it, but it obviously tasted absolutely dreadful, and no amount of marketing was going to persuade people otherwise. It was a massive, costly failure from which Watney as a brewer never really recovered. For three years it was by far the biggest spender on advertising in the beer market, and that spend failed to get people to love the brand. CAMRA denies orchestrating any large-scale consumer campaign against the brand – this was people acting independently. Watney's Red failed because the brewer could not get away from its modernist progression logic at a time when people were starting to reject it of their own free will. There is a point beyond which people will not go no matter how slickly rubbish is presented, and those who assume we can be forced into drinking crap by slick marketing alone are mistaken.

CAMRA's main strength is also its Achilles' Heel: to many of those that love it, beer is more than just a drink; it's a hobby. Hobbies are very English, very male, and increasingly seen as eccentric. That's not a problem if your hobby keeps you in the garden shed, but in public, the more passionate someone is about their hobby, the more they tend to put you off joining them in it.

Old-fashioned beer hobbyists form an increasingly small minority within the army of people who love real ale, but boy, you notice them. For a start they stand out from the crowd, and not in a good way. It's a depressing cliché to hear some besuited yuppie git sniggering into his Pinot Grigio about the bloke with a bird's nest in his beard, a bunch of badges on his jerkin, thick, heavy rimmed glasses that are misted over either by accumulated filth or sexual excitement at having got his hands on a half of an award-winning Mild, stained Oliver Reed tribute T-shirt straining over a sagging belly, shorts with a personalized pewter tankard hanging off a lanyard from his belt and – always – sandals with calf-length black socks. But unfortunately, when you finally convince the yuppie that he's wrong and persuade him to go to a beer festival, these people are there in abundance, farting silent-but-deadlies at each other across the room. If you were to count them they are a tiny minority compared to the huge number of perfectly normal people in the room. But if you move in circles in which you can easily go a year without seeing one person like this, it can be disconcerting to find yourself sandwiched between two or three of them at the bar.

Rejecting image and claiming it doesn't matter does not stop you from portraying an image of yourself – good or bad, there's nothing you can do about that. If you decide that image is unimportant, you're less likely to take care of the image you portray. And so, for much of its existence, CAMRA imbued real ale with an image of the socially inadequate middle-aged man who takes beer far too seriously, the beery equivalent of the trainspotter.*

---

* In fact, buried deep within the subculture of real ale appreciation, there

Pluck up the courage to talk to one of these relics though, and it's often more than their appearance and social skills that are unpleasant. Many of them love real ale because it's traditional. That's not the problem – the problem is the binary world view in which anything *not* traditional is seen as evil. They don't just choose to not drink lager, they *despise* lager – often even perfectly made Czech and German pilsners – and then get into a lather about how we should drink real ale because it's British and that other stuff is foreign muck and you're transported back to the questionable level of political discourse of the 1970s, when CAMRA began. You come away feeling that some of these people wish it still *was* 1973.

You can ignore these people if you like, or just not go. But because they care more about real ale than you, they are more actively involved in it than you. Thus CAMRA policy, decided by a National Executive and an Annual General Meeting, is often the policy of the geeks rather than the broad membership.

The notorious recent example of this is the cask breathers

---

is such a thing as a beer trainspotter – the ticker. These guys are often looked down on even by other beer geeks. They meticulously catalogue every single beer they have ever sampled, and compete as to who can tick the most different beers. At the hardcore end the 'scoopers' don't even have to drink the beer – they'll settle in pubs with a bag full of paraphernalia including funnels and empty pop bottles, order a half and pour it into a bottle before carefully labeling it. In this way they can work in pairs, each partner taking a string of pubs, then swapping samples and collecting new beers twice as fast. We're talking geek squared here. But a documentary film about tickers, shot by filmmaker Phil Parkin in the ticker Mecca that is Sheffield, revealed them to be warm, engaging, interesting people. Well, some of them.

debate. A cask breather is a gadget that injects carbon dioxide into the top of a cask as beer is drawn from it, leaving a blanket on top of the remaining beer that prevents oxygen from getting to it. Oxygen is the enemy of beer and makes it go stale, so a cask breather can extend the life of a tapped cask of ale by a few days. This is brilliant news for a pub that doesn't sell much real ale, one that supports slow-selling styles such as Mild, or one that has an issue with stale or mouldy air in its cellar that you wouldn't want getting into the beer. But CAMRA asserts that the method produces subtle changes in the character of the beer, and that CO_2 going into the cask is the same thing as artificial carbonation in the beer itself. Even though the CO_2 sits on top of the beer rather than interacting with it, even though every cask ale brewer who expresses an opinion on the issue rejects the notion that cask breathers change the beer's character, and even though in repeated blind taste tests CAMRA members are unable to distinguish cask breather beer from non-cask breather beer, they maintain that the beer has been somehow degraded.

The real problem of course is not that cask breathers change the beer, but that they are not 'traditional', not 'natural', and are therefore bad. Which begs the question: when did progress in brewing become a bad thing? It was scientific innovation which gave birth to modern real ale in the late nineteenth century. At what year should we draw the line and say 'anything that improves the flavour and quality of beer before this time is good, but anything that comes after it is bad'? If you think I'm overreacting, just Google 'CAMRA cask breathers' and be alarmed at the incredibly aggressive language some CAMRA branches use on what is to any sane person a minor technical issue. CAMRA states in its aims that it represents all beer drinkers, and that it exists to promote good quality real ale in pubs. Here, militants are actively obstructing the spread of real ale to swathes of pubs, on grounds that the vast majority of beer drinkers would know or care little about.

The reality of CAMRA is that it is a broad church with many differing points of view. It's inaccurate and unfair to generalize and state that 'all CAMRA members believe the earth is flat' or 'All CAMRA members have nests growing in their beards'. But some of them do. And often they're the loudest, most visible ones.

Reasons to be cheerful

And yet, despite that handful of militants, over the last decade both real ale and CAMRA itself have managed to change their image and move into the twenty-first century. In the early noughties, new executive officers, including a very bright and engaging full-time CEO, began to transform CAMRA into both an incredibly effective lobbying voice on beer issues, and a body that the ordinary beer drinker shouldn't have any problem with being associated with. CAMRA finally recognized that image matters in beer choice, and ran a number of publicity campaigns aiming to increase its membership and to promote the image of real ale in general. They weren't always as clever and engaging as they tried to be, but they were effective: over the first decade of the twenty-first century, CAMRA doubled its membership. Given that the number of sandal-wearing, beer-bellied geeks showed no noticeable increase over that period, you can only agree with CAMRA when they claim that this image simply is not an accurate representation of the modern real ale drinker.

And what about the running sore that was the Great British Beer Festival?

I continued to go every year, and to hate it every year. And then one year, it moved to larger premises in Earls Court. While some visitors felt lost inside this vast hangar, and those trying to listen to announcements could only despair at the acoustics, something more than the venue had changed. The festival is still organized by region, but the programme is way more user-friendly, and the *bieres san frontiers* stall is bigger every year, now an integral fixture. The staff are still volunteers, but they seem to have been sent to some kind of miraculous charm school – they are slick, professional, and every single interaction with them is full of pleases and thank yous. Remembering past experiences at the bar, last time I attended I overheard the following conversation:

Barman: 'Yes, sir, what can I get you?'

Customer: 'Oh, er, um, I, er . . .'

Barman: 'Can I help you make a choice?'

Customer (relieved): 'Oh thanks, yes, I don't know where to start.'

Barman: 'OK, well would you say you prefer lighter, hoppier, refreshing ales or darker, maltier, chewier ales?'

Customer: 'Oh, lighter and refreshing I think.'

Barman: 'OK, have a little taster of this one and let's see how we get on.'

If it wasn't guaranteed to send all manner of wrong signals, I'd have leaned over the counter, grabbed the barman by his cheeks, pushed his face in to make him pucker up, and given him a big, wet, sloppy kiss on the lips.

CAMRA will always tie itself up in policy knots and frustrate as many people as it delights. The increasingly loud voice of drinkers asking the organization to campaign for all decent beer is regularly answered by the official, 'We'd love to, but the clue is in the name – we're the campaign for real ale.' But this is conveniently forgotten when CAMRA also actively promotes real cider, and spends campaigning resources supporting traditional Czech and Belgian beers in their home countries. Not to mention the fact that if they wanted, CAMRA could always change its constitution, its aims, or even the very definition of real ale if it wanted, given that they created the term. But the fact that some of its flat-earthers now grumble that it has become too slick, modern and image-conscious is the best possible evidence of the fact that CAMRA has changed for the better, and does speak increasingly on behalf of anyone who loves decent beer.

At the time of writing real ale is thriving. The Great British Beer Festival has record attendances, and smaller beer festivals throughout the country are selling out way in advance.* But real ale has a lot of catching up to do, and remains far behind where you'd think it should be given that it's a natural, traditional, flavourful, locally-sourced, well-crafted, quintessentially British product in an age where each of these concepts is very important to us.

The trouble is, the clichéd real ale enthusiast had his biggest reaction against the idea of image at exactly the same

---

* We'll come on to the non-CAMRA-specific reasons for this towards the end of the next chapter.

time as most of us decided that image mattered to us a great deal; when the age of big branding dawned not just brightly, but with NEW, ADDED, ULTRA-BRIGHTNESS! which was preferred by nine out of ten consumers, and made traditional ale start to look very dull indeed.

Chapter Twelve

'Drinking the advertising'

The age of the mega-brands

Drinking and the Dark Arts

In January 2010 the Parliamentary Health Select Committee released a report savaging Britain's alcohol culture, claiming that we were drinking ourselves to death and bankrupting the country while we did so. Among its many attacks, it reserved particular vitriol for the role of alcohol advertising. It pointed out that in 2003, £600–£800 million had been spent on booze ads, claimed these ads targeted children and encouraged them to drink, and said the system of regulating alcohol advertising desperately needed to be strengthened.

A closer reading of the report raised obvious questions, such as how come not one study cited by the report could actually establish a causal link between advertising and under-age drinking?* If the regulations were so lax, why

---

* The main study it used to make pronouncements about the link between advertising and under-age drinking in the UK was actually a

couldn't they name a single example of an advert on British TV that had youth appeal? And why could a 2009 parliamentary sub-committee only get its hands on estimates of figures from 2003, when these figures are in fact freely available on an annual basis?

If alcohol advertising really is trying to get young people to drink, it's not doing a very good job. Because despite all those millions being spent, the number of children who have ever drunk alcohol and the number who drink it on a regular basis today both show consistent declines in every single survey on the topic over the period being discussed by the report (though of course, the report doesn't tell you that).

I'll admit that when I was a kid, I loved beer ads. I watched them all, chatted to my mates at school about them, recited the catchphrases. But they didn't make me want to drink beer. Until I was fifteen I only drank very watery lager and lime, half a can with Sunday lunch, offered to me by my parents. And after that it was my schoolmates, not the adverts, who made me think drinking beer might be cool.

But I have to make a confession. When I was nine, running around the playground chanting 'Stop, stop, we're going round in *circles*!' * little did I know that beer ads would have far graver consequences for my moral development.

They didn't make me want to drink beer. It was much worse than that.

They made me want to work in advertising.

If my fellow admen and I were trying to get people to

_____

survey of students in two schools in South Dakota. (And that study concluded that causal effects were unclear).

*   It's the punchline to an old Heineken ad – you had to be there I guess.

drink more booze, we clearly failed spectacularly. My only consolation is that the people who succeeded us are doing even worse: the amount of alcohol consumed in the UK declined by over 12% between 2004 and 2009. In 2009 itself, when £66 million was spent on beer advertising (not to mention the extra millions on sponsorship, online marketing, PR etc) beer sales in the UK fell faster than at any time since 1948 – in other words, faster than at any rate since before TV ads were even invented.

Beer ads don't make people drink more. But they do have a profound effect on *what* we drink, and *how* we drink it. Through the course of this book, we've seen how the dominant forces in society at any point in history shape our drinking habits as much as any other aspect of our lives: religion, patriarchal power structures, trade, industry, colonialism and political ideology have all played their part. But over the last half-century, nothing has shaped our boozing habits anything like as dramatically as the force that now defines our entire social landscape: brand marketing.

The triumph of branding

Brands have been adding an emotional aspect to our purchasing choices over and above the physical attributes of products for at least a hundred years and, as we have seen, beer led the way. In 1876, Bass registered the first trademark in the UK as a way of guaranteeing that any beer carrying their mark would be of a certain quality. In the 1970s, Heineken revolutionized how brands worked. But in the 1980s people actually *got* brands. We worked out that the intangible dimension was the thing that made the difference, and recognized that our emotional attachment to brands was heavily influenced by advertising and marketing. But when we realized how our tastes were being manipulated, we didn't throw up our hands in horror and sue advertisers for trying to brainwash us. We joined in the game. It was enjoyable; if brands were all about image, we could co-opt them to help build our own image. Once we understood how the emotional, intangible dimension worked, in markets where image played a role it became more important than the physical product itself.

This new understanding of the power of brands and how they worked would subsquently result in frequent condemnation of the 1980s as the decade of style over substance. As we have become increasingly adept at understanding brands, we have learned to manipulate them, to be more subtle in our use of them, even to subvert their intended meanings. But in the 1980s it was enough simply to wear the badge in an obvious way that would be considered quite vulgar by today's standards. The Beastie Boys wore VW car badges around their necks, and kids up and down the country were suddenly vandalizing any Golf or Polo left unattended. T-shirts with slogans became a form of self-expression after Katherine Hamnett's 'Frankie says . . .' designs. Designer labels moved from inside the necks of garments to be emblazoned where they were most visible. Yuppies carried Filofaxes and students who bought imitation ones, mere 'personal organizers' from W. H. Smith, were ridiculed for it.*

---

* Well, I was anyway. I know, I should let it go.

Brands were so powerful that advertising could actually change the way something tasted. Pepsi famously demonstrated that people who said they preferred Coke consistently favoured Pepsi when they were asked to sample the two products unbranded and side by side. Pepsi trumpeted that this meant their product was better. True, but it also meant their brand was much weaker. Beer was the same. Brewers conducted blind tastings in which respondents ranked several beers in order of preference, and that order would change once the identities of the brands tasted were revealed. It's what some rather thoughtful adman once referred to as 'drinking the advertising'. And lager, with its lack of discernible differences between products, was the drink that led the way. The relationship we had with beer began to have much less to do with the taste and character of the product, and a lot more to do with its image. That's why, if you look along the bar in a typical pub today, resting your gaze on each font on the counter and each bottled brand in the fridge, it's almost a museum of every cultural trend and fad that has afflicted our social lives for the past twenty years. And after Heineken, it was that one on the bar with the big red 'F' inside a blue oval that led the way.

Fostralia

Australia has been a big beer market since the middle of the nineteenth century. Contrary to the cheerfully xenophobic British popular myth, the country was not colonized entirely as a result of the UK transporting all its convicts there. There was a gold rush in the 1850s that led to 400,000 Brits with no serious criminal record dashing to the other side of the planet of their own accord. And where the Brits went, their beer had to follow. This was good timing for British brewers, who had already built up profitable export operations supplying the British in India. As we all know from that classic of modern cinema *Crocodile Dundee*, the Australian climate is harsh, unforgiving and very, very hot, and this led to an insatiable demand for beer. The colonists relied on pale ales such as Bass, and kept them in underground cellars to protect them from the heat. It was not ideal.

Australian drinking culture as we know and love it really took off when Gambrinus, a brewer from Germany, set up shop in Melbourne in 1885. They brought refrigeration with them, and with refrigeration came lager. Unsurprisingly, it was a hit. The American Foster brothers soon set up a second lager brewery in the city, and Castlemaine started to brew in Brisbane in 1889. When the German submarines killed off British pale ale exports for good in the First World War, Australia became and remained a nation of enthusiastic lager drinkers.

By the 1980s Elders IXL dominated Australia with a few large brands, one of which was Foster's lager. Just like Carlsberg and Heineken in their own markets, Elders were in a position where they couldn't grow much further locally and had to look to exports to continue their growth. They recognized that, while obviously nobody could touch the Aussies in terms of the sheer gusto with which they sank pints, the Poms weren't too bad at it. At any rate, we were better drinkers than we were cricket players, and we were getting a bit of a thirst for lager. Elders realized that to break into this market they needed tied houses, and that meant they needed an alliance with a British brewer.

Back in Britain, lager was lager was lager. The leading brands looked and tasted the same, and they all came, allegedly, from somewhere in Europe, where Teutons or Scandinavians had supposedly been brewing them for centuries. Their unimpeachable Continental heritage was the serious bit we took out of the thirty-second gags, the sell we agreed to take with us in return for being entertained. There were some lagers that just went for the 'all lads together' theme, but the ones that seemed to have staying power in people's minds, the ones that were considered to have some notion of quality, were the ones that had a European connection.

At the start of the 1980s Watney Mann was selling large volumes of Carlsberg on draught, and had the market-leading brand in the small but profitable premium bottled lager market with Holsten Pils. But there were nearly thirty brands competing in the European heritage market, most of them with names ending in berg, brau or meister, and mostly brewed in sheds in the Home Counties by people with no more knowledge of German than my mate Paul at school.* Drinkers were jaded by everyone insisting they were the best, and anyway, no matter how the drinker felt, Watney Mann couldn't launch another European-based standard

---

* We both started German when we went to Big School aged eleven. After a few weeks I asked Paul who took his class for German, to which he replied, 'Well, he calls himself Herr Woodward but he won't tell us his real name.'

lager brand without damaging their Carlsberg business. But they still wanted a bit more of the lager action. If only there was another country with a serious lager heritage . . .

Foster's and Watney Mann were a perfect match. Foster's already imported small volumes in large cans, and had a cult reputation in the UK. Here was a lager brand that was different. It was Australian. That meant it had a genuine lager culture behind it, but brought with it a fresh, new personality. Having said that, at the time of the Foster's launch in 1981 we were not exactly in love with Australia. There were those jokes about convicts and, like Canada, it was a place where dodgy relatives had gone to live. Australian soaps were the height of tackiness; *Sons and Daughters* and *The Young Doctors* were on ITV in the afternoon dead zone before kids' telly started, and had acting and sets that made the infamous *Crossroads* look Oscar-worthy. Still, anybody was better than the Germans.

Watney Mann used Paul Hogan, a little-known comedian with a late-night sketch show, as the launch spokesperson for Foster's and the embodiment of the brand. He was the naive Australian abroad – like the brand, a visitor to Britain. In each ad he would encounter a traditional British institution and would, apparently, not quite get it, preferring instead to just drink the good old 'amber nectar' (which tasted 'like an angel crying on your tongue') and reflect upon the absurdity of Britain as seen from the outside. There was the time he went to the ballet, and sat bemused until the male principal dancer wafted onto the stage in his tights and codpiece, forcing Hogan to splutter, 'Strewth! There's a bloke down there with no strides on!' and cover the eyes of his lady friend. Or the time he was outside the Tower of London and asked one of the beefeaters* what was inside. When the beefeater replied, 'The Bloody Tower,' Hogan, affronted, retorted, 'I was only asking.'

The ads worked. People associated Australia with a macho drinking culture at a time when lager was still seen by some as effeminate. This, combined with Hogan's outsider stance, meant Foster's was edgy and different. Research said it was 'the most youthful, trendy and masculine brand around', and sales soared.

And then – well, talk about timing. Suddenly, Australia became the trendiest place on earth. Hogan took the character he had used in the Foster's ads to Hollywood, made *Crocodile Dundee* and became a global superstar. And those midweek afternoon soaps seemed to disappear in a muddle of embarrassed coughing and mumbled apologies, to be replaced by a show that recognized tackiness and gloried in it, having worked out that their key audience was kids looking for a bit more life and more convincing acting – though not too much more – than they were getting from their cartoons. Seemingly from nowhere, *Neighbours* became the biggest-rating programme on British television. Soon we were all doing dodgy Oz accents, saying things like 'Let's throw another shrimp on the barbie' and falling around laughing at how clever we were.†

Australian-ness just seemed to *fit* so well. It felt genuine, because Australians really did brew and drink lager, but it also felt a bit more lively than all those European brands.

---

* Who was actually Arthur Fowler out of *Eastenders*, for all you *Before They Were Famous* fans.
† Well, I was anyway.

It was foreign and exotic, and yet Australia was more 'like us' than any other country. This went down very well with a new generation of lager drinkers. As Foster's grew, brands like Carlsberg and Heineken were increasingly seen as the beer your dad drank.

Allied Breweries recognized this. With Skol they had been one of the pioneers of lager brewing in the UK, and they were now aware that, in the young drinker's eyes, the only thing worse than a dull European lager was a British lager pretending to be a dull European lager. They wanted a new brand to take advantage of the booming market.

At the time Allied had a minority shareholding in the Australian brewery, Castlemaine Toohey's. When they checked things out, they realized that Castlemaine XXXX, not Foster's, was the biggest-selling brand in Australia itself. Here was the brand and the strategy. Foster's might be the Australian abroad, but XXXX was the beer really drunk in the outback.

The brand launched on TV in 1984. One of the first ads shows two guys stuck in a shack in the middle of the outback. One of them, Bill, is seriously ill, sweating feverishly in a sodden bed with flies buzzing around. The second guy, Bruce, is on the radio to the flying doctor, expressing concern that his friend is 'real crook', asking if there is anything he can do before the doctor gets there. The doc tells Bruce to get the patient something cool to drink, anything, or else it could get real bad. All Bruce can find is a solitary can of XXXX. Bruce opens the can, takes a long, refreshing drink, and says querulously, 'He says it's going to be real bad, Bill.' The ad ends with the punchline 'Australians wouldn't give a XXXX for any other lager'. The British gave a XXXX what the Australians drank, and consequently Castlemaine gave Foster's a run for its money over which was the coolest Australian lager for the rest of the 1980s.

Provenance – country of origin – had become at least as important to lager drinkers as taste. Ten years previously, people had expressed themselves by drinking lager rather than bitter. Younger drinkers could now set themselves apart from those lager pioneers with an extra layer of image management.

A new folk demon hits the streets

In 1987 and 1988, reports grew of unrest outside pubs at closing time. Fights outside pubs were nothing new, but what was different was that these disturbances were not taking place in Sheffield or Newcastle, but in tranquil villages and towns in the south, where people had money. In June 1988 the Association of Chief Police Officers published a report which stated that in 1987 there had been two thousand arrests in incidents in country towns and villages, half of them happening on Friday and Saturday nights, almost all of them involving people who had been drinking. Genteel Gloucester was dubbed as 'Thug City' by one local paper. If nice middle-class people were scrapping, there was obviously something badly wrong with society. Something Had To Be Done. Douglas Hurd, home secretary at the time, summed up just how worrying the situation was for Middle England:

> You do not find much poverty or social deprivation in these parts. What you do find are too many young people

with too much money in their pockets [and] too many
pints inside them.

Lager was still regarded as premium to bitter. It was more
expensive, had a more sophisticated image. Although it
was growing rapidly across the country, for a long time it
was definitely drunk more in the south than in the depressed
north.* Putting two and two together, tabloids and Tory
politicians concluded that lager, rather than rural affluence,
made people violent. They ran sensational stories on 'rural
riots', and the 'lager lout' was born.

In 1992 the Social Issues Research Centre carried out a
comprehensive study in search of the lager lout. They carried
out three thousand interviews across the country, with young
drinkers as well as the Friday night supporting cast: cabbies,
kebab van owners, beat police and bar staff. Many of these
people said that fights outside the pub were just part of
Friday night, always had been, and that there had been no
discernible increase in such incidents. Even in Banbury, the
location of the 1988 rural riot that allegedly kicked off
the whole lager lout debate, drinkers, observers and even the
police claimed the whole thing had been a misunderstanding.
Police had intervened in a small-scale fight, then mounted
police appeared from nowhere. People felt the police were
overreacting, and waded in. But it turned out the horses
were only there because they happened to be out on a training exercise. Taken alone this explanation might sound a

* To any pedants reading, yes I know that 1988 was a time of economic
boom rather than recession. But this was kept a secret from people in
northern towns and cities, who thought that the recession in the early
nineties was simply a continuation of the one from the early eighties.

little contrived, but the report studied many incidents in England and abroad. The conclusions are clear: if there is an expectation that things will kick off after a few pints and if people are treated as thugs, they will behave that way. In all the trouble spots, a constant factor was an intimidating police presence *before* trouble ignited. In places such as Italy and Spain young men drink just as much, but because there is no expectation of violence, it rarely occurs.

The SIRC suggested that the phenomenon was just the latest example of society needing a 'moral panic' to get exercised about. From the 1960s, the moral panic had been football hooligans, and the lager lout phenomenon was a close reworking of the same debate. No academic study into football hooliganism found drinking to be a major factor. There are football fans who get trolleyed at the game and don't fight, and there are people who commit violence at matches who don't drink. In fact many of the hooligan 'firms' that arose in the 1980s made a point of not drinking, so they could stay sharp and focused enough to slash their adversaries. But this was the Thatcher era. Football support-ers were lumped in with striking miners and Irish republicans as the enemy within, and treated accordingly. As drinking on the terraces was stamped out, corporate hospitality, com-plete with free booze, prospered, and drinking at games with more middle-class appeal, such as tennis, rugby and cricket, remained unchallenged.

It was just the same with rural and suburban drinkers on a Friday night. Only a tiny minority of pissed-up lads get into fights, so there must be factors other than drink at work. Nevertheless, lager louts joined football hooligans in the folk demon category, just as mods and rockers had before them.

Designer beer

Whatever the truth behind the lager-lout scare, it left the stylish urban drinker with a bit of a problem. Suddenly, asking for a pint of lager was a sign that you were looking to kick something off rather than that you were a sophisticated drinker. No matter how discerning your taste, once you'd got a pint of lager in your hand it was a glass of fizzy, piss-coloured liquid, and no one could see what a cool choice you'd made. If there had been a brand on the bar called Pacifist or Above That Sort Of Thing it would have been indistinguishable from what the yobs were drinking once you'd bought it. The most obvious solution was a drink that was clearly labelled and badged.

Bottled beers were hardly new. Until the 1960s they had been growing thanks to the fact that while they might not have tasted as nice as a well kept pint of draught beer, they beat the pants off a badly kept pint. When keg bitter came along and reproduced the advantages of bottled beer in a good, manly pint glass, bottles went into decline. Bottled lager bought in a pub was also less than appetizing. Remember that until the mid-1980s most pubs still had shelves rather than fridges behind the bar, which meant bottles were served at room temperature. But the popularity of lager and the trend towards all drinks being served colder meant that fridges started to appear in the more stylish bars, and eventually became ubiquitous. Landlords could now stock a wide range of bottled lagers, rotating their stock easily and cheaply, trying out new and different brands.

In a climate where there was such emphasis on style

and being different, drinkers were not just going to settle for bottled versions of existing draught lagers. They wanted to experiment with different images and pursue new avenues. Between 1986 and 1993, 144 new beer brands were launched into Britain's pubs, from all over the world. The Brits were finally losing the parochialism that had characterized so many of their decisions and attitudes. Food and drink from across the world ceased being 'foreign muck' and became a sign of culture and discernment.

With new brands launched every week, bottled beers went in and out of fashion at a furious rate. And because it was all about packaging, fads and gimmicks that would have been embarrassing a few years previously became sickeningly common. There was Sapporo, with its weird, ultra-modern can from which you pulled the whole top away. Then there was Sol, which suddenly had everyone insisting that you drank it with a wedge of lime in the top of the bottle. Why? To enhance the taste of the beer? To disguise it? To keep the flies out? Just because the Mexicans did it? The debate raged up and down the country for the few brief weeks of summer 1988 when it was OK to drink the brand. And then there was Grolsch with its funky flip-top cap. Not too gimmicky in itself perhaps, but sadly this very decent beer fell foul of the fact that your beer choice says so much about you. For a whole generation of premium-lager drinkers, choosing Grolsch meant you were a Bros fan, after the ill-fated, queasily Aryan proto-boy band 'endorsed' the beer and captured the zeitgeist by wearing the bottle stoppers as fake buckles on their nice black patent-leather loafers.

Another huge change had taken place: the countries whose beer it was hip to drink were no longer just those with a bit of brewing credibility. It was no longer about the beer, it was simply about where it came from. People were buying the glamour and otherness of the country and the attitude of the people, maybe hoping that American cool or Japanese sophistication or Latin spirit would rub off on them. The process that had started with Foster's bringing the Australian 'no worries' attitude into play had come full circle. People paid more for a 33 cl bottle of beer than they did for a full draught pint. They drank from the bottle, being careful to hold the label outwards so everyone could see what they were having. Bottles did still count for quality to some extent, as they had always done – beer from a bottle meant the barman wasn't watering it down or serving you the slops tray when you were too drunk to notice – but really the product was irrelevant.*

Eventually though, drinkers did begin to tire of the gimmickry. People were increasingly weary of marketing hype, and increasingly educated by it. As the dawn of a new decade prompted its usual bout of reflection, people began to reject the conspicuous consumption of the 1980s and look for

---

* If you think you can appreciate the flavour of beer straight from the bottle, I'm afraid you're wrong – you really can't. We often use 'taste' and 'flavour' interchangeably. In fact taste is a mere component of flavour. There are only five tastes – sweet, sour, salty, bitter and umame (savoury) – and these are pretty much the only flavour components the tongue can identify. But there are an infinite number of aromas, which contribute most of the depth, subtlety and character to what we think of as flavour. If you drink straight from the bottle you're cutting your nose out of the equation and therefore missing 80 per cent of the total flavour. It's exactly the same as trying to taste something when you have a cold. Next time you're drinking beer from a glass, hold your nose and you'll see what I mean.

something with a little more authenticity. This wasn't a simple case of rejecting labels, more a case of reducing the size of them. The truly hip no longer needed to broadcast their brands; genuine style was being able to spot them when they were discreet. Style was still important, but empty style, with no genuine quality behind it, started to look a little lame.

The end for bergs, braus and meisters

Premium lagers were much more likely to be imported, and this meant they were brewed to the 'proper' lager strength of 5 per cent ABV common in the rest of the world rather than being bastardized to suit the British predilection for quantity over strength. Also, people were visiting the places where the best lagers supposedly came from, and they came back a little pissed off. Yeah, there were great beers on the Continent, just like the brewers had told us, so how come they were serving us watery piss back home? Drinkers increasingly acquired a taste for premium-strength lager.

Once their cover had been blown, the weak, pseudo-continental lagers such as Skol, Heldenbrau and Hofmeister started to look embarrassing. European lager brewers maintain that it is impossible to get a true, rounded lager taste below 5 per cent. By the early 1990s, we were starting to agree with them. These old brands started to disappear, until they became the ones you found tucked at the back of your gran's fridge a month after Christmas, or the stuff you took to a party and dumped in the kitchen before nicking someone else's Stella. Lager and lime and lager shandy became heinous crimes.

Around this time it also began to look like we were giving up on beer altogether. The total volume drunk in the country dipped, and then accelerated into a nosedive, falling from nearly 40 million barrels in 1989 to just over 36 million by 1994. There was the trend towards smaller volumes of stronger beer, not to mention a recession, but as the decline continued it became obvious that there was something else going on.

By now lager accounted for over 50 per cent of the beer market. As we've seen, lager brewers finally got going when they realized that younger, affluent drinkers in the 1960s wanted something different, and since then lager had continued to be associated with the young. Although there were a far greater number of middle-aged blokes drinking beer than there were kids under the age of twenty-five, the under-twenty-fives packed far more away in a session, and therefore accounted for a hugely disproportionate volume of the total beer sold. The big brewers were increasingly leaving older drinkers to their own devices; the money was now in youth. The trouble was, these young people had started getting their kicks elsewhere.

As raves sprang up in warehouses and fields outside big cities, pubs and bars emptied. Young people hadn't stopped drinking beer as such, but on the weekend nights when pubs were accustomed to shifting the most volume, the people they relied on were off their tits on something better and cheaper. Obviously reliable figures are difficult to come by, but in 1993 the Henley Centre, a leading consultancy in the forecasting of cultural trends, estimated that one million people a week were going to raves, spending an average of thirty-five pounds a time, half of which went on Ecstasy, amphetamines and LSD. Richard Carr of Allied Breweries admitted that, 'Youngsters [could] get Ecstasy for ten or twelve pounds and get a much better buzz than they can from alcohol.' On top of this 'buzz', raves went on all night and were characterized by feelings of intense camaraderie. It was all a far cry from being chucked out of the pub pissed and staggering just after 11 p.m. to fight in the streets. Friday and Saturday night pub culture suddenly looked very lame.

Style *and* substance

We never stopped drinking altogether, but when we did fancy a beer, we were becoming a little more choosy. It's now a recognized fact that, in a recession, people trade up in the little things because it makes them feel better about not being able to afford the big toys any more. Added to this, our knowledge of what was good and bad was getting a lot better thanks to all this sophisticated marketing. In the early 1990s we started to buy freshly squeezed orange juice instead of pasteurized gunk made from concentrate, ciabatta bread instead of Homepride white sliced, as well as Pringles crisps, Pret A Manger sarnies and Haagen Dazs ice cream.

And we traded up in lager. The Porsches may have been repossessed, but even a giro could stretch to a few expensive beers. But people now wanted value with their status symbols, and many drinkers who had acquired a taste for premium lager realized they could be drinking almost twice as much of the stuff for the same price if they left the bottles alone, worried a bit less about the label and ordered a pint of premium draught lager. Through the 1990s, the fixture that quietly appeared on bar tops almost everywhere was Stella Artois.

Stella Artois had been brand leader of the tiny premium draught lager market for years, sitting in a corner and largely minding its own business. In many ways it was the antithesis of the fabricated 'Continental' standard lagers of the 1970s. The Artois brewery, one of Belgium's largest, has a history stretching back to 1366. Artois brewed its first lager, a dark beer called Bock Artois, in 1894. Stella Artois was first brewed for a limited period in 1926, and was intended as a Christmas beer. This seasonality, plus its unusually bright, crisp appearance, earned it the Stella name. The beer proved so popular it ended up staying around after the decorations came down and became the brewery's main product. It grew in popularity through the 1930s, and established a reputation as a decent but everyday lager in a country full of weird and eclectic brews.*

Stella was first introduced into the UK in 1937, sold, as were all the lagers at that time, in bottles only. Over the decades that followed, as other lagers tried every trick in the book to make us love them, Stella doggedly carried on selling the full-strength product instead of producing a weaker,

---

* You might think Belgium is boring, but when it comes to beer they are *out there*. They still have Trappist monks brewing Lambic beers, fruit beers, you name it. In the 1920s, when many countries were toying with variations on the theme of prohibition, Belgium decided to ban gin but not beer, so Belgian brewers simply started brewing really strong beers. If you ever get one of their squat, ugly bottles in your hand check the ABV before you neck it – it's not uncommon for them to be anything between 6 and 9 per cent. You need to show them a bit of respect.

inferior version more in line with British drinking tastes. This immediately placed it in the specialist, high-strength sector where, by the 1970s, it was rubbing shoulders with such illustrious company as Carlsberg Special Brew.

When lager finally started to take off, Stella signed a deal with Whitbread, who launched it on draught in their pubs. It never had that much competition because, with beer duty determined by alcohol content, premium-strength draught lager had to be sold at a far higher price than mainstream bitters or standard lagers. For years, Stella was ultra-premium, regarded as ludicrously expensive.

Stella also garnered a formidable reputation for potency. At 5.2 per cent it was fairly typical for a decent-tasting Continental lager, and was not that much stronger than bottled pils brands. The difference was, we were drinking it in pints. Several generations had passed since pints this strong were normal, and we had become accustomed to drinking large volumes of relatively weak beer. When you're drinking, you know this stuff is stronger and should be treated more carefully, but ingrained behaviour takes over. You might sip from your designer bottled beer, but the correct behaviour with a pint is to address the glass with a manly swig. People who tried this with Stella soon learned the folly of their ways. The brand came to be regarded as dangerous, and earned the affectionate nickname, 'wifebeater'. People became convinced that it was somehow more potent than its claimed 5.2 per cent ABV would suggest, little realizing it was their own drinking habits that were condemning them to 'travel by rail'.*

---

* Give up? OK. It's a phrase that derives from being so drunk that you can only proceed by hanging on to things.

Stella never was the most finely crafted beer of its kind (famously, it was regarded as quite an ordinary lager in the surrealist beer paradise of its native Belgium) but it was the first lager brand to talk openly about things like maturation time and the quality of its ingredients. Thanks mainly to its alcohol content, it really was much more expensive than other lagers at the time, and it highlighted aspects of its production that were true (at the time), but not unique, to do this.

Over the course of the 1980s, if you had money, you flaunted it. If you didn't have money, you pretended you did and still flaunted it. Stella Artois was onto a good thing. In 1982 the tag line 'Reassuringly Expensive' was discreetly added to the ads, and Stella became a symbol of the era of excess. The brand's volume grew five-fold over the course of the decade. But all those bottled-lager launches started to hurt Stella, and Whitbread decided to move the brand's advertising over to television to compete. Their ad agency understood that linking the beer to a place that had values to which the target audience aspired was a winner. But with Stella they decided to fudge things a little. Given that most people don't really aspire to things Belgian, they gave the beer a general, French-speaking provenance. Or Provence, to be more precise. Leuven is nowhere near Provence, but in the early 1990s the south of France had just been discovered by middle-class Britain, so it didn't matter. Peter Mayle, himself an ex-adman, had just foisted his cosy Provençal books on the nation, and we couldn't get enough. Property prices in Provence shot up to London levels as it became de rigeur for posh Londoners to take a holiday home down there. For those who couldn't afford that, the shelves were buckling under Provençal cookery books and terracotta kitchenware. And for those who didn't fancy cooking, there was Stella Artois.

The reasoning behind locating Stella Artois in Provence was the desire to portray it as a lager of supreme quality and worth. The way this was brought to life was to think about how the French revered wine and to write an ad about that, substituting a pint of Stella for the finest burgundy. *Manon des Sources* and *Jean de Florette* had just been huge cult cinema hits, and they inspired the campaign. The ads were big-budget affairs, cinematic in scope. A new one came out each year, and each time the sacrifice for the pint of Stella became a little more extreme, until French peasants were giving away priceless works of art and betraying their mothers, their priests, even their dying fathers, to get a pint.

All other lager advertising was brash and in your face, because lager is all about going out and having a good time, right? Stella was laid-back. Youth culture analysts everywhere were going on about postmodernism and the fractured narrative, irony and self-referentialism. Stella told an old-fashioned story with a beginning, middle and end. While 'dumbing down' became a common phrase, Stella ads remained in French with no subtitles. Viewers could pick up the odd word and follow what was going on, so watching a Stella ad made you think you were better at French than you had realized. In a small way, they rewarded your intelligence.

Although the advertising was great, luck and timing played a big part, and the fashion for all things Provençal was not the only factor. Everyone suddenly wanted to know about premium draught lager, they wanted something genuine, and Stella was a brand in the right place at the right time. Around the world Heineken and Carlsberg are revered as brews of the highest quality, but in the UK in the 1960s and 1970s they had compromised to secure a quick entry into the British beer market. The fact that these brands came to be regarded by the British lager drinker as weak and pissy meant that even when the companies promoted the proper beers here as export-strength versions – the beers which have always been sold everywhere else in the world – they were wrongly perceived to be weak and pissy beers with added alcohol rather than the fine-quality brews they actually are. Whether you prefer the taste of Heineken, Carlsberg Export or Stella Artois, they are all perfectly acceptable, high-quality, authentic European lager beers. But Stella was the one with the reputation for quality and worth in the UK which the others could only dream of. Because of its consistency, it was seen as the most genuine brand, exactly what the new premium draught lager drinker was looking for.

Premium lager conquers the country

Writing in *Arena* magazine about the premium lager phenomenon in 1997, Nick Compton offered another reason for Stella's success. He referred to the 'creeping Hornby-isation' of traditional male pursuits. In the wake of the enormous success of *Fever Pitch* men wanted to demonstrate that they were men, with proper manly interests, while remaining thoughtful and considerate and not getting too boorish in front of the ladies. Compton argued that this was something that transcended class divisions, and had lager at its heart:

327

Just as the scaffolder and the architect can speak with one voice in support of Arsenal or Man United . . . so they can both enjoy a night with the boys, drinking Stella and watching the away matches at the local sports bar. Once-distinct class pursuits are collapsing into and on to one another, dragging each other up and down in the process.

Men had begun to successfully play different gender roles in a way that women had been doing for years, combining the strength of traditional macho man, the sensitivity of the reviled New Man, and the playfulness of the once fashionable but increasingly loathed New Lad. Premium lager allowed men to think they were as discerning and thoughtful as a real ale drinker, only with a much cooler image. As Chardonnay became linked with thirty-something girls in search of Mister Right and the Bridget Jones-clone books they read, wrote and featured in, blokes who enjoyed a glass of wine could escape for a pint without being accused of regressing. And those less enlightened blokes who thought wine was for girls could trade up a bit and still be men. At first, it happened in the affluent southeast more than anywhere else, but as the 1990s progressed, premium lager became the beer of choice across the UK.

Football nation

The football fever that accompanied the foundation of the Premier League and the subsequent 'Hornbyization' of British male culture provided a lucrative way for some non-premium lager brands to survive. As we've seen, brewers granted loans to football clubs in the early days of the game's mass appeal. By the 1970s, despite a great deal of unease on the part of the FA, sponsorship was gradually becoming the preferred financial arrangement between beer and the beautiful game. The first to take advantage of this was Watney. In the middle of their ill-fated Red Revolution, they launched the Watney's Cup for football league teams.* In the 1980s, rules regarding the sponsorship of team shirts were relaxed, and the names of beers and brewers were soon clearly visible beneath the permed mullets of the country's top players.

In the 1990s sponsorship really became part of the fabric of the game. Worthington sponsored the League Cup, Carling sponsored the Premiership, and Tennent's sponsored the Scottish Cup. What's particularly scary is that at the time these brands were all owned by the same brewer, Bass, whose Premiership sponsorship alone was costing it a million pounds a month. And it worked. In 1998, the brewer declared, 'When football succeeds, so does the brand.' Carlsberg came in to pick up what was left. In 1992 they began to sponsor Liverpool's kit, and subsequently became the 'official' beer of the FA Cup, the European Cup Winners' Cup, the UEFA Cup and the England team.† The trend was

---

* As if the brand wasn't already reviled enough, it was this tournament that introduced the penalty shoot-out to British football.
† Part of a brilliantly meaningless trend in sponsorship. What does 'official beer' mean exactly? We all have to drink it while we're watching the game? Squads of heavies will come round your house and bundle you away if you're found in front of the telly with a can of Heineken? What? My favourite example of this trend was in North America where M&Ms were the 'official snack' of the Millennium. How can you be the official snack of a date for God's sake? Does this mean that M&Ms are Jesus'

only halted when Foster's tied to sponsor the FA Cup, and a massive outcry declared that enough was enough.*

Brands such as Carling and Carlsberg should arguably have faded along with the rest of their standard-lager brothers. But with no particularly noteworthy brand-building advertising campaigns, they remained current simply by aligning themselves with football, once again reaffirming the almost mystical power of the union between beer and the game. They are like one of those cantankerous old couples who often seem to hate each other but who you simply can't imagine ever parting.

'Portfolio drinking'

Initially it might seem surprising that it was standard rather than premium lagers that dominated football sponsorship. But there is a good reason for this. Despite constantly changing our preferences, we never quite got away from our predilec-

---

favourite sweet? And since when have a bastardization of Smarties counted as a 'snack'?

* Since then, sponsorship has become far more important, and some people have started to take this 'official beer' thing way too seriously. In the 2006 World Cup in Germany, Budweiser – a beer that would be laughed at and have sand kicked in its face by any beer brewed to the *Reinheitsgebot* (the German beer purity law) – was the only beer for sale in or around the football stadia. In one infamous incident, hundreds of Dutch fans wearing orange trousers featuring the logo of a Dutch beer brand were ordered to strip and leave their trousers outside the stadium or be refused entry. Anheuser-Busch, brewers of Budweiser (and now part of AB-Inbev) labour under the corporate slogan 'making friends is our business'. You might need to think again about how to best do that, guys.

tion for drinking pints. And if you're going to stick to pints, you just can't drink premium-strength lager all night. Three pints of it and you really feel the effect, so you pace yourself and switch to something else, maybe the odd pint of standard lager or John Smith's mid-session. Previously, people had been thought of as either lager drinkers, bitter drinkers or stout drinkers. If this had ever been true, it certainly wasn't any longer. By now people didn't just drink, they *used* different drinks to control the arc of their inebriation, a process referred to by those who analyse drinking behaviour as 'portfolio drinking'.

This meant that there was still a role for standard lagers, just not quite so many of them as there used to be. The importance attached to specific brands was no longer as great as it had been – no standard lager was really going to be the ultimate in pub cool because they now existed in the shadow of premium brands. Credibility was still important, but this meant that now only the biggest and best brands were required. The early 1990s saw another round of mergers and reshuffling which resulted in the Big Six brewers retrenching into the Big Four: Scottish Courage, Bass, Whitbread and Carlsberg-Tetley. They each had more standard lagers than they needed, and many of the first wave of lager brands finally disappeared from the bar. Three or four big ones remained: Carling, Foster's, Carlsberg and Heineken, with Tennent's holding its own in Scotland. They were still promoted and people carried on drinking them when another pint of Stella would have tipped them over the edge a little earlier than they were planning, but it became rare for anyone to make them their first-choice beer.

The beer market was now dominated by ever fewer brands

and any brewer who didn't have one of these brands felt it was missing out. In their search for a slice of the market, they turned again to fads and gimmicks to try to grab the drinker's attention for two minutes

'Dry' beers made a big entrance and then mumbled vaguely about being cleaner and crisper. No one really got what the point was and they soon disappeared again. As soon as they'd gone, in came 'Ice' beers, some of which were taken down to −5 degrees C in brewing so ice crystals formed, leaving a beer that was stronger in alcohol with even less flavour than the original beer. Apart from some funny ads featuring ants, these two are now almost forgotten. Once more, despite what some real ale purist anti-lager conspiracy theorists might believe, marketing and gimmickry alone can't persuade us to drink something we don't really want – no matter how many millions are spent behind it.

Whazzup?

Portfolio drinking isn't just about alcohol content. Now that your choice of drink said so much about you, the type and format of drink you chose made at least as much difference as the brand itself. Lads who thought a pint was fine in a pub with their mates decided it looked a little uncouth in a club, as well as being impractical if you wanted to shuffle out onto the dance floor and groove the ladies. Just as there was still a role for standard lager, there were also still occasions when only premium bottles would do. But, again like standard lager, there was no longer any need for so many brands. Premium bottled lager became a much smaller market than premium draught, but it came to be dominated even more completely by one brand than draught was by Stella.

In 1857 Adolphus Busch, a German businessman, had arrived in St Louis and married the daughter of Eberhard Anheuser, a local brewer whose beer was described by *American Mercury* magazine as 'so inferior that St. Louis rowdies were known to project mouthfuls of it back over the bar'. But Busch was an amazingly talented (or absolutely ruthless, if you prefer) salesman, and the brewery prospered. In 1876 he discovered Pasteur and found a great pilsner recipe in the Czech town of Budweis, and Budweiser beer was born. Over the next century, Anheuser Busch turned it into the biggest beer brand in America, and ultimately the world.

Budweiser made several unsuccessful attempts at cracking the British market before they finally got it right. Like so many brands before, it had reached saturation point at home and saw Britain as a logical place to go. But when it first landed here Bud made several horrible mistakes. One was launching it as a lager for women. Then they launched it as a draught pint. Ever wondered why you only see Bud in bottles? Pour it out into a glass and it looks really weak and watery. It's significantly lighter than other lagers, and by comparison looks less appetizing. And then they did an ad campaign which featured a young Robson Green ripping off that scene from *Top Gun* where they all sing to the woman with the bad perm in the bar. Understandably, nobody was interested.

But Anheuser Busch were not going to just accept this and walk away. One way or another they were bloody well going to grab a slice of the UK beer market. They realized that a presence in the fridge was easier to get than a place on the bar, and decided to focus on bottles. They made sure this strategy worked, quite simply, by spending far more money on advertising and promotion than anyone else.

The advertising itself simply dripped Cool America. We'd grown tired of the glitzy, Hollywood–New York axis of Americana; Bud gave us the gritty, rootsy underbelly, the genuine America, with blues artists, trains crossing the desert and Native Americans driving cement trucks. The endline of the ads, 'The Genuine Article', said it all.*

Bud became synonymous with bottled lager and the up-for-it partying occasions on which it was drunk. It rapidly became ubiquitous, and the environment in which it was served helped. In crowded clubs and fashionable bars people drank in large groups. To keep the order simple for the poor bastard who was about to try to fight his way to the bar and get a round, people would ask for a Bud simply because they knew it would be there.

Back in the States a curious battle was going on at Anheuser Busch. The company had largely been kept in the family, and by the 1990s was being run by Augustus Busch III, known as Three Sticks by those who wanted to pretend they had his measure. Knowing the value of a good name when he had been given it, Three Sticks kept the family tradition alive by naming his own son Augustus Busch IV.†

---

* Demonstrating the value of a good thesaurus. Coca-Cola ads at the time represented the smiling, vacuous corporate face of America with ads that signed off with the line 'The Real Thing'. Clearly 'The Genuine Article' is a totally different thought to 'The Real Thing', and these two giant US corporations are not in the least bit alike.
† Who wisely decided against asking people to call him One Stick and a V and stuck with plain Augustus IV. Or Gus. Or The Fourth, maybe.

Gus IV, as I like to think of him, was the young marketing director of the company, eager to make his mark, while
Dad was the patriarch who had presided over the brand as it
had grown into the world's biggest beer. Gus IV started to
commission hot ad agencies on the West Coast to make the
brand feel cool and contemporary. Three Sticks wasn't interested in cool. He felt the main messages that people needed
to hear were about the quality of the barley and the smoking
of it over beech wood. He ignored his son and commissioned
advertising of his own that featured fields of barley and
Chesterfield horses. Indignant Gus IV was still marketing
director though and still had a budget, so he decided to teach
his dad a lesson and bought some really weird ads featuring
talking ants, talking frogs and, subsequently, talking lizards
moaning about how the talentless frogs were getting all the
limelight. Everyone close to Three Sticks thought the ads
were rubbish. Then the ads became world famous. They were
so successful the only problem was how to follow them. Luck
was with the ad agency, who saw a short film of some cool
urban black dudes shouting 'Whazzuuuuuuuuuuuuuup' at
each other. The agency asked the guys if they would like a lot
of money in return for letting their idea be adapted into a
Bud ad, and the next campaign, even more successful than
the frogs, was in the bag.

When they hit the UK, the campaigns became the most
talked-about advertising of their time. People aged from
three to eighty-three said they were their favourite ads, and
commercials briefly regained their place as the source of the
playground catchphrase of the day. But neither campaign was
sustainable. They burned brightly and briefly before people
tired of them, and didn't really seem to help sales of Bud,

which had started to go into a gentle decline. Having said that, the whole bottled market was now in decline, and Bud's sales were falling much slower than the rest. As a result, with millions of pounds behind them, the ads consolidated Bud's position as the runaway leader in bottled lager.

And then . . . things started to go wrong.

The gradual shift from pubs to home drinking meant that supermarkets increasingly became the battleground where brand loyalty was won and lost. And the brands concerned started to fight this battle with entirely the wrong weapons.

Years of successful brand marketing meant that while blokes may have had one *preferred* brand, they had a set of four or five leading brands that were perfectly trusted and acceptable if their favourite wasn't available. In pubs, this meant that if you went up to a bar that stocked Carling and you were a Foster's drinker, or Kronenbourg and you were a Stella drinker, you'd give a slight shrug and order what was there rather than storming out and going down the road to the next pub.

In supermarkets this 'acceptable choice' mentality had a profound effect. Incredibly, in an age when sexual equality is by and large a simple reality, women still do most of the weekly shop (just as men still change fuses and light bulbs). A woman knows her partner will be happy enough with any leading brand, so she simply looks for the 20-can slab that has the best price promotional deal on it. Supermarkets use beer as a 'footfall driver' – it's heavy in bulk, and shoppers are driving. People might switch between supermarkets based on the deals advertised, but they know they're going to buy beer before they go in. This is why beer is always at the back of the store, so you have to walk past everything else before you get to it and always come out with a much fuller basket than you had intended. It's also why the average browsing time in the beer aisle fell lower than that of any other part of the store – supermarket category managers came to feel that even dog food was a more interesting bit to work in. The supermarkets that offered the best deals on beer got the highest traffic, and the price cuts on beer became more aggressive, to the point where at peak times such as Christmas, beer could cost less per litre than mineral water.

The beer marketers themselves didn't help. On the pricing issue they had little choice – if they didn't agree to steep price cuts they knew they'd be delisted in favour of their bitter rivals. But brewers reacted to the new importance of supermarkets by hiring marketers who knew or cared little about beer, but knew a lot about selling 'fast moving consumer goods' (FMCG) such as washing powder and confectionery. They began to treat beer as little different, ignoring the unique bond drinkers felt for their favourite brands and for beer generally. They were hardly helped by ever-tightening restrictions on ads, but they began to look for differentiating product attributes instead of emotional connections with beery blokes and great gags, invented them where they found none, and began to appeal to the brain rather than the heart. 'Insight mining teams'* spent tens of thousands of pounds and came back with the earth-shattering news that lager drinkers liked their beer cold, so brewers duly spent thousands installing new equipment in pubs so we could drink 'extra cold' beers – a meaningless concept by the time

---

* I can't for the life of me now remember why I was so desperate to get out of advertising.

the beer had been poured into a hot glass straight from the washer in a busy pub. Or they did research that showed people thought lager was gassy,* and offered us smaller bubbles in our beer for a smoother texture.

In 2007, the newly appointed president of one of Britain's largest brewing corporations declared that his organization was not a brewer, but an FMCG marketer that happened to sell beer. Employees who actually cared about beer and what it stood for found they no longer fitted in, and faced the choice of jumping ship or waiting to be pushed out with a decent severance package.

Shorn of its trendy image, mainstream lager itself was revealed as quite a boring drink. It was still an important part of relaxing on the sofa in front of the telly or meeting up with your mates before the match, but increasingly blokes were just as happy to switch to wine with meals or in mixed company, because it had a more sophisticated image.† Even cider – drunk by generations of teenagers on park benches before they graduated onto other drinks, and by tramps on park benches when they moved back down into a similarly undiscerning state – began to look much more interesting in comparison to lager.

Throughout the noughties, lager sales endured a steep

---

* I know – beer marketing researchers will be discovering the cure for cancer and cracking the Middle East peace process if they carry on like this.

† This image was arguably undeserved. When a bottle of Pinot Grigio is chosen for its light, easy drinking character, bought from the supermarket on the basis of a price deal and drunk so cold that what little flavour is present is masked by the temperature, it's only really the alcohol content that makes it any different from Carling.

decline. And the biggest loser was the once unbeatable Stella Artois.

At the dawn of the new millennium Stella was in double-digit growth and was having its cake, eating it, and keeping the money it bought the cake with into the bargain. It was seen as a discerning, individualistic choice by millions of drinkers, each of whom thought they were being classier than the other millions around them who were drinking exactly the same thing. It walked a brilliant tightrope between ubiquity and specialness. And then it fell off, headfirst, into a particularly deep and smelly pool of ubiquity.

The brand's owners, Interbrew, went on a global buying spree and became Inbev, a massive brewing conglomerate that was desperate for cash and thought this would be an excellent time to start cutting costs on the brand. The recipe was cut with maize, a cheaper grain than barley, which produces less flavour, and what had once been seen as a challenging, full-flavoured beer became strong but bland. By 2008, this 'quality' lager had either watered down or completely thrown out every single one of the product or process points discussed in a beautifully written 1980s press ad about what made it so special. The ABV was reduced. The beautiful embossed can was replaced by a bog-standard can. The supermarket bottle quietly shrunk in size. And the supermarket price war became frenzied. Inbev would later protest that other brands were price cutting way more than Stella did, which was true – but not one of those other brands had built their popularity on the back of a long-running 'Reassuringly Expensive' message.

Stella's higher alcohol strength, coupled with its ubiquity, started to earn it the unpleasant nickname 'wifebeater', and it became seen as the drink of choice by people who thought wearing as much Burberry tartan as possible was a really good idea. Double-digit growth promptly flipped into equally dizzying decline. New variants were launched and quickly withdrawn. The advertising stopped being subtle and rewarding in favour of simple and browbeating. In a final attempt to shake Stella's headbanging image, Inbev launched a 4 per cent version – a curious move given that they had also just launched a 4 per cent version of Becks (which by now had, bizarrely, more flavour than the full 5 per cent Stella) and used the success of the lower strength version to mask the continuing decline of its once-great parent. At the time of writing, Stella's owners have announced brewery closures and swingeing job cuts, claiming no one is drinking beer any more.

Stella is still market leader in premium lager, but where lager itself had once seemed cool and stylish, it increasingly became dull, bland and commoditised.

Pure genius: the sequel

But even now, decades after we were finally persuaded to drink the amber nectar that makes up 95 per cent of global beer sales, the story of British beer – and great beer brands – isn't just about lager. Back on the bar top, there is one font that we have hardly yet touched on, a beer that is virtually ubiquitous. It wasn't just lager that benefited from selling a country to push sales in the 1980s and 90s. The brand that used provenance to best effect, the brand that stood head and shoulders even above Stella Artois in terms of the regard in which it is held, was Guinness.

Since Arthur Guinness first started brewing in Dublin in 1759, the beer he created has been one of the world's most powerful and enduring drinks brands. It has propagated a romantic image of Irishness and the Irish drinking experience that, in the 1990s, became a whole market in itself. Irish drinking is synonymous with stout, and Ireland is the only country in the world where stout is the most popular type of beer. Guinness *is* Ireland. Not bad for a beer that started off as an idea nicked from the big London brewers.

As television took off, Guinness followed the rest of the big brands into broadcast advertising. Some of the ads look embarrassing now, but in their time they were always innovative. From 'Friends of the Guinnless' in the 1970s, through Rutger Hauer talking bollocks in the late 80s and early 90s, to the late 90s 'Surfer' ad (voted by Channel Four viewers the best ad for any product of all time) to 2009's ad showing Guinness drinkers becoming cheeky, affable gods creating a whole new planet, Guinness has always been one step ahead of the competition. But curiously Guinness's appeal remained firmly rooted in its Irishness. Although the ads rarely mentioned Ireland, the brand itself is tied up with Gaelic romance.

Like Stella Artois, in the early 1990s Guinness was a brand in the right place at the right time. As the Provençal fad faded, we looked for somewhere else romantic, and fell seriously in love with Ireland. And so we suffered *Riverdance* and the inexplicable success of the Corrs, and a thick Irish vein running through every sentimental product oozing out of Hollywood. Fake Irish pubs colonized not only the UK, but the entire planet. You went on holiday specifically to get a drink somewhere, anywhere other than your local

O'Neill's, and there they were: Van Morrison on the jukebox in the heart of the jungle, Guinness on tap in the middle of the desert.*

In this context Guinness was a brand *idolized* by beer drinkers; the only problem was, many of these drinkers didn't actually like the taste of it. Market research revealed that more people claimed to drink Guinness than any other brand. But the sales figures said that couldn't be true – it wasn't selling nearly as much as the leading lager brands. If we had been drinking as much Guinness as we claimed, the streets would have been running with a reddy-black deluge that would make the Meux brewery tragedy look like a little bit of beer that got spilled on the way back from the bar. This was provenance and branding gone insane. We liked the brand image so much, we 'bought' the brand without actually buying the beer itself.

The Irish fad got so huge that eventually the big brewers actually spotted it. Bass realized that people liked Ireland but didn't like stout, and launched Caffrey's bitter on St Patrick's Day 1994. Initially it looked like they were going to walk away with the entire beer market as a result. They might have done, if only they'd spent a little bit more time thinking about the product.

The Caffrey's strategy was brilliant. They took a mundane, failing bitter, pumped it with nitrogen to make it creamy and swirly, and served it chilled, combining the smoothness and stillness of Guinness with the more palatable flavour of bitter and the cool bite of lager. The ads showed people in hip, trendy New York bars ordering a Caffrey's while making

---

* OK, I'm exaggerating to make a point. Or am I?

meaningful, possibly homoerotic eye contact with each other, then being magically transported back to the Ireland of green rolling hills and wild horses running through the streets, the Ireland of Enya and Hollywood.

People loved it. Everybody who drank beer went out and spent a thoroughly enjoyable night getting riotously hoonered on Caffrey's, telling each other what an absolute *craic* the whole thing was, to be sure. The trouble was, all but the most hardy or masochistic of drinkers only did it once. The combination of its smooth, easy-drinking taste, 5 per cent ABV and all that nitrogen meant that the Caffrey's hangover was one of the worst comedowns this side of heroin. People still loved the beer, but would only ever drink one or maybe two pints of it in a session, which immediately limited the volume that could be sold to a level far below Bass's expectations. By the time they figured out what was wrong and reformulated the beer to a lower ABV, the Irish fad had faded.

Guinness remains. Like Stella, Guinness outlived the fad for its mythical homeland.* Guinness is a slow, smooth beer, from a sleepy, slow-moving country, and has to be drunk on slow, mellow drinking occasions. Oh yes, and on St Patrick's Day. Even though the complete infatuation with Irishness eventually left us, this important festival has remained. Every March the English celebrate St Patrick's Day with far more gusto than they do St Georges's Day a month later.

---

* I hope this doesn't sound too cynical about the whole Irish drinking experience. Most of this chapter was written before I'd actually been to Ireland and sampled the Guinness there. If my opinion counts for anything, I'd just like to add my voice to the chorus that maintains that Guinness in Ireland tastes different to Guinness over here.

Each year's celebrations are bigger than the last. Paddy's Day is the biggest pub event of the yearly calendar, and sales almost double as tens of thousands of drinkers switch from lager to the dark stuff. The black pint with the white head has become an icon, inextricably bound up with St Patrick's Day. The occasion and the brand feed off each other, and in doing so have transformed our drinking calendar.

From Mega to Micro

In the first decade of the twenty-first century the brewing industry finally went global.

Beer isn't like other consumer products. While almost any brand choice says something about us as individuals, beer does so even more. And because we drink it when we're being sociable, it can also say something about what kind of group we are. And if it does that, it can ultimately be a badge of recognition for us as a nation. When Americans drink Bud, Belgians drink Jupiler, Aussies drink VB and Brits drink Carling. While brands like Heineken and Guinness are sold around the world, there's still no beery equivalent of Coca Cola or McDonald's – a leading brand that's recognized and thought of in similar terms wherever you go.

In the decade of globalization, the world's largest brewers gave up trying to get people in other countries to like their beers more than their national brew, and simply bought up the local favourites instead. The pace of mergers and acquisitions was dizzying and, by the end of it, Britain's brewers had been through a transformation that would have left even

Eddie Taylor scratching his head and making indignant puffing noises.

By the close of the noughties the former Big Six had become the Big Four. Interbrew bought Whitbread, shortly before it merged with South American giant Ambev to become Inbev, and then merged with arch-rival Anheuser Busch to create AB-Inbev, the largest brewer in the world, owners of both Stella and Budweiser. American brewer Coors came in and bought most of Bass' brewing interests, after Interbrew was prevented from doing so by the government. They later merged with Canada's largest brewer to become MolsonCoors, bringing Carling's prodigal odyssey full circle. The corporation once known as Allied breweries dropped the 'Tetley' from its name to become simply Carlsberg UK. Globally, Carlsberg and Heineken carved up Scottish & Newcastle between them with Heineken taking the UK operation, acquiring Kronenbourg, John Smith's and Foster's. And somewhere a little below the radar of the Big Four (from an English if not an international perspective) South African Breweries bought America's Miller corporation, and as SAB-Miller quietly started building up a nice UK business with brands such as Peroni and Pilsner Urquell.

These five global brewing corporations hold 80 per cent of the British beer market between them, and not one of them is British-owned. Almost our entire brewing industry fell into foreign hands. In a sense, it was the logical conclusion of our love affair with beers from other countries. But it raised questions as to how well these corporations understood the British drinker and catered for their needs. The continued commoditization of mainstream lager was actively accelerated by global companies who wanted the world to look neat and tidy, and premium lager sales collapsed, falling quicker than almost any other beer style in the latter half of the decade.

But people didn't stop drinking beer. And they didn't stop looking for a beer that felt special. Stella's voluminous carcass was nibbled at by scores of smaller brands surfing a second wave of novel 'global' beer brands from somewhere we hadn't had beer from before. Budvar and Baltika, Staropramen and San Miguel, Paulaner and Peroni – from Asahi to Zywiec, novel brands got away with charging 40p more than the usual pint. In some cases, after that novelty wore off we realized the beer was actually pretty poor compared to old standards like Kronenbourg. But others, particularly those that were genuinely imported from their claimed country of origin, rather than brewed in a shed just off the M4, showed that lager could still brush up well. Heineken took the brave – some might say incredibly stupid – step of finally ditching its weak, cooking lager British bastard offspring, killing dead Britain's fourth biggest beer brand. It relaunched as a genuinely imported full strength beer from Holland which eventually – after years of effort and millions of pounds – became seen as the premium beer it always wanted to be.

Increasingly though, British beer fans decided there was more to life than lager. Drinkers in their late twenties who had once considered Stella to be challenging and sophisticated now looked at lager and the occasional pint of Guinness and asked 'Is that it? Is that really all beer has to offer?' And they realized there was so much more. In the late nineties a pale, cloudy beer served in a chunky glass bucket, sometimes with a wedge of lemon, began appearing in the kind of pubs that eschewed swirly carpet in favour of pine floorboards. Hoegaarden, a Belgian wheat beer, created a new 'speciality beer' segment of the market. Leffe, a sweet, blonde Abbey ale, and fruit beers such as Liefmanns Kriek, brewed with cherries, paved the way for a controlled explosion of eccentric Belgian beer styles in the UK. Boutique beer bars and speciality shops catered to the needs of a growing band of beery explorers. Import wholesalers seized the potential of the Internet and began offering mail order mixed cases to connoisseurs and foodies who realized that beer needn't be an exception in a world where ciabatta and focaccia now competed with white sliced, the artisanal cheeseboard replaced Kraft cheese singles in the fridge and people started to talk about how well hung their beef was.

And finally, in this climate of culinary exploration and appreciation, cask ale got the reappraisal it so richly deserved. As mainstay brands like John Smiths, Tetley's and Boddington's had their advertising budgets quietly pulled and their Smoothflow beer made ever colder and blander by their lager-loving global brewing conglomerate owners, the much trumpeted terminal decline of ale revealed itself to be nothing of the sort. The decline of papery, characterless ale was one thing. But a flood of new beers swept into the bar to take their place. Regional brewers such as Marston's and Greene King indulged in a little merger and acquisition activity of their own and became sizeable brewers with national reach and a couple of thousand pubs in which to stock their cask ales. After recognizing that they could never compete with their bigger rivals' multi-million pound marketing budgets they stocked the lager brands of the multinationals, but first and foremost each of these 'super-regionals' was an ale brewer. Brands like Marston's Pedigree, Fuller's London Pride, Bombardier and Greene King IPA signed sponsorship deals with rugby and cricket, and even dipped a toe into TV advertising. As the dominant smoothflow brands fell silent and withdrew, even though real ale was still smaller in volume its distinctive tall handpumps gradually came to symbolize what ale was all about, and ale finally began to appeal to people as a contemporary, credible beer style.

And at the same time, there was the microbrew revolution.

In 2002, Chancellor Gordon Brown introduced Progressive Beer Duty (PBD) to the British brewing industry. As the headline rate of beer duty continued to increase well above the rate of inflation, PBD meant anyone brewing les than 30,000 barrels of beer per year paid a lower rate of duty on that beer. Brew less than 10,000, and you paid even less. Less than 5,000, and you paid less still. This meant someone brewing homebrew in his garage could potentially supply beer to his local pub at a lower price than big rivals benefitting from economies of scale.

The result was immediate: everywhere you looked, waves of small new breweries declared themselves open for business. Some of them were hobbyists who brewed absolutely dreadful beer, and used PBD to turn their hobby into a frankly unjustifiable career. Others inspired fury in the established regional and traditional family brewers by using all the benefit of PBD to sell their beer at rock-bottom prices to pubs who then stuck scribbled beer mat labels onto the front of handpumps supplied and maintained by the bigger breweries, inspiring wars of words between 'parasites' and new 'big corporates'.

But many micros use PBD to brew wonderful beer. Some small breweries that had struggled for years to get by used the duty savings to invest in new equipment, hire salesmen and marketers. Others combined amateur enthusiasm with natural talent and began to push ale in new directions. As we've seen, ale brings with it a reverence for tradition, and looks back to how things have always been done. But this new wave combined a reverence for tradition with a willingness to experiment. Old, extinct styles such as porter, Mild and traditional full-strength IPA began to reappear. American hops with fuller, more pungent citrus aromas spiced up fresh golden and pale ales that offered a new alternative to the bored lager drinker who wasn't quite ready for something thick and chewy.

And brewers such as Dark Star, Thornbridge and Otley simply tore up the rulebook and began creating new beer styles, learning and often collaborating with craft beer brewers in other countries, borrowing techniques, styles and ingredients from Belgium, Germany or the USA, and experimenting with new techniques such as ageing beer in whisky casks. In 2007, one of the founder brewers from Thornbridge left to set up Brew Dog with a pal from his native Fraserburgh in Scotland. Within two years they became the only brewer whose every action was reported by the national press and, more importantly, could be named by my mum, thanks to an irreverent and often ill-advised PR campaign promoting beers that were sometimes dreadful but most often stunning. Zephyr was a 13 per cent IPA aged for a year in whisky barrels on a bed of strawberries and made the very notion of dessert wine irrelevant. The notorious Tokyo claimed on its label to be a meditation on 'the irony of existentialism, the parody of being and the inherent contradictions of post-modernism' which was 'inspired by a 1980s space invaders arcade game played in Japan's capital'. In fact it was an 18.2 per cent Imperial Stout brewed with cranberries and jasmine and aged in oak barrels. Whether you wanted to explore the outer limits with Brew Dog, or simply relax with a quenching blonde beer like Wye Valley's HPA, ale started to appear in new places and look far more interesting than it ever had. By the end of 2009, there were more breweries in Britain than at any time since the Second World War.

This was all given added impetus by a new wave of beer enthusiasts with a beer glass in one hand and a laptop or iPhone in the other. They didn't just want to drink exciting beer, they wanted to tell everyone else just how exciting it was. In Wikio's rankings of UK beer and wine blogs, about sixteen of the top twenty are about beer rather than wine. With every quality newspaper in Britain carrying at least one wine column a week and not a single one carrying regular beer coverage, British craft brewing claimed blogs and social networking sites as its own. It's notable that Brew Dog achieved notoriety without ever running a traditional ad campaign – before the inevitable backlash towards the end of 2009, their online fans spread the word about their beers with missionary zeal.

In the final month of the first decade of the twenty-first century, premium lager showed an annual sales decline of about 7 per cent. Over the same period, cask ale showed an annual volume of growth of 0.04 per cent. That may be about as small as small can get, but growth is growth – the first for 25 years.

British beer has moved beyond the age of mass marketing

that defined it in the final third of the twentieth century. The big, generic lager brands brewed by multinational companies, often marketed by people who don't even *like* beer, will continue to dominate thanks to their corporate might and economies of scale as well as the fact that most beer drinkers are happy with something cold, refreshing and mildly intoxicating. But as we grow increasingly weary and cynical of the age of big branding, those brands no longer define us in the way they once did. The beer advert is no longer the shop window for the creative ad agency. In our new century we rate substance over style, and people who are passionate about beer have an unprecedented range before them: more imports from exciting brewing nations like Belgium and the USA, coupled with a British brewing industry in which small is often very beautiful, an industry that is rediscovering confidence in beer styles that are justly revered around the world and – finally – in their country of origin.

It's a great time to be alive and drinking beer.

Chapter Thirteen

'It was like anywhere and nowhere'

The local goes national

The 'death' of the English pub

If there is one thing that can get serious beer enthusiasts foaming at the beard as much as the scandal of What They've Done to Our Beer, it's the absolute bloody outrage of What the *BASTARDS* Have Done to Our Pubs. Pubs, it seems, are in a terrible state, and it's not as if we haven't been warned. As early as 1912, Hilaire Belloc in his essay *On Inns* warned:

> From the towns all inns have been driven; from the villages most . . . Change your hearts or you will lose your inns and you will deserve to have lost them. But when you have lost your inns drown your empty selves for you will have lost the last of England.

Thus forewarned, CAMRA and beer lovers everywhere have been fighting against such a thing coming to pass, but just as beer was being assaulted, so the prognosis for the English pub started to look bleak. In his 1978 book *Pulling A Fast*

One, Roger Protz was as eloquent and passionate on the subject of pubs as we know him to be on beer itself:

> Trendy young architects are ... ruthlessly engaged in the business of 'modernisation'. The regular users of street-corner locals find to their horror that their pub has been re-designed as a large pineapple, a sputnik or a Wild West saloon to attract the gin-and-tonic and lager-and-lime trade. Public bars are ripped out and replaced by lounges* with soft lights,† soft carpets,‡ wet-look mock leather§ – and several pennies on the price of a pint.

But back then he hadn't seen the half of it. Because just as what we drink has undergone fundamental change, so has the nature of the places we drink it. And the biggest symbol of this change, the phenomenon that goes hand it hand with cheap lager as the antithesis of everything CAMRA hold dear, is the theme pub.

When is a pub not a pub?

The grumbling over theme pubs is the continuation of an argument that began with the campaign for the Improved Public House in the 1920s and 30s. Faced with temperance pressure on the one hand and falling demand on the other, the brewers felt something had to change, and built fewer, larger pubs with better facilities. Some of these were hideous

---

* No!
† Never!
‡ The horror! The horror!!
§ OK, so he might have a point.

and excessive, and lived short lives. Others thrived and are now regarded as classic pubs. But at the time the whole movement was derided, and seemingly sensible initiatives such as bar food and comfortable seating were lumped in with miniature golf courses and Shakespearean plays as an abomination against the idea of the pub. Many beer historians look back on the whole thing scathingly, while other beer enthusiasts are passionate about some of the pubs born in that period.

After the Second World War there was a gradual, inevitable shift in the attitudes of the big brewers, and (eventually, as we have seen) they started to think of themselves as property owners. As building materials became less scarce and rationing eased, a great programme of rebuilding got under way. Much of this rebuilding took the form of 'special treatment' or 'theme' houses. The first of these was Whitbread's Nag's Head, which opened in Covent Garden in 1948. It was swiftly followed by many others. According to an official history of Whitbread, the idea was to theme the decoration of the pub around the life, entertainment, work, sport or history of the local area, using collections of prints, trophies or other forms of decoration.

Many so-called traditional pubs date back to this period, and in their day they were just as much theme pubs as the most garish marketing efforts of today. Remember that at one time pubs were simple utilitarian drink shops with a bar, beer pumps and, if you were lucky, somewhere to sit. As soon as a pub was decorated in anything other than a style reflective of current local design, effectively you had a theme pub. If you buy this, it means that today a 'heritage' pub, such as an authentically preserved sixteenth-century tavern in Wiltshire or a lovingly restored Victorian gin palace in the centre of London, is actually a theme pub. The theme may have direct relevance to the heritage of the public house, but it is a theme nonetheless.

So if the principle of theming pubs is not the problem, the issue really is over what makes an appropriate theme or style for a pub. It is a debate that seems to have intensified recently. One reason for this is that the themes being chosen for pubs have changed, and the palette of what is deemed acceptable by pub owners has stretched quite far from the traditional oak beams and horse brass template so beloved of tourists. Although you'd probably be hard pressed to find a sputnik or a pineapple supplanting your local boozer, we're all familiar with concepts based around exotic locales, sport, music, film or entertainment. And where you find these concepts, you also find fans of the traditional pub bitterly opposing them.

Beer writer Barrie Pepper got himself tied up in the theme pub conundrum in a 1998 newspaper article:

> At one time names like the New Inn, Royal Oak, Commercial and Bay Horse were the most popular in Yorkshire but now such weirdoes as Scruffy Murphy's, Tap and Spile and Hogshead are rapidly taking over ... That is not to say there are not still some very good pubs around ... In Leeds the Adelphi at Leeds Bridge and the Garden Gate in Hunslet remain fine examples of turn of the century pubs with tiles, glass and woodwork all preserved or carefully restored ... Others have followed. In Knaresbrough's Market Place, Blind Jack's is a medieval recreation out of an ancient chemist shop. It won a

national architectural award and the judges expressed surprised delight that this pub was less than two years old.

I'm sure Barrie's favourites are really nice pubs that serve excellent beer but it seems strange that a pub themed around the Irish drinking experience (Scruffy Murphy's) is less acceptable than a pub themed around the Victorian drinking experience (the Garden Gate). One may well be executed better than the other, or be run by people who care more, but as *ideas* for pubs they have equal merit and are both themes. And it seems ironic, when the whole idea of theme pubs is derided, to then say that a brand new pub built from a medieval chemist's shop is somehow exempt. In some circles, theme pubs are an irredeemably bad thing unless, of course, the theme is one they like.

Arguments like these aside, the search for the best pub theme continues apace. This search has now, inevitably, come full circle. In the trendiest parts of London, the latest theme that pubs have adopted is: the pub. It's difficult to explain if you haven't seen one, but try this as an analogy. I still have a definite northern accent despite the fact that I'm now trying to pass myself off as a posh southerner. Real posh southerners often mimic my accent, usually delivering a badly mangled imitation which sounds more like a Mancunian suffering constipation than my manly Yorkshire brogue. Oh, how we laugh. If I go home to Barnsley my accent gets stronger, and sometimes if I get drunk it gets stronger (and louder) no matter where I am. But sometimes when I get drunk, rather than simply reverting to my native accent, I fall in with everyone else and start doing a bad impression of the bad impressions that the drunken southerners are doing of me. So even though I really do have a Yorkshire accent, I find myself speaking in a bad imitation of one. Still with me? Well that's what the latest theme pubs are like. Rather than simply being pubs, they act like something else pretending to be a pub. It's like they've seen pictures of pubs but forgotten what they are supposed to feel like. Bars are filled with bulk-bought Victorian junk, with no understanding of why it's actually there and no serious attempt to create the atmosphere of how these pubs used to be.

A few years ago I appeared on a BBC TV programme on the history of the pub. One of my fellow contributors was a builder who had been employed by pub chains in the 1970s to rip out the Victorian interiors from pubs being modernized. He was told to just throw all the mirrors, vintage beer ads and ornately carved wooden shelves and snug partitions into the skip. Instead he rented warehouse space to preserve them. Since then, he has made his fortune selling this irreplaceable treasure back to the same pubs he ripped it out of.

The heart of the community?

This lack of decisiveness about whether we want our English pubs to look like French bistros, American sports bars, medieval apothecaries, early eighties Wham! videos or, God forbid, English pubs mirrors our broader concerns about image in a world that has accelerated and interconnected to a point where we have access to an infinite amount of imagery and associations from any point in history and any place in the world, and we have trouble fitting it all together.

Pubs are a reflection of the community they serve. While some mourn the passing of the 'community pub', the truth is it's simply changed its colours. When I first wrote this book, I believed that communities of interest – sports fans going to sports bars, real ale fans going to real ale pubs, randy twenty year-olds going to Walkabout and shouty old men going to Wetherspoons – were the new community pubs, and that this was fine. I still think this holds, but the community pub as it always was is still going strong, and I now recognize that it tends to be a bit more pleasant all round than any of the above examples because it makes an effort to cater to everyone. My local, the White Hart in Stoke Newington, is great for families on Sunday lunchtimes thanks to its decent Sunday lunches and well-kept ales, ideal for freelancers during the day with its coffee and free wi-fi, and perfect for Stokie's trendies on a Friday night with its bottled lagers and DJ spinning the decks in the corner.* The nature of our communities has changed, so the nature of the pub has changed. But whichever way you look at it, the pub is still at the centre of our communities – all the communities we each belong to.

We've already talked about how the public house is a curious combination of the security of the home and the excitement and freedom of being out. There's a tension in this, and different pubs sit at different points on the scale between excitement and security. If you think about what a

---

* Or twiddling with his iPod. I don't know. I don't go in on Friday nights – it's too loud for the dog.

pub actually is and the role it performs, there's a wide range of styles theoretically suitable. Bearing this in mind, it's worth going on a brief pub crawl around the different haunts available to the contemporary beer drinker.

The traditional community boozer is usually found off the main road. It's quiet. These days it may even proudly advertise the fact that it has no jukebox or gaming machines or plasma screen. It will have a lot of features that remind you of home, but the colours will be a little bolder, the space a bit more open. It's the homeliest of pubs. The drinkers will probably be older on balance, but the important thing about the community boozer is it's just that: a place for the local community. And despite all the changes that have taken place, these pubs are still common. Down most back streets and in many small villages, away from the glitz of the town centre, many pubs are essentially the same as they have been.

But nowadays there's an increasing chance that the traditional pub has been turned into a gastropub. It may be styled very differently from the traditional community pub, with stripped floorboards, oddly matched furniture and white plates the size of car wheels, but it's still all about the same thing: a place to relax, chill out and spend time with your friends. It's merely catering for a different audience. Functionally, the gastropub is still a community pub, reflecting the community of which it is a part. It's the local if you live in Islington or Leith rather than Barnsley or Abergavenny. The sofas, Sunday papers and chalkboards pushing organic burgers are arguably far more appropriate here than horse brasses and pictures of fox hunts.

Increasingly, as this new style of food-led pub becomes more established and settled in, there's a scale between the two, and a 'gastropub' can be a very traditional-looking pub that specializes in food. Whereas the first wave of gastropubs eschewed beer and pubbiness for wine and a continental feel, many discerning food-led pubs are now increasingly stocking a great range of world lagers, speciality beers and cask ales. The term 'gastropub' will always evoke reactions from an embarrassed wince to a raging boil, but there's nothing intrinsically wrong with a pub deciding great meals and a decent wine selection rather than twelve real ales and a pickled egg, or a full variety of flavours of WKD and some posh crisps (that no one, if their honest, really likes as much as Seabrooks) is the way to stay in business in a tough economic climate.

Then there's the pub with the big screens for the footie. Beer's sponsorship of sport is huge, and with good reason. Many of us may not know our neighbours' names any more, but we all go down to the pub when the big match is on. As old ideas of community increasingly fragment, we go for these unifying events with greater gusto. Each time the World Cup or the European Championships come around more of us watch them. And even though many of us now have satellite and cable access, we still choose to go and watch it on the big telly in the pub. It's not even necessarily about having a pint with the game.* In 2002 when the World Cup games were broadcast in the morning, UK time, pubs opened early. Although the opportunity was there to celebrate our glorious 0–0 draw against Nigeria with a few snifters, most people drank tea, coffee or orange juice with their bacon rolls

---

* Although let's be honest, you'll probably have a couple, just to keep up appearances.

instead. The important thing was to be able to watch it in the pub, not to get drunk. These are the events that draw us together. In this way, the pub becomes the focal point of the new, more loosely knit community.

Moving along, out on the high street and towards the other end of the continuum between home and out, there are the town centre 'circuit pubs', so called because we follow a route between them having one drink in each before always moving on to the next, in search of something. These pubs, or bars, have fewer home-like features, and are the most likely to have novel themes to keep young people interested. They try to create a party atmosphere in order to get onto the circuit and, once they've got people in, to make them stay as long as they carry on spending money. Promotions and happy hours are commonplace. These pubs make the most money, but only as long as they stay at the forefront of what's exciting and new. Consequently they are redecorated and revamped more than any other kind of pub, and reflect most directly the fashions of the day. Because they are so much more wrapped up in short-term trends, these are the pubs that can quite often get it badly wrong. They parallel fashion itself: the more you try to stand out and be different, the bigger the risk you're going to get it completely wrong and look like a twat. When a theme is stylish and resonates with the times, we flock to it. When a designer gets a theme hopelessly wrong, it dies a quick and costly death. We've all seen them, the poorly thought-out 'fun pubs' with their garish colour schemes, cheesily named cocktails, and overall ambience that reminds you for some reason of 1980s chart-toppers Black Lace. We maybe visit once, by mistake, but then we hurry past in embarrassed silence as they put on happy hours and party nights in increasingly desperate bids for our custom, until one morning the windows are white-washed once again.

Looking at pubs this way, it is entirely reasonable for a sleepy community pub to look traditional, and it is equally legitimate for an urban high street bar to look stylish and modern. Things only go wrong when pub operators don't know which market they're in. The most common mistake they make is to go for the modern style bar when they shouldn't. It's like people. Someone in their fifties or sixties can look very cool – think of Sean Connery or Robert de Niro – but if they dress like a teenager and go clubbing they're going to look dreadfully sad. So it often is with pub refurbishments.

Here's an example from my own experience. The Talbot in Mapplewell, the village outside Barnsley where I grew up, was a lovely mock-Tudor pub* that served a great pint of cask John Smith's. Lots of us young blades went there for a few pints on a Friday night, and again on Wednesdays for the quiz, when the top prize was, of course, a mixed grill.† In five years of going to that bloody pub quiz we never won it, and Anthony Andy (his real name) won himself no friends when he defected from our team to join the swotty couple who usually did. But I digress. On Saturdays we'd go into

---

* Yes, yes, I know that 'lovely' and 'mock Tudor' don't sit well together in the same sentence, but that was the magic of the Talbot: it managed to be both. Or maybe at seventeen I just didn't know any better.
† I don't know why, it's just one of those things; the same way that it has become 'traditional' for London pubs to serve decent Thai food over the last fifteen years, so a Yorkshire pub really can't hold its head up in public if it doesn't have a pub quiz where the top prize is a mixed grill.

town to the busy circuit pubs, quite reasonably expecting to pull women, and believing that our ability to do so would be enhanced by putting 'Black Betty' on the jukebox on constant repeat and standing by the soundsystem speakers in a big, nodding, mullet-headed group, drinking Castlemaine XXXX. Anyway, in an attempt to get our custom on Saturdays as well as Fridays, the landlord of the Talbot decided he needed to jazz the place up a bit, so he painted the walls pink and the oak beams a darker shade – I suppose you'd call it mauve – and turned the music up. He'd completely missed the point. Of course he pissed off the older regulars, who probably blamed this vandalism on us young 'uns, but we didn't like it either. We went to the Talbot when we wanted a quiet drink, and we went into town when we wanted to pull.*

Within the spectrum that ranges between community pubs and circuit pubs there are many variations, all of them direct reflections of the people who drink in them. There's the housing estate pub, which looks so rough from the outside that you'd never dream of going in if you happened to find yourself passing by, but which on the inside is the beating heart of its community, a place probably closer to the old ale house than any other modern pub, where business is transacted, meetings are held, karaoke is taken very seriously, and everyone really does know your name – or if they don't, you shouldn't be there. There's the family pub, recognizable because it probably has an area called something like 'Wacky Warehouse' or 'Charlie Funston's Funny Big House of Fun', complete with a special kids' menu, lots of stuff made out of

---

* As far as I am aware, no one has *ever* pulled in the Talbot. Not even if they won the mixed grill.

lurid plastic and, if you're lucky, a bloke in a clown costume that could probably do with a wash. And although changes in our economy are killing it off, there are still many places where you can find the working men's club, still ploughing its own furrow, immortalized by Peter Kay's *Phoenix Nights*.*

Then there's the nice country pub. In many rural parts of the country restaurants are almost nonexistent, because there's no way they could compete with the classy pub in which people book tables and drive to for a nice meal. The food may be traditional,† but if you fancy a steak, a pie or a nice piece of gammon, there really isn't much point going anywhere else.

When we walk into a place we take in all the cues straight away. Are there locals sitting at the bar? Carpets or bare floorboards? Music or not? Are there hand pumps on the bar? And we choose different pubs for different occasions: the big old food pub for lunch with your parents; the trendier gastropub for Sunday lunch with a group of friends; the Australian bar when you want to get pissed and throw up on a Friday night;‡ and the back-street local for a quiet pint with a book when you want to feel like part of your community or watch old men shouting at each other. All of them can feature in a week's drinking for the contemporary chap

---

* I could wax eloquent about the club, but since *Phoenix Nights* there's no point. My mum thought it was a fly-on-the-wall documentary.

† One of my favourites has a section called 'foreign food' stuck away at the bottom of its menu, where all those dodgy dishes such as chicken balti, chilli con carne and spaghetti bolognese are lumped together where they won't cause any trouble.

‡ Because, as we all eventually discover, this truly is a sure-fire way to impress the opposite sex.

or chapess about town. Some pubs even change their function at different times of the day, particularly now since pubs decided to start trying to attract women. So the pleasant food pub for an afternoon glass of Chardonnay before your hair appointment can be a cattle market with bouncers on the door six hours later.

Whether you love them or hate them, the alternative to theme pubs, gastropubs and Continental-style café bars is not a return to an idyllic never-never land of oak beams, horse brasses and jolly landlords. Pubs don't change just to spite their customers, however difficult that might be to believe sometimes. They change in ever more desperate attempts to stay in business. We are drinking less beer. As further leisure alternatives continue to proliferate, pubs are fighting for our diminishing custom, and are simply trying to furnish themselves in a way they think we will like.

Drinkers in chains

The debate over what pubs should look like will continue for as long as there are pubs. But having said that, a new issue has emerged over the last twenty years that has changed things profoundly, and led to the arguments becoming far more intense. Our drinking landscape is undergoing a profound change. Critics of theme pubs no longer talk just about the latest abomination visited upon their particular local. Themes now are being executed on a much larger scale, with previously individualistic pubs giving way to chains of identical pubs and bars. The theme has gone national.

Pub chains can be traced back to the emergence of casual

dining in the 1970s and the golden age of Berni Inns and Beefeaters – big pubs that families would drive to on a Saturday night to enjoy the princely fare of scampi or chicken in a basket. Fine, if that's what you wanted from a pub, and if you didn't, you could clearly identify them and avoid them. But the idea of branded chains is now transforming pubs and bars of all kinds. This has happened because, in the 1990s, the whole structure of the brewing and pub industry changed fundamentally. Yes, again. It all started with a piece of government legislation designed to increase consumer choice and – surprise! – ended up having the opposite effect.

By 1985 the Big Six owned 73 per cent of the country's beer output and 73 per cent of the tied houses. Concern mounted that the brewing industry was increasingly oligopolistic, with the big operators creating conditions that made it impossible for new players to enter the market. Without decent competition, the big companies could make lots of money without having to worry about keeping their customers happy.

In 1986, after a steady stream of inquiries which grumbled about the state of the industry but got nowhere, the Monopolies and Mergers Commission decided to have a look. They concluded that the tied-house system was the main culprit in stifling competition, just as the big Continental lager brewers had realized decades before. If the big brewers owned the outlets that sold their beer, nobody else could get into the market without doing a deal with them. The MMC investigated and deliberated for three years, and in 1989 they produced the Beer Orders.

The Beer Orders promised to shake up the entire structure of the industry, breaking up the cosy party the big brewers had been having for the best part of a century. They required any brewer owning more than 2,000 pubs to get rid of half of those in excess of 2,000 before 31 October 1992. From May 1990, the remaining tied premises were also to be allowed to stock a 'guest' cask ale not produced by the owning brewer, and to buy drinks other than beer from suppliers outside the tie.

These measures were to have a big impact, but clearly the main task for the Big Six, who had tens of thousands of pubs between them, was to dispose of many of these in less than three years. And although the MMC's intentions were fine, they didn't seem to have given much thought to the question of who was going to buy all these pubs. Sure, some went independent. Across the brewing industry, many of the old hands who actually cared about beer took advantage of the huge reorganization, took voluntary redundancy, and bought a pub or even a small chain of pubs. But in the short time available before the deadline there simply weren't enough small buyers around who could stump up the required amount of money.

The big brewers were faced with a choice. They could no longer both brew and sell beer, so which would they rather do? In the 1970s the Big Six had merged and allied themselves with companies across a broad spectrum, diversifying into wines and spirits, food and general retailing, getting into hotels, restaurants, bingo and leisure centres. Scottish & Newcastle even decided that buying Center Parcs was a good idea. These were no longer simple brewers; they were providers of leisure opportunities and owners of real estate. It wasn't a difficult choice to make. Through the 1990s the oldest names in brewing called time on making the stuff, sold off the brewing parts of their corporations and focused on retailing.

But even with such an organizational upheaval, there were still thousands of pubs up for sale, and only a company with massive capital could afford them. Overnight, the Japanese investment bank Nomura became the largest pub landlord in the country, and other financial institutions soon followed suit. Morgan Grenfell Private Equity and Alchemy & Partners joined Nomura as some of the UK's biggest pub owners. These companies knew that pubs didn't offer the massive capital growth that they were used to, but they were solid, dependable assets that could provide a steady stream of income. CAMRA, who had for so long regarded the big corporate brewers as the enemy, suddenly faced something far more worrying. These were companies who didn't even pretend to have a link to Britain's proud brewing heritage, had no reason to view their pubs as anything other than retail outlets, and were interested solely in maximizing the return on their investment and shedding unprofitable units. The nineties and the early noughties saw frenzied buying and selling between breweries, investment banks and pub companies, with hundreds of pubs at a time being picked up, sorted through and kept or rejected like playing cards in an apocalyptic, steroid-crazed game of Rummy. By the middle of the decade a new hierarchy had emerged. Punch Taverns and Enterprise, each of which had formed as new companies in the wake of the Beer Orders with a few hundred pubs, ended up with over 15,000 pubs between them. When smaller players such as Admiral, Scottish & Newcastle Pub Enterprises and Mitchell & Butler's were added into the mix, the concentration of pub ownership into fewer hands was actually higher than it had been before the Beer Orders.

The Beer Orders, designed to increase consumer choice, ended up causing a big reduction in the choice of brands available. In the old days an individual pub had to sell the beers which were made by the brewery that owned it, but there were a lot of breweries around, each with its own brands. So if you went into a Whitbread pub the lagers were Stella and Heineken, the bitters were Boddington's and Flower's, or before that Whitbread Best and Trophy. Go to a Courage pub and in their place you had Foster's, Kronenbourg and John Smith's, and so on. But now you had chains of thousands of pubs which could cherry-pick brands from whichever brewer they saw fit. They were large enough to demand huge volume discounts (which they forgot to pass on to their customers) and so only the biggest brewers, with the strongest brands and greatest economies of scale, could compete. Throughout the 1990s weaker brands disappeared and bars across the country began to look remarkably similar. And it wasn't long before homogenization spread much further than just what was on the bar. Existing chains of food pubs such as Harvester and Beefeater were beefed up, sometimes even with their own advertising campaigns, and the town centre suddenly saw the King's Head turn into a Firkin, Hogshead, Scream, Wetherspoon's, Walkabout, Edward's, O'Neill's or Yates's.

But the chain that symbolized the biggest change in our drinking culture was All Bar One. The original strategy behind this Bass-owned pub chain was to tap into what was still a largely under-exploited market: women. Bass's market research showed that young women wanted to go out and drink just as much as men, but found pubs quite unpleasant. They didn't necessarily want to drink beer, and were baffled by the fact that the only wines on offer were Liebfraumilch and Lambrusco at a time when excellent wines were available in any supermarket for under five quid a bottle. They were put off by the dark, murky atmosphere, intimidated by having to fight through the old soaks perched at the bar to get served, and generally found the smoky, jukebox-and-fruit-machine atmosphere altogether too boyish.

So All Bar One was designed specifically for women. And unlike previous attempts to lure the fairer sex into our drinking dens, it was executed in a way that wasn't patronizing. It served a large range of decent quality wine by the small or large glass, or by the bottle. There were no stools at the long, open bar. There were big bright windows so you could see inside as you were walking past. Large tables catered for bigger groups, such as birthday parties or even just the office crowd after work. And with its fancy menu and its olives and cashew nuts and newspapers, it felt a bit more stylish than the local boozer.

Bass had created a modern, stylish drinking environment that also managed not to be too pretentious. Amazingly, this seemed to appeal to men as well as women. You might argue that a drinking establishment full of young women is sure to be a magnet for blokes whichever way you look at it, but All Bar One's aspirational, Continental-style bar culture was a refreshing change for both sexes of a generation for whom the pub had been running out of ideas.

It was a great concept. So good, in fact, that many other pub groups slavishly copied it. The frustrating thing was that they simply looked at All Bar One and aped its style, rather than going through the difficult but potentially more rewarding process (for pub owner and customer alike) of identifying a specific type of drinker and doing something different to cater to their needs. Pale wood, big tables, sofas and decent but overpriced wine became ubiquitous. Most of these bars were nice enough, but you felt that they'd maybe missed the point a little, and had merely replaced one type of homogeneity with another. And it didn't seem to matter to the developers what role the pub played – All Bar Ones worked so well because they were on high street sites, perfect places for groups to meet up before deciding what to do with the rest of the evening, and suitable during the daytime for a meal or a glass of wine while out shopping. The model wasn't necessarily right for a sleepy suburb or back-street boozer, but sod that.

And so you got somewhere like Hogshead. This was a branded chain that had been doing a fair job of making old-style pub culture look a little fresher and more urban, even cool. It had bare stone floors and tables made out of old barrels. It was a bit more mature and mellow than the screaming, garish circuit pubs, and had a decent range of real ales and Belgian beers at the bar. Then they decided they wanted to be more like All Bar One, but seemingly on a budget. So they put in louder music and painted the walls pink and lime green. I won't go on, because all I need to say is this: just after the Hogshead in Islington was done up in this way, I went in for a drink and spotted a celebrity in there who seemed at home. It was Su Pollard.

I know what I like and I like what I know

The fact that more pubs are being turned into national chains reflects the homogenization of the high street in general, as business becomes bigger in scale and society becomes ever more interconnected. Bill Bryson identified this trend in his book *Notes From a Small Island*, in which he travels from one end of Britain to the other in search of the defining essence of Britishness. By the time he reaches Aberdeen he is quite dispirited:

> It was like anywhere and nowhere – like a small Manchester or a random fragment of Leeds ... It wasn't that there was anything *wrong* with Aberdeen exactly ... then I realised the problem really wasn't with Aberdeen so much as with the nature of modern Britain. British towns are like a deck of cards that have been shuffled and endlessly redealt – same cards, different order ... I could get exactly the same things, the same shops and libraries and leisure centres, the same pubs and television programmes, the same phone boxes, post offices, traffic lights, park benches, zebra crossings, marine air and post-Indian-dinner burps anywhere else.

Increasingly pubs are a part of this, and they succeed because homogenization has its advantages. When you go into a retail chain pub, you know exactly what to expect. Let's say you're in a town you're not that familiar with. You're a businessman and you've had a meeting there that's finished early, and you've got an hour before your train. There's a pub called the Green Man just by the station:

whitewashed walls, metal bars covering the opaque windows, one empty trestle table outside on the pavement. You can't tell what's inside. Your local is also called the Green Man and you like it in there. It serves a decent pint, it's got Sky for the footie and, most importantly, there's no Simply Red on the jukebox. But you once went into a pub called the Green Man on holiday and there was a man at the bar who looked disturbingly like Father Jack out of *Father Ted* who never stopped leering at you, it still served Double Diamond, and the whole place unaccountably smelt of offal. What will this Green Man be like? Are those bars on the windows a necessity or just decoration? Are you feeling lucky?

Across the road there's an All Bar One, with its dangling ivy and elegant lettering, neat, understated chalkboards and stripped pine clearly visible through the large windows. You used to go to All Bar One quite a lot when it first opened and the ground beef and coriander burger on ciabatta is really nice, and they do those lovely sun-blushed tomatoes on the side. It's a bit passé now there are so many, but it's still where you normally meet up with people, whether it's Sophie before you go out for a meal or the guys before you go on somewhere else if you're on a night out in town. There's probably a better pub if you knew where to look, but this is fine and you'll be on familiar ground, so you go for the easy option.

These chains would not succeed if they didn't offer us something we wanted. The growth of nationally branded chains of pubs is simply a continuation of the trend that started when the first ale wife realized people would rather drink her ale than their own home brew, and put up a big stick above the door to let people know it was ready. When real-ale enthusiasts fondly recount tales of Samuel Pepys travelling miles to get a pint of Alderman Bide's fine ale, they are talking about an early form of brand loyalty. It is the same motivation that drives the growth of branded pub retail chains today: the value of emotional reassurance in deciding what to buy.

For all that, only someone without a soul could argue that Britain's pub landscape would be improved if every King's Head and Dog and Duck were replaced by an O'Neill's or All Bar One. And to be fair, the chances of that look very unlikely. Just as in the world of consumer brands, beer lacks the global uniformity of fast food, soft drinks or fashion, so in the British high street many pubs stubbornly resist the trend towards homogenisation. Of course every town has its Wetherspoons and Walkabout, but the vast majority of pubs retain their independent character and feel. Even the large regional brewers with their modest but still sizeable chains mean the dialect of the pub changes as you wander across the country, as Fuller's pubs in London are replaced by Shepherd Neame boozers to the south, and Wadworth's or Hall & Woodhouse to the west. As you go north, Wells & Young's merges with Greene King, which is then overtaken by Everard's, which then gives way to Marston's, and so on up and across the country. When the shops in Aberdeen and Aldershot look identical, the pub, its customs and the beer it sells are increasingly the only clues as to where you are in the UK.*

The problem with big chains is that their modern, share-

---

* Well, apart from bread rolls. I mean teacakes. Or do I mean cobs, or stotties?

holder-driven business is very short term in its approach. You can make *more* money by identifying a particular target group, adapting your offering to suit their particular tastes, and catering for their every need so you get their undying loyalty and most of their money over the long term, delighting them in the process, so everyone is happy. But you can make *quicker* money by just appealing to the basest instincts in everybody.

Making ends meet

The thing is, whether the branded concept is right or wrong, the big pub chains are doing it to stay in business and make money, and that's something which is becoming increasingly difficult. The amount of beer we drink is in long-term decline. Since the 1970s leisure markets have been fragmenting, and just like in the 1920s and 30s, the pub has been steadily elbowed out. Clubs, coffee shops, wine bars and leisure centres have grown. Shopping has become a hobby, an end in its own right as brand names have gone from being emotional symbols of reassurance to religious icons for blank-eyed, celebrity-worshipping zealots. We seem to be getting healthier and more sensible; the breathalyser was introduced in 1967, and since then we've grown increasingly aware of the consequences of drinking and driving. We've started jogging, running marathons, joining gyms and eating healthier food, and as we have become more aware of the effect of beer on the waistline we've got into wine.*

---

* Even though we're misguided in doing so: a 250ml glass of red wine

Wine drinking is not just about being healthy though. It is the most visible aspect of a change in society that has not done beer culture many favours. As we saw earlier in the century, beer drinking is concentrated in areas where manufacturing industry is strong, real working-class heartlands. Beer therefore declines if there is an industrial recession. In the 1979–81 recession, the amount of beer drunk fell off a cliff and never recovered. As Margaret Thatcher's economic policies systematically destroyed Britain's manufacturing base, unemployment rose from one million in 1979 to three million in 1985, and was highest in industrial areas in the north and Midlands – areas where the heaviest beer drinkers lived.

And just in case anyone entertained notions that this was anything less than a vendetta against working class pursuits, duty on beer was raised by *90 per cent* between 1978 and 1982, at the same time as VAT on beer was increased from 8 to 15 per cent. As a result, as people lost their livelihoods, the retail price of beer rose by 80 per cent. Duty had doubled again by 1986. And just to rub it in and really show who was boss, duty on wine was heavily reduced over the same period. We may all supposedly be middle class now (at least those lucky enough to get a decent education), but this was only made possible by a full-scale assault on working-class lifestyle and culture, and beer was a significant casualty.

We do still drink beer, of course. The premiumization of lager, together with the more successful of the lifestyle theme

---

contains 170 calories – the same amount as an average pint of bitter. Per 100ml, beer has fewer calories than wine, gin and tonic, cider, coke, orange juice, even milk.

bars, has reinvented the concept of the pub for a more middle-class nation, and that's fine. But we are drinking less beer, and when we do still choose beer we're increasingly likely to drink it somewhere other than the pub. The number of licensed premises in the country is increasing, but the number of pubs is declining, as clubs and restaurants become our new drinking hang-outs. We're also increasingly fond of drinking at home. Off-licences have proliferated and all supermarkets now stock booze.

The supermarket beer price war meant the average price of beer in the off-trade actually fell marginally over the same period as it almost doubled in pubs, accelerating a shift to home drinking which means that for the first time in our history, we are now drinking marginally more beer at home than we are in pubs.

Then there was the reality of our increasingly ridiculous-looking licensing laws. But slowly, our closer ties with the continent we fought for in World War One gradually helped loosen the ties that had constrained pubs since that war. Seventy years after the end of the war, British licensing laws were looking increasingly silly next to those of our neighbours. Even the police favoured longer opening hours, and pressure for reform increased through the 1970s and 80s, particularly after successful experiments in Scotland. There used to be a much more extreme reputation for heavy drinking north of the border, and pubs had more severe licensing restrictions. They would close at 10 p.m. and scenes would ensue that rivalled Australia. Bars were closed on Sundays and only 'bona fide travellers' were allowed to drink in hotels. This absurd law led to the magnificent spectacle of coach loads of piss heads travelling from one side of a city to the other.* In 1976 licensing laws were relaxed, bars were allowed to stay open much later, and Scotland, over the last twenty years or so, has become one of the best places to drink. The bars are pleasant and the late-night atmosphere in city streets is much lighter and less threatening, almost Continental compared to England.

It became increasingly evident that something had to change, and in the late 1980s it did. But the final impetus for change wasn't a desire to sort out this nonsensical situation for the British drinker; British licensing laws were upsetting the tourists, and we couldn't have that could we? Afternoon opening was permitted in 1988, and in 1995 it was extended to Sundays. Finally, in 2005, pubs were granted the freedom to open when they liked. The eleven o' clock limit and the mad scramble and swill it invariably prompted was abolished, at the same time as the right to grant licences was moved to local magistrates, and the police were given tougher powers to deal with late night disorder.

This introduction of 'twenty-four hour drinking' was condemned by fearmongering right-wing tabloids who predicted a wave of booze coming along to drown Britain. In fact, only 7,000 of Britain's 105,000 licensed premises hold

---

* This practice was also prevalent south of the border until it was abolished as part of the licensing restrictions in World War One. A fantastic example of the lunacy this provoked featured in 'Diary of a Nobody', published in *Punch* magazine in 1892. A Mr Pooter and his three companions walked on a Sunday afternoon from Holloway in north London a couple of miles across the Heath to a pub in Hampstead. Pooter is asked where he has come from, and is barred when he replies. Then his colleagues approach: 'I heard the porter say: "Where from?" When to my surprise, in fact disgust, Stillbrook replied: "Blackheath," and the three were immediately admitted.'

24-hour licences, and the majority of those are hotel bars for whom it just makes that whole serving guests after 11 p.m. thing a little more straightforward. Only 12 per cent of 24-hour licences were granted to pubs, clubs and supermarkets, and the average pub now puts the chairs on the tables a mere 27 minutes later than it once did.

But it means that pubs can open for as long as feel they need to, and those in busy late night locations can open into the small hours, and there's less of the awfulness that used to blight town centres when every pub threw its drinkers out at the same time into streets with inadequate public transport, not enough taxis and no public toilets. The government was at worst a bit naïve when it spun the idea that working class British pub boozing would instantly transform into a delightfully continental café culture. But while the tabloids continue to insist that '24 hour drinking' has 'turned many of our town centres into no-go areas for normal people', the truth – according to data from the Home Office, the police and the Office of National Statistics – is that late night crime and disorder, and rates of binge drinking and 'harmful' drinking have fallen since the legislation was introduced. And anyone who actually cares to visit a town centre pub late at night can see that they are more pleasant places than they were during the days of the eleven o'clock swill.

The bigger problem for pubs though was that beer drinking and, more broadly, total alcohol consumption, resumed a steady decline from 2004 after a brief upwards blip around the Millennium. And that fall happened far quicker in pubs than in supermarkets. What the Labour government gave pubs with one hand, it took away with the other. In 2007 the smoking ban in public places was introduced. While the ban had broad popular support, it was catastrophic for pubs, prompting on-trade beer sales to fall off a cliff as many drinkers simply opted to stay at home. There were legions of other people who realized that now they could drop in for a glass of wine without leaving smelling like an ashtray, they could visit pubs more often. But the smokers had been much more regular drinkers, and the influx of middle class, middle aged people – particularly women – who had been forecast to replace them never quite materialized.

Not content with this disaster, Chancellor Alastair Darling declared war on the pub industry in a way Thatcher would have heartily applauded. He announced a duty escalator on beer that would guarantee an increase well above the rate of inflation for three years. When the banking-led financial collapse led to a global recession, he piled on more duty. When he reduced VAT to help struggling businesses through the recession, he popped an extra tax on beer to ensure it was the only sector of the British economy not receiving financial help. As he agreed to government-owned banks using public money raised from struggling people to pay billions of pounds in bonuses to the inept millionaires who had caused the crash, the VAT rate returned to normal and the extra tax on beer to cancel out its temporary reduction remained in place. Then came yet another annual duty increase. In eighteen months, duty on beer increased by more than 20 per cent. It's enough to make you suspect a barman stole his girlfriend at university, and he bided his time to become chancellor simply to exact his revenge.

As pub closures hit horrific heights of thirty, then thirty-nine, then fifty-two every single week, Britain hemorrhaged more than 5 per cent of its total pubs in a few years. When the industry pleaded to government for a break in the punishment, they were hit with rafts of new legislation and red tape until it was estimated that the average landlord had to spend half a day of every busy week dealing with bureaucracy. When the industry pointed out that people were abandoning pubs in their droves and drinking cheap beer from supermarkets, the government responded with a mandatory code to crack down on the supposed binge drinking problem with six measures aimed at curbing excessive drinking in pubs – including banning promotions such as the 'Dentist's Chair', which in reality only ever took place at one shithole pub in Newcastle – and imposed no restrictions whatsoever on the freedom of supermarkets to sell beer as cheaply as they liked.

Apart from the government's seeming determination to destroy one of Britain's few remaining industries that actually makes stuff, an industry that contributes £28bn to the economy every year and employs over 600,000 people, there were yet more factors that persuaded us that we'd be better off drinking at home. And sadly, in relation to some of those factors, the pub could often be its own worst enemy.

The total package

Picture your home now compared to how it was, say, at the turn of the millennium. Try to work out what's in it that wasn't there back then. You've probably got a big plasma screen telly, which has a DVD player and a games console attached to it. You can probably watch that telly in High Definition, and if there's more than one thing on that you want to watch you can set your box to record two channels simultaneously to the one you're watching, or even just ask it to record every episode of your favourite series. You've probably got at least one computer in the house, and it's probably got high speed, wireless internet access in any room. If you don't fancy watching yet more telly on it, you can listen to pretty much any music you can think of on Spotify, download entire movies illegally in a matter of minutes, watch that video of the sneezing panda or the sinister hamster on YouTube, or entertain yourself for days with social media sites such as Twitter and Facebook instead of old-fashioned face-to-face relationships, as well as the more traditional pursuits of playing computer games or surfing for porn. You've probably got more cookbooks in the kitchen than you had back then, and a bit more proficiency in using them to turn the vast array of quality produce from the local farmers' market, or home-delivered from the posh deli bit of the supermarket, into something your friends and family will be genuinely impressed by.

Most of this stuff simply didn't exist in 2000. The home has undergone its most radical transformation since the introduction of heating, electric light and the wireless in the 1920s – and do you remember what happened to pub-going back then?

Forewarned, a decent publican needs to counter all this stuff by giving you new reasons to visit his pub. So over the same period as this incredible change indoors, how has the pub changed?

If you're lucky, it might have had a lick of paint or a couple of new dishes on the menu.

Pubs simply failed to respond not only to the revolution

in the home, but to the plethora of new entertainment options outside it. A pub landlord who complains he's losing business to the new coffee shop up the road really has no business running a business if he fails to install a coffee machine and offer wi-fi in response. Pubs are quiet during the afternoons. Many people – not just beer writers – work independently and on the move. Is there any excuse, ten years after wi-fi became universal in Starbucks and Costa Coffee, why most pubs still don't have it?

One of the most unintentionally hilarious phrases in British smalltalk is 'One day I'd like to retire and run a pub'. You wouldn't say 'I want to retire and run a supermarket'. You can do one or the other. But there's a residual notion, a dream, that after a lifetime's slog you can simply open the doors of a cosy little boozer and enough business to make a living will simply walk through them. If that ever happened, it no longer does in reality.

The other big problem afflicting pubs is the common complaint that you just can't get the staff these days. In the 1970s the big brewers were attacked over the rate at which pub prices were rising above inflation.* They replied that when you went into the pub for a pint you weren't just paying for the liquid in the glass, you were paying for a package, a total experience that included not just the heat and light and a place to sit, but also the ambience, the music and the service. It's a fair enough argument, but it obliges pubs to actually deliver the rest of that package, and staff play a key part in this. However, working behind a bar has

---

* Not a new phenomenon then – who'd have thought?

become a McJob. Most bar staff are young, work part time, and receive minimal training.

If, like me, you develop a passion for real ale, going into a pub and trying to get a pint of it can be a depressing experience. I once went into a real ale pub where the staff were obviously new and unsupervised. I asked for one of the brands clearly advertised on a chalkboard behind the bar and the barmaid looked at me blankly. When I pointed to the board she looked confused and said they didn't have it. I pointed to another beer on the bar and asked for a pint of that, but she couldn't pour it properly because she didn't know how to work the hand pump. Someone came to help her, but then it ran out after half a pint and I was told I couldn't have it because even though they had more in the cellar, no one on duty knew how to change the barrel. Between us we managed to get a full pint of my third-choice brand, London Pride. I had to stop her putting a slice of lemon in it. Then she had to be shown how to work the till. You get the idea. It's a common enough experience. It would be ironic if the owners of these pubs were the same people complaining about how you can't make any money off beer these days, wouldn't it?

An increasing number of bar staff are Kiwis and Aussies, because at least they don't require special training to be polite and friendly to people – they already know how. But in many cases you get 'served' by the same sullen spotty teenagers you find in Burger King. As a result, the pub is losing a lot of its special character. At closing time it's rare now for someone to call last orders and time. They just turn the lights up at 11.00, or maybe 10.55 if they're bored and waiting to go home. And don't we all love it when, in return for their sparkling wit and conversation, you get your change slapped down on the bar in front of you on a 'silver' tray, with the clear indication that you should be leaving some of it there as a tip.

People in management at some of the big pub chains shrug their shoulders helplessly. They say this is a consequence of our part-time, flexible, tight-margin economy. What's the point giving them proper training when they only stay a few months? How can we afford to pay them more when two minutes ago you were moaning at us to keep the price of a pint down? It is tricky, but go somewhere like Pret A Manger and wonder why, in a similarly competitive market, they have staff who are similarly aged and with similar training and qualifications who seem much more friendly, efficient and happy in their jobs.

Last Orders?

It would be a tragedy if the traditional British local disappeared entirely, and not just for tourists. But pubs do have to change. When it's done properly, the pub is still a wonderful place, quite unlike anywhere else. It is a vital part of our heritage, and at the same time has modern relevance. But every pub owner needs to keep an eye on the times. Our houses, workplaces, shops and restaurants all change, their style continually evolves. Why should the pub be an exception? As traditional communities fragment, younger drinkers are looking for environments that reflect their more cosmopolitan outlook. We're increasingly searching for authenticity under the glitz, but that doesn't mean pokey or twee bars that could serve as locations for costume dramas. Authenticity isn't about hankering for a past that was never that great anyway. New types of pubs will emerge to reflect our lofty aspirations (and our baser urges), and we'll find places that we love. And despite the need for modernization, there will always be a place for the traditional English pub. As society becomes ever faster, more fragmented and virtual, even younger drinkers look for an escape to a place that reassures them with continuity, tradition and heritage. Let's just hope that when the big chains decide to rip their ideas off and do them on a national scale, they don't screw things up too badly.

Despite all its problems, the pub is still the focal point of British beer culture. For every pub that's failing because of a combination of shocking trading circumstances, supermarket prices and government legislation mixed with a total absence of any entrepreneurial spirit, there are many more that will stay in business because they are run by someone who understands what business means. In an age of shocking pub closures, you don't have to look too hard at all to find pubs that are booming. With some it's because they offer stunning food. In others it's because they stock a world-class range of real ales and keep them in perfect condition. In others still, it might be the fact that they do a pub quiz on Monday, live music on Wednesday, pie and pint night on Thursday and karaoke on Saturday, giving you a new reason to pop in every night of the week. The numbers of pubs and pub-goers may have declined, but no alternative has emerged to challenge its place. It seems highly unlikely that anything will. We now drink half as much beer as we did in the Victorian era and more than we did between the wars. We might drink more beer at home these days, but it's the pub that sets the standard. The pub has been the defining feature of British social life for a thousand years; it would be both deluded and arrogant to imagine that it's about to disappear in the next decade.

Market researchers Mintel produce regular reports on our drinking attitudes and behaviour, and when questioned the vast majority of us say that we prefer to drink there. It's in the pub, with its combination of home comforts and 'being-out' excitement, that we still have the best times. You don't go into work and say, 'Ooh, you should have seen us last night; we sat in front of *Corrie* and drank twelve cans each and got absolutely stocious by the time *I'm a Celebrity Get Me Out of Here* came on.' That would be sad. Whereas to do it in front of strangers, paying about double for the same amount of booze, is still what we spend the whole week looking forward to. The pub's the place where life actually *happens*.

Chapter Fourteen

'Haven't you got homes to go to?'

A sort of epilogue

When I first completed this book in spring 2002, this final chapter began like this:

> In July 1991, *The Times* announced that the British Women's Temperance Association had decided to disband. Where once there had been five hundred branches and over eighty thousand teetotal members, there were now five branches with less than a hundred ladies between them. The last president of the association, Margaret Duncan (84), said that it had become impossible to attract young members. Drinking had become a normal part of everyday life for most women. Pubs, once a place where they simply could not be seen, had become a regular haunt where they felt just as at home as men.

It felt like a nice way to end the story of thousands of years of struggle, conflict, misunderstanding and bad management. We'd reached the point where drinking and pubs had become accepted as a harmonious part of ordinary life – or so I thought.

If by some chance Ms Duncan lived to celebrate her centenary (and let's hope she did), she would no doubt have been delighted by the sudden and dramatic change that happened in British attitudes to drinking in the decade that eventually became known as the 'noughties'. Perhaps it was something to do with that nickname, but all kinds of naughtiness came under scrutiny, and none moreso than drinking.

The first time I re-read the early chapters of this book, I was shocked at how carefree and celebratory they were about our nation's drunken behaviour. The best part of a decade later, that attitude seems naïve, perhaps even irresponsible. At the time, the book reflected our cheerful acceptance of our fondness for boozing. But things changed very quickly. After a decade on the sidelines letting other moral panics have a go at scaring us into the kind of numb terror that can only be alleviated by barricading ourselves in our homes with a constant diet of top brands at great prices from Tesco and Celebrity Morris Dancing on TV, the lager lout returned to terrorize us in a far more threatening and omnipresent form: the binge drinker.

Gay binge drinking asylum seekers have sex with the memory of Diana

The binge drinker is the strange child of an unholy three-way union that tells you the entire story of the end of the last millennium and the first ten years of this one. Those three parents are 'The Nanny State', the *Daily Mail* and celebrity culture. And the man who got them all so turned on? None other than John Daly.

Remember him? No? Well, Daly was the American golfer who seemingly appeared from nowhere to win the British Open in 1995. His sudden success seemingly led him astray, and he spiraled into what the tabloids have always referred to a 'booze and drugs hell' for a few years before reappearing clean, straight, and determined to get back to winning ways. In 1997, and again in 1999, he spoke to the *Mail* about his 'drink binges', giving that newspaper its first two features containing references to binge drinking. They clearly liked the term: by 2000, women – and in particular 'ladettes' – were also being warned of the danger of drink binges, with scare stories about how even the regulation number of alcohol units per week could give you breast cancer, malnutrition, foetal alcohol syndrome, mental health problems and worst of all, bad nails.

For all the *Mail's* alarmism though, there was a common understanding what a drink binge was – it meant going on a sustained and long term session of single-minded alcohol abuse, probably over a few days, something all of us could recognize as extraordinary and potentially damaging. As 'binge drinking' took hold as a common term in the paper (two stories containing the term in the late nineties, thirty in 2001, 68 in 2003) apart from the ladettes, it was only people like England footballers, Chris Evans and Robbie Williams who indulged in such behaviour.

Official advice on alcohol units then changed that.

To understand where the whole units thing came from, we need to go back to competing theories on how best to deal with alcohol problems in society. Most of us have heard of the Alcoholics Anonymous theory that alcoholism is a disease, a theory which is very popular in the US. As such it is a medical problem, which therefore obviously has to be dealt with by the health service. In Britain that's bad news, because with a population that's living longer and longer, the health service is falling apart.

The thing is, there is no scientific evidence whatsoever – not a shred of proof – that alcoholism is a disease. As Andrew Barr perfectly puts it, 'It is scientific only in that it was originally articulated by a scientist'. So the British establishment rejected it and instead adopted the Ledermann Theory. This states that the higher the overall level of alcohol consumption in a given society, the greater the amount of alcohol-related harm. If you think about alcohol abuse this way it's a societal issue rather than a medical one, which means that instead of simply dumping it on the health service, it's something government and sociologists can get involved with. Various government-sponsored bodies were pulled together to form Alcohol Concern, and legislative and public information measures to help reduce overall alcohol consumption were drawn up, including the creation of safe levels of alcohol unit consumption.

The problem was, there was no hard evidence for the link between the level of overall consumption and the level of alcohol abuse either. Different studies around the world show that measures to reduce overall alcohol consumption – such as increasing prices and reducing availability – could just as easily lead to diverting alcohol from legal to illegal channels, and make the problem worse. Don Steele, a sociologist in charge of a body called Action on Alcohol Abuse through the 1980s, later admitted that the group had gained attention by being 'outrageous', and that the case the body made 'was true – but much of it was unverified fact'.[*]

The invention of safe limits for alcohol unit consumption was one such 'unverified fact'. A unit is ten millilitres of ethyl alcohol, the amount the average healthy adult can break down in one hour. In 1987 the Health Education Authority and Alcohol Concern agreed that units were a good way of teaching people about alcohol consumption, and recommended that men should drink no more than twenty-one units a week, and women no more than fourteen. Above that level, they claimed, the risk of alcohol-related harm increased exponentially.[†] What they didn't see fit to mention was that only five years earlier, the Royal College of Physicians and the British Medical Journal had been advising that the safe limit for men was fifty-one units a week. There was no new research to back up the reduction to twenty-one units five years later, and no reason given for doing so. Later Richard Smith, then Deputy Editor of the British Medical Journal and a member of the working party that established the new safe limits in 1987, admitted 'We just pulled them out of the air'.

Despite the fact that these arbitrary safe limits have no scientific foundation, and are based on a sociological theory that isn't universally true, they went on to form the bedrock of the entire approach to countering alcohol-related harm. In 1995 the government realized that even though people were beginning to understand the concept of units, they would

---

[*] How a 'fact' can be a fact if it is, in fact, not factually verified is perhaps something a philosopher is better qualified to try to make sense of rather than a sociologist such as Steele.
[†] They've since retracted the 'exponentially' bit and become much more vague about precisely how much the risk increases.

'save up' their weekly allowance for one blowout session at the weekend. In other words, the concept of safe weekly limits was actually *encouraging* people to binge drink rather than drink moderately throughout the week. So they simply divided the weekly total by days, and changed the story so that men should drink no more than three or four units a day, and women no more than two or three.

With that in place, the government then decided that if you drank more than double your daily recommended unit allowance, this constituted a 'binge'. There is no global consensus on what level of alcohol intake becomes dangerous – partly because it varies massively from individual to individual and culture to culture. But with a definition of 'binge drinking' in place that now included anyone who drank more than three or four pints of beer in one day – not even in one session, but one day – official figures suddenly revealed that it wasn't just Gazza and Robbie and Chris who were binge drinkers – about one in four of us were.

This was gold dust to the fearmongers, and binge drinkers became the new folk demons of our age, taking their place alongside asylum seekers, devil dogs, paedophiles, knife-wielding hoodies, teenage single mums on benefits, video nasties, violent video games, bird flu, swine flu, Chris Morris and mad cow disease as a grave threat to society that was about to coming knocking on our doors.

Like some of its colleagues in this rogues gallery, there was a real problem to be tackled. But as in every other case, that problem was grossly overstated and didn't affect the vast majority of the population.

Maybe it wouldn't have been so bad – but this definitional tinkering coincided with a brief upward trend in alcohol consumption, rises in alcohol-related hospital admissions, and the announcement of the new Licensing Act that would usher in '24-hour drinking'.

The number of binge drinking stories in the *Mail* went up from 68 in 2003, to 87 in 2004, to 129 in 2005, the year the Act came into force. More than one story every three days told us not about celebrities on drink binges, but about town centres that were out of control, a population drinking itself to death and crippling society along the way. Comparisons were made with the gin epidemic of the eighteenth century. Perhaps you'd expect nothing better from a paper that thrives on creating fear and distress in its readership, but *The Times* – which mentioned binge drinking a total of 49 times in the two centuries from 1785 to 1985 – was even worse – it ran 300 binge drinking stories in 2004, and just under one every day in 2005.

When the Licensing Act didn't precipitate the social melt-down we'd been promised, the fearmongering slackened off a little in the next couple of years. But this didn't spare us the ridiculous articles on the first anniversary of '24 hour drinking' complaining about how Britain's pubs had not instantaneously transformed into pavement cafes full of people drinking Pastis and black coffee while reading Sartre.

Within all this, one drink was singled out as the bane of society. Can you guess what it was? Alcopops, which teenagers were supping on park benches? Strong cider, the drink beloved of alcoholic tramps? Don't be silly – on every 'Binge Britain' TV programme, every scary newspaper report, the accompanying visual seemed to be a pint of beer. A study of the BBC's website coverage of negative drinking stories in 2008–09 revealed that beer was featured as the accompanying illustration on over twice as many occasions as any other drink, and real ale featured more than lager. *The Sun* even ran a story about under-age binge drinkers accompanied by a shot of that favourite teen drinkers' hang-out, the Great British Beer Festival. And no matter how often self-declared binge drinkers explained that they 'pre-loaded' on cheap supermarket booze before going out, everyone agreed that pubs were the heart of the problem.

The smoking ban in 2007 gave new impetus to the neo-prohibitionists. The health service professionals and government departments who successfully engineered it were hardly keen to volunteer for redundancy afterwards, and after seeing smoking fall dramatically, they applied the same pressure to drink. The smoking ban was supported by the public because over decades, public opinion had been turned against the filthy habit. If drinking could be made similarly socially unacceptable, went the thinking, Britain could be persuaded to accept measures such as a ban on alcohol advertising, minimum pricing, a return to stricter licensing controls, a reduction in the number of licences, and after that ... who knows?

And so, the last few years have seen report after report on the dangers of drinking and the damage it is doing to society. Figures such as a £55bn cost to the economy were seemingly plucked out of the air, with no balancing figure for the beneficial contribution alcohol makes by keeping most people who drink it happier than they otherwise would be in modern society. The cost to the NHS supposedly doubled between 2003 and 2007, which turned out to be nothing more than normal NHS inflation coupled with more reliable data. Binge drinking was reported as having increased when the Office of National Statistics had in fact merely changed the method of calculation. Their protests that this one-off increase did *not* represent a rise in binge drinking were ignored just as enthusiastically as the 'increased' figures were quoted.

And all this time, the actual NHS and government data on which this hysteria was based showed consistently falling numbers for harmful drinking, drink-fuelled crime and anti-social behaviour, drunk driving, alcohol consumption and under-age drinking. The media didn't want to let the truth get in the way of a good story – bad news always sells – and from left to right, tabloid to broadsheet, newspapers simplified and distorted data that had already been twisted by those with an anti-alcohol agenda, and wrote obsessively about Britain's fictitious 'binge drinking epidemic' and 'rising alcohol problem'.

The beer and pub industry, punch-drunk from being blamed for everything from litter and public urination to rape, domestic violence and early mortality, had no unified voice to fight back. If they disputed the figures they were hit with claims of 'well they would say that, wouldn't they,' even as bodies such as the official sounding Institute of Alcohol Studies – in reality a front organization for our old friends the Temperance Alliance – were quoted without question.

As well as a good story, it gave us an excuse to indulge in bashing the poor and the young, and ideally the young poor. Everyone agreed that these were the real binge drinkers. Nowhere was this more evident than in January 2010, when Conservative shadow home secretary Chris Grayling actually said out loud that the reason the Tories opposed a minimum price per unit on alcohol was that 'it puts up the price of a bottle of sherry, a bottle of wine, so responsible drinkers will end up paying more.'

And so I finish this revised version of the story of beer and pubs when both are under the most concerted attack for a century, when medical professionals have stated on the record that they wish to persuade us that drinking is not natural. It's a sombre place to end the story, but I don't think we'll fall for it. I think in our hearts, we know it *is* natural, and that beer – far from being the villain of the piece – is relatively the healthiest, most enjoyable form of mild intoxication there is.

We don't just drink beer to get drunk – it would take an awful lot of effort compared to downing shots and shooters. We drink beer because the gods gave it to us so we could get over the fact that we're going to die. Yes, we drink beer because it intoxicates, but it does so in a way that is gentler than many other drugs, while still making a nice change from stone-cold sobriety. Like the old ad for fresh cream cakes, beer for the most part is 'naughty, but nice'.

We drink beer and wine because they are good for you. This was even more the case before we developed proper sanitation. For most of its history beer in particular has been food as well as drink, full of nutrients, proving itself vital in ways that other booze, or other drugs at large, simply could not. And if you had to drink something potentially intoxicating, it was easier to stay on top of things drinking weak beer rather than wine. Beer was more adaptable to the various demands of everyday life.

The British drink beer because, around the world, people ferment whatever they can find with naturally occurring sugars in it, and we just happen to live where barley grows better than, say, grapes. We drink it because it makes you a man,* because it makes you truly British, and because it tastes nice.†

In summary, we drink beer because we will always want to get out of our brains somehow, and despite all the problems that drinking can cause, it remains the most sociable, laid-back, communal way of doing so. What we drink, the way we drink it and the places we drink it will continue to evolve, but drinking culture has been a constant of civilization throughout history. We not only relax and entertain ourselves by it; we define ourselves through it. And we will continue to do so.

During the last millennium our lives and culture were dominated by beer and by the places we chose to drink it. And throughout that time, through the ages of alehouses, taverns, inns and gin palaces; through fads for sweet old English ale, newfangled hopped beer, porter, IPA, mild and lager; through wars, taxes, drinking epidemics, industrial and social revolutions, no one with any interest in the pub has ever, not for one second, stopped bloody arguing about it. We argue about what the pub should look like, what it should serve, when, and in what quantities. Gourvish and Wilson, in their definitive economic history of the brewing industry between 1830 and 1980, wrote:

---

* Which is incredibly important if you are a man. And quite handy if you're not.
† Well, it does eventually. As Winston Churchill once said, 'Most people hate the taste of beer to begin with. It is, however, a prejudice that many people have been able to overcome.'

The opinion of one industrial analyst in 1988 that 'The UK brewing industry is currently at a cross-roads' could have been advanced equally well in 1830, 1907–9, 1915, 1932, 1959 or 1969. Common elements at all these dates include brewers' anxieties about government regulation, the excise, the changing level of demand, and the maintenance of public house custom.

So next time someone moans that the Great British Pub is disappearing, or that the beer is not as good as it used to be, remember that people have been saying that for as long as beer's been around. The pub is not going to disappear; it's the most resilient feature of English cultural life. Pubs were a vital part of the community when people lived in castles and went off to fight in crusades, and they're still here. But the nature of the community is changing, and the pub is a reflection, a physical embodiment, of the community at any given time. British pubs today are more multicultural, more branded and flashy, more varied and diverse, and less certain of what they are and where they are going, because that's what we're like as a society. For better or for worse. A researcher who helped write *Passport to the Pub*, a guide to pub etiquette aimed ostensibly at tourists, noted that the footie team in his Oxford local consisted of one head of a university department, a bricklayer, two solicitors, a postman, a financial consultant, two self-employed builders, a biochemist, a maths teacher, a factory worker, a computer programmer, a salesman, three unemployed, an accountant, a roofer, a tiler, a town planner, a shop assistant and himself, a research manager. Which says it all, really.

So. Anyone fancy a pint?

As I'm sure you'll understand, writing this book has given me a bit of a thirst. It's got to the stage now where I can't really concentrate unless I've got a nice glass of beer in front of me, to keep me company and spur me on. All those years ago, when I first started researching this book, I was a straightforward lager drinker. But the incredible story of beer spurred me to seek out examples of the beers I was writing about, and hopefully reading this narrative has made you want to do the same. Following the book's publication I carried on exploring and tasting and learning, and as I finish this revised edition I find myself in the absurd situation of being an authority on the subject, with a cellar full of so much beer that to drink it all before it goes off would kill me. I have to give it away to make room for the new stuff a beleaguered but very fit postman delivers on a weekly basis. Since I finished *Man Walks into a Pub* the first time around, I've drunk successive beers that, at the time of drinking, were the strongest in the world. I've had Danish-brewed Imperial Stouts, American IPAs, and Finnish spruce beer. I've drunk a beer that was 139 years old at the time we drank it, and beer fresh from the fermenting vessels in brewery cellars. I've had beer that tastes like whisky, beer that tastes like wine, beer that tastes like port, sherry or Madeira, beer that tastes like cough syrup, beer that tastes like Bovril, and beer that tastes like nothing you could ever put into words. I've raised a glass with multi-millionaire entrepreneurs in mansions, prostitutes in Brazilian dockside bars, household names from off the telly, and Filipino sailors on a cargo ship in the mid-Atlantic. After all that, when someone asks me my favourite beer – which they constantly do, shortly after declaring me the luckiest bastard in the world – I'm struck dumb every time.

And so I come full circle, back to the straightforward yet multifaceted delights of the pint of lager. The ode to that pint with which the first edition finished seems as relevant as ever.

I realize the importance of the pint glass itself. It's the perfect vessel, the ideal amount. You know that there is enough for you to take a long, indulgent pull to clear the dust and cobwebs from the back of your throat and cool you down, and still have a satisfying amount left to savour more slowly after this initial greedy rush. The long straight glass holds enough volume, in the right proportions, for you to be able to properly contemplate the colour of the liquid. The colour gold has deep-rooted associations that stretch back to the dawn of civilization. It represents power, luxury, wealth, the utmost height of achievement, the fulfilment of dreams. These associations are enhanced on a really hot day, when condensation forms in fat droplets on the outside of the glass, dimpling the perspective and creating the illusion of beaten metal rather than flat liquid. Capping this liquid is the thin, white, foamy head, and with a perfectly poured pint there's a short time when it remains in perfect proportion to the body of the beer. As the head thins out and disperses, it leaves imaginary white continents of bubbles floating on a sea of gold. Steady streams of bubbles, a constant source appearing magically from nowhere, rise up through the body of the pint to join those at the top in streams that become hypnotic, deeply calming, if you watch them for a few seconds. And when you gaze past the bubbles, through the glass at the world beyond, your vision is distorted, twisted, as if you're already hammered, suggesting perhaps that anything is possible through the glass.

Cheers.

Further reading

If you've read this far then it's probably obvious that *Man Walks into a Pub* is not intended to be a comprehensive, definitive, academic business or social history. I'm not a historian. I'm merely skimming the surface of a lot of work done by a lot of people. If you want to find out more, please look at some of the following books.

Intoxication

Inglis, B., *The Forbidden Game*, Coronet, 1975
Rudgley, R., *The Alchemy of Culture*, British Museum, 1993
Williamson, K., *Drugs and the Party Line*, Rebel Inc., 1997

Beer mythology, history and lore

Barr, A., *Drink: An Informal Social History*, Bantam Press, 1995
Brown, P, *Hops and Glory – One Man's Search for the Beer That Built the British Empire*, Pan Macmillan, 2009

Buhner, S. H., *Sacred and Herbal Healing Beers, the Secrets of Ancient Fermentation*, Brewers Publications, 1998

Cornell, M., *Beer – The Story of Britain's Most Popular Drink*, Headline, 2003

Dunkling, L., *The Guinness Book of Drinking*, 1992

Eames, A., *Secret Life of Beer: Legends, Lore and Little Known Facts*, Storey Publishing, 1995

Gourvish, T. R. and Wilson, R. G. (eds), *The British Brewing Industry 1830–1980*, Cambridge University Press, 1994

Hackwood, F., *Inns, Ales and Drinking Customs of Old England*, Bracken Books, 1985

Hawkins, K. H. and Pass, C. L., *The Brewing Industry, a study in Industrial Organisation and Public Policy*, Heinemann Educational, 1979

Matthias, P., *The Brewing Industry in England 1700–1830*, Cambridge University Press, 1959

Millns, A., 'The British Brewing Industry 1945–95' in Wilson, R. G. and Gourvish, T. R. (eds) *The Dynamics of the International Brewing Industry Since 1800*, Routledge, 1998

Monckton, H. A., *A History of English Ale and Beer*, Bodley Head, 1966

Paul, W. and Haiber, R., *A Short, but Foamy, History of Beer – the Drink that Invented Itself*, Info Devel Press, 1993

Protz, R., *The Great British Beer Book*, Impact Books, 1987

Smith, G. and Getty, C., *The Beer Drinker's Bible: Lore, Trivia and History*, Brewers Publications, 1997

Vaizey, J., *The Brewing Industry 1886–1951*, Pitman, 1960

Walton, S. and Glover, B., *The Ultimate Encyclopedia of Wine, Beer, Spirits & Liqueurs*, Hermes House, 1998

Wilson, R., 'The British Brewing Industry since 1750' in Richmond, L. and Turton, A., *The Brewing Industry, a Guide to Historical Records*, Manchester University Press, 1990

Young, J., *A Short History of Ale*, History Workshop Pamphlets, 1972

The history of the public house

The Brewers' and Licensed Retailers' Association: The Story of the Pub, 1996

Haydon, P., *The English Pub, a History*, Robert Hale Ltd, 1994 (Reprinted in 2001 under the title *Beer and Britannia, an Inebriated History of Britain*, Alan Sutton)

Monckton, H. A., *A History of the English Public House*, Bodley Head, 1969

Taylor, J., *From Self-Help to Glamour, The Working Man's Club 1860–2*, Leisure Studies Association seminar, Edinburgh, 1982

Pub customs and appreciation

Brewers' Society, *Pubwatching, with Desmond Morris*, Alan Sutton, 1993

Fox, K., *Passport to the Pub, the tourist's guide to pub etiquette*, BLRA, 1996

CAMRA and the fight against the brewers

Hutt, C., *The Death of the English Pub*, Arrow Books, 1973

Pepper, B. and Protz, R. (eds), *Beer Glorious Beer*, Quiller Press, 2000

Protz, R., *Pulling a Fast One, What the Brewers Have Done to Your Beer*, Pluto Press, 1978

Protz, R. and Millns, A., *Called to the Bar, 21 Years of CAMRA*, CAMRA, 1992

Van Munching, P., *Beer Blast, the Inside Story of the Brewing Industry's Bizarre Battles for your Money*, Random House, 1997

Various authors, *Advertising Works*, Vols 1–11, Institute of Practioners of Advertising, 1890–2000

Beer and sport

Collins, T. and Vamplew, W., *Mud, Sweat and Beers, a Cultural History of Sport and Alcohol*, Berg, 2002

Lager louts

Social Issues Research Centre, *Drinking and Public Disorder*, 1992

Brewery histories

Owen, C. C., *The greatest brewery in the world – a history of Bass, Ratcliff & Gretton*, Derbyshire Record Society, 1992

Pudney, J., *A Draught of Contentment, the Story of the Courage Group*, New English Library, 1971

Richie, B., *Good Company, the Story of Scottish & Newcastle*, James & James, 1999

Whitbread & Co., *Your Local*, Whitbread & Co., 1947

Whitbread & Co., *The Story of Whitbread's*, Whitbread & Co., 1964

Beer in World War II

Glover, B., *Brewing for Victory, Brewers, Beer and Pubs in World War II*, Lutterworth Press, 1995

Eddie Taylor

Rohmer, R., *E. P. Taylor – The Biography of Edward Plunket Taylor*, McLelland and Stewart, 1978

Slang

Green, J., *The Cassell Dictionary of Slang*, Cassell, 2000